AM I GETTING PAID FOR THIS?

Also by Betty Rollin

First, You Cry

A Romance about Work

AM I GETTING PAID FOR THIS?

by
Betty Rollin

Little, Brown and Company   Boston—Toronto

FIRST EDITION

The names and identities of certain people in this book have been changed out of respect for their privacy.

The author is grateful to Cowles Broadcasting, Inc., for the material on pages 164–168, from "Love Letters from Beverly Hills," © 1969 by Cowles Broadcasting, Inc., which originally appeared in *Look* maga-zine, August 12, 1969. Reprinted by permission.

Library of Congress Cataloging in Publication Data

Rollin, Betty.
  Am I getting paid for this?

  1. Rollin, Betty. 2. Journalists—United States—
Biography. 3. Authors, American—20th century—
Biography. 4. Actors—United States—Biography.
I. Title.
PN4874.R56A3 070'.92'4 [B] 82–7766
ISBN 0–316–75454–4   AACR2

MV

Designed by Janis Capone

Published simultaneously in Canada
by Little, Brown & Company (Canada) Limited

PRINTED IN THE UNITED STATES OF AMERICA

FOR ED

PREFACE

I don't want to mislead anyone. This is not a celebrity autobiography. First of all, I wrote it myself. Secondly, although people stop me in the street sometimes, it is more often than not to ask directions to Bloomingdale's. And third, I have never slept with anyone famous. I did, once, sleep with the son of someone famous (page 13), but as you can see, I don't even say who.

Rather, this is a story about someone who happens to be me, but might as easily have been someone else, someone who is neither a movie star nor a Watergate burglar, but who is no nine-to-fiver, either. It is about someone for whom work, at some point along the way, became more than a matter of paychecks, vacations, and health benefits. It's about someone for whom work became like love. And by that I do not mean only the moon-in-June part of love, but the grainier side as well—the not sleeping or eating, the waiting for the phone to ring, the caring more than you want to, the just plain caring.

Men have always cared about work. Women have not. And now that's changed. Now women care about their work as much as—sometimes more than—men do, and probably for the same reason. For more and more women, work isn't just something they do. Rather, it's become part of who they are.

Some people think this is bad, some think it's good. But whatever anybody thinks, there, undeniably, it is. It's happened. It's happened so fast, moreover, that I think some women are caught by surprise (I was) when they find themselves feeling things like passion and excitement—and grief—in what seems like the wrong room, i.e., the office. These days, a broken-hearted woman is as likely to be a woman who has lost her promotion as one who has lost her man.

I found myself all worked up over work before most women I know. That's because in my pre-liberation twenties, I missed the first boatload of husbands and was forced to occupy myself, and earn a living, until the next one came along. (Then I missed that one, too.) I made the third boat—I did get married—but by then work had become my husband, too. So now I practice bigamy, all around a fine solution.

Romance has always been a mix of pleasure and pain, but the kinds of work I got stuck on—acting, writing, and television—have had a particularly high dosage of both. As a result, next to cancer, work has been the most interesting thing in my life.

So that's my excuse for writing a book about my career. Plus I figure what I always figure when I write about myself: that I'll get the straight story (and, some of my news colleagues might add, the story straight).

AM I GETTING PAID FOR THIS?

CHAPTER
1

I never had goals. I had vague notions. One was that I didn't want to be a secretary. Another was that I would do something "artistic" (my mother's word). Less vague than the preceding two was the notion that I'd get married and have children. I guess I figured when I got married I'd be artistic on the side, like coleslaw.

I went to Sarah Lawrence College, where I spent four years, from 1953 until 1957, being as "artistic" as possible. There were no required courses at Sarah Lawrence. No one mentioned that it might be nice to know when the Spanish–American War was, let alone that Keynesian economics has something to do with fiscal policy. Nor did anyone mention that if I didn't find out these things then, I probably would never find them out. So, oblivious to all, I diddled at painting and Dance (never dancing: Dance) and, predictably, Theater. That I actually got a part in an off-Broadway play the day, the very day of my graduation, did nothing to hasten my acquaintance with reality. I was excited, to be sure, but I also supposed that that's how things were out there in the world— or, at least, that's how they would be for me.

The way it happened was, in the early spring of my senior

year I had a leading role in one of those plays by García Lorca about suffering peasant women, which were very big at Sarah Lawrence. An agent saw me, called me, sent me to an off-Broadway audition on Bleecker Street, and, incredibly, I got the part. It was to play (are you ready?) Miss Dainty Fidget in William Wycherley's *The Country Wife*. The starring role it was not. Mostly, I stood around in a bustle, looking perplexed while the other actors did and said all kinds of lively and interesting things. (The director had given me a large feather to hold, so that I'd have something to do with my hands.) But never mind. The ink was barely dry on my diploma and I had a job! Not only a job: a profession! Actress! Not as good as Wife! But better than Secretary!

It was a wonderful summer, that summer of '57. I sublet an eccentric, high-ceilinged apartment on St. Luke's Place in Greenwich Village with two other Sarah Lawrence girls, and tried to convince my parents that the derelicts who slept in the doorway would not hurt us.

One of my roommates was black and sane. The other was white and a fruitcake. I didn't mind. In those days, being a fruitcake meant you were deep. But whenever I had a date, she'd answer the door in her leotards, which were flesh-colored, and I minded that a lot. But I didn't know how to tell her to stop. That was probably because I thought it was wrong to mind. In those days, pre-psychoanalysis, pre-practically everything, I thought most feelings I had were wrong.

Anyway, the problem solved itself because the summer sped by, as summers always do, and on August thirty-first the lease on the apartment ran out, whereupon the sane black roommate went off to marry a Jewish law student and the fruitcake went back to college. Meanwhile, the play closed and suddenly—very suddenly, it seemed—it was fall.

I scrambled fast and, through someone who had been in the play, found out about an actress going on the road who wanted to sublet her apartment. I didn't know for sure if I could swing eighty-five dollars a month plus gas, electricity, and telephone but I did know my parents would bail me out if it came to that. So I went to have a look, and took it on the spot.

The apartment was on the fourth floor of a small commercial building on West Forty-fourth Street. The floors slanted and the plaster in the bathroom had bulges and cracks and there was a hole the size of my head in the wall under the sink; but there were a lot of nice pillows in the living room— Indian, I think—and, in the bedroom, a large canopy bed.

My parents helped me move my things from St. Luke's Place and refrained from saying anything about the apartment. My father did say, "Well . . ." a couple of times, then stopped and shook his head, and as the moments went by, my mother's silence thickened. But we all focused efficiently on the business of unpacking, and when it was done they put on their coats. "Well," said my father (again), "tomorrow's labor day!" which was what he said every Sunday. "Come on, Leon," said my mother, not looking at either of us. "Lock the door!" called my father from the other side of it. *"Okay!"* I shouted back, and did. Then, for no particular reason, I stood still inside the door and listened to their footsteps going down the stairs.

When I couldn't hear them anymore, I went into the bedroom and sat down on the canopy bed and listened to the car horns, which sounded farther away than they were. "The apartment's in the rear," the actress had said, "so it's very quiet."

I looked at the clock. Not quite bedtime, I thought, wishing it were.

That was September 1957.

I didn't work again until the following July. The oddest part of it was, given the profession I had chosen—if chosen is the word for it, which I think it probably isn't—there was nothing odd about it. *Most* actors, it turned out, don't act. One striking difference between actors and other people which, when you're new at it, hits you right away is that although you have a profession you probably don't have a job. Another is, although you probably don't have a job you probably have some money because, assuming you had a job at some point, as I had, you can collect unemployment insurance. If you haven't worked and you can't collect unemployment insurance, you can still *call* yourself an actor, even though you spend your working days and/or nights waiting on tables or sitting behind mahogany desks in carpeted reception areas saying things like "Who shall I say is calling?"

Third, whereas you do all the things that other people do when they get up in the morning, since you're not going anywhere, you take longer to do them. Most people get out of bed, go to the bathroom, brush their teeth, wash, fix breakfast, eat it, make the bed (optional), get dressed, and go to work—all in about an hour. An actor learns to do all of that in two hours and after he's had a few years' practice, he can, in all likelihood do it in three. (In California, he can probably get it up to four because of the extra hour spent doing something with or to the body.)

By noon, one is geared up for the obligatory call to the agent. But the agent has "gone to lunch" or he's "in a conference" or he "my-he-was-here-a-minute-ago-he-must've-just-stepped-out." If you're lucky, as the secretary devises the lie, she'll put you on "hold," thereby allowing you to kill another five minutes.

With half a day safely gone, you can relax a bit, take a walk and buy a newspaper—two newspapers, actually: *The New York Times* for your general interest, if you still have any; and *Show Business* or one of the other casting rags, where you can expect to find a job if you still believe in the Easter bunny. It's been twenty years since I've looked at *Show Business*, but little has changed. In a recent issue, a play called *Animals* was listed as needing an actor to play the role of "Thaddeus: man who's been around, not too bright, but with unsurpassed sense of loyalty. Sympathetic and comic." And for a play, *Flea in the Ear*, an actress was "still being sought to play CAMILLE: 20s to 30s, secretary and cousin of Victor Emmanuel, has cleft palate, is extremely funny."

It takes a certain kind of person to call a producer and say, "Hi, I've been around! I'm not too bright, but boy, am I loyal! And I feel sorry for people, except for the thousands who find me amusing!" Or "Hi, I have a cleft palate! And the minute I open my mouth, you'll bust your buttons!"

There are actors like that and they survive and, occasionally, they even work. That's because they are willing to do two things necessary for survival in show business: lie and nag. I never got the hang of nagging. I could not successfully affix myself to people who, I knew, would just as soon I dropped into the nearest elevator shaft, and not make too much noise on the way down. But lying was different. That I learned to do.

Actors are not the only people who lie when they're looking for a job. Civilians, too, exaggerate credentials; and who among us, when confronted with a horse's ass who is in the position of granting us employment, has not, at the very least, smiled insincerely? The difference is, most civilians job-hunt only occasionally. Actors do it every day. Even when an actor gets a job, how long does it last? If it's a television show, a week or so; if it's a play, *maybe* longer. A long-running play is the exception, not the rule.

The horses' asses in the theater, by the way, are usually not the directors, but the people you have to see before you get to see the director—if you ever do—people like casting directors, agents, and production assistants. It is probably true that they were not monsters when they were small babies, but, like some guards in state penitentiaries, get that way from having more power than talent or brains.

There was, I found, a cumulative effect of spending most of your waking hours presenting yourself before such people and pretending to like them and trying to make them like and, more to the point, buy you. After a while, I began to feel like those girls on five-inch heels in doorways on Eighth Avenue. Except, I couldn't help noticing, the girls on the heels got more work.

The second kind of lying you have to do is less damaging to the soul, but equally wearing. It takes only a few auditions to find out that an actor's talent has little to do with whether he or she gets a part. Nor, as far as I ever knew, does it have anything to do with gymnastics on the casting couch. Most often, an actor gets the part because the people who do the hiring think the actor *is* the part, that he *is* the character in the play. When, on rare occurrences, I got an acting job, it was never, I soon realized, because of my ability to act, but rather because I was "right," as they say, for the part. I was hired, simply, to be myself—or whoever they thought "myself" was. (Often, in those days, they had a clearer idea than I did.)

This is where the second, more advanced, kind of lying came in. When you catch on to the system, you realize that you must pretend not only to act the character, but to *be* the character—to enter the room dressed as the character and say how-do-you-do as the character would.

Once, I heard about a casting call for the role of a French

girl. I called my agent, who told me that they were interested only in seeing actresses who were French. "Does she have to speak French?" I asked. "No," said the agent, "it's just that they want to make sure the accent is authentic." My French was rotten, but as it happened, my French accent could have won prizes. "Tell them I'm French," I said to the agent.

I couldn't afford taxis in those days, but I took one to the audition so that I could practice on the driver. "Feeftyth Street, pliz," I said throatily. Then, when I had settled back in the seat, "My, eet ees a beauteeful day, n'est-ce pas?"

"Yeah," said the driver.

"I luv zee fall," I said, pressing on. "Zee leaves, zey are zo beauteeful, no?"

"Yeah," said the driver. New York's only monosyllabic cabbie was also, to my chagrin, New York's speediest driver, and we arrived at the theater before I had even warmed up.

I paid the fare and walked down an alley to a backstage door, pulled open the heavy stage door, and then, without going inside, let it close. I had just been struck by a paralyzing thought. *What if someone in there spoke French?*

As any criminal knows, to pull off a heist you must feel confident. Once again, I pulled open the door and walked inside and onto the stage, but I did not feel confident. I felt like jelly. I did all the "zo nize to zee yous," but in a faint voice, waiting for what I now knew was inevitable: that I would be addressed in what was most assuredly not my mother tongue. As it happened, I flattered myself. No one spoke to me in either language; but the mere expectation of French did me in. By the time my turn came to read, I was mumbling so, the accent could have been Hungarian. . . . I did not get the job.

I used to love the Astor Hotel on Times Square. When I felt particularly rotten after botching up an audition, I'd go into one of the phone booths in the lobby, pull the glass door shut, lift the receiver, face the back of the booth, and cry. Then I'd wipe the mascara from my cheeks and head for Forty-fourth Street or for whatever, at that moment, I happened to be calling home.

I went to a lot of auditions that jobless, formless first year out of college, and spent a lot of time in phone booths in the Astor Hotel. I also began to do the one thing other than a job that makes actors feel respectable: Class. "Class" (like "Dance" at Sarah Lawrence) was more than acting lessons. It was a reminder that, whatever the life of an actor was, acting itself was an art. And Class made learning the art seem important.

There is probably very little going on in the universe that is, in fact, less important than an actor's learning to act. But, as anyone who has ever taken a class (in anything) knows, it can get to *feel* important—particularly if it's a good class.

I had engineered my way into a formidable biweekly gathering of professionals only, taught by Sanford Meisner, who, along with Lee Strasberg, Uta Hagen, Stella Adler, and a few others, was one of the teaching stars in those days. My classmates were a diverse group, ranging from dour, dark men in black chinos to Pat Boone, who was the cleanest person I'd ever seen. Class soon became the center of my life. Not that I had any other life to speak of in those days. Never had the notion of husband-and-children seemed more remote.

Class, too, served as protection from the crude commerce of the outside world. In Class you didn't have to sell or lie, or enter contests. You had only to practice the art, to act.

In between classes we were assigned homework. We were expected to rehearse at least twice during the week with a partner, which, among other things, used up one's afternoons nicely. At the beginning, classes consisted mostly of improvisations, which are grown-up versions of games children play: I'll be the mommy, you be the daddy, I want to break your neck, or whatever. Improvisations taught you to act without relying on words given to you by the playwright. You had to make up your own words, which, if you were doing it right, would evolve from the emotion you felt during the improvisation. Later, the same technique—emotion leading and words following—was supposed to work for scenes in plays. The emotion itself came from your own personal "bank," from which you would make appropriate "withdrawals."

If you're playing Medea, for instance, you can't know what it's like to have murdered your children; but perhaps once when you were a child you tortured your gerbil or smashed a firefly or pummeled your kid brother—it doesn't matter what, as long as it made you feel terrible. So before doing the scene you close your eyes and, through what is called a sense-memory, try to recall how you felt and armed with that feeling go out and play the scene.

You couldn't cheat, either. Meisner always knew if you were pretending. If you did—God help you—pretend, Meisner would stop the scene and, after a short, punishing silence, snarl at the offender: "Don't *show* us what you're feeling. *Feel it.*" Another silence. "Then," he'd add contemptuously, "we might believe it."

Naturally, I loved the man. I was desperate, simply desperate, to please him. When I didn't, it made me practically sick. It wasn't his fault. It was not his intention, I know, to have such a hold on anyone. To his credit, Meisner's demeanor was entirely businesslike. He wore suits and ties and kept his professional distance. I'm sure he had no interest in being anyone's guru, and probably didn't even notice that he had become mine.

Once you are in a cult frame of mind, some kind of self-flagellation is almost inevitable. Whatever you do isn't good enough, whatever you *are* isn't good enough. You try hard, but you never try hard enough, and so on and on. This does not improve your acting any more than chanting Hare Krishna improves your singing voice. But what did I know? When one of my acting partners—the son of a Western movie star—told me that the reason that I wasn't "hitting the emotional peaks" in my acting was that I wasn't having sex with anyone and hinted, furthermore, that he was available, I bought it.

This, for the record, was my—I could still count them on one hand—Third Time. Although I'm never sure whether to count the first, which happened in the middle of my senior year at Sarah Lawrence after I had decided, simply, I *had* to do it. My best friend had done it (twice), and it just seemed like something I should do, too. Besides, graduation was coming up and I didn't feel right about graduating a virgin. Unfortunately, instead of choosing some young lout, who would have pounced on me, and that would have been that, I chose a sensitive pre-med student who played the flute and stuttered. A friend of his lent us his apartment in New York. At the appointed hour, we went there. Jonathan, his name was, couldn't find the right key for the downstairs door. Then he found it. Then we went inside and found the bedroom. We hung our coats up and I looked at the bed. I remember thinking it was probably the girl's job to take off the bedspread, but I wasn't sure. I started taking it off and he helped me. We folded it together and put it over the back of a wing chair. He started to unbutton his shirt. This startled me. But, after all, that was what was supposed to happen, wasn't it? I started to unbutton my blouse. . . . It was like a doctor's appointment, except at a doctor's appointment you're not so tense, because you know what's going to happen.

He got down to his shorts (white) and his socks (navy blue); I, to my bra and half-slip (underpants still on). We looked at each other and tried to hug. The skin of his middle on my middle felt strange. There was too much light in the room, but I wasn't sure if it would be too forward to say so. Before I got a chance to decide, he pulled me down on the bed and kissed me. We both had our eyes open. We stopped kissing and looked at each other. "Maybe we shouldn't do this," I said. "Okay," he said. We sat up and put on our clothes and left the apartment, locking the doors behind us. I never saw Jonathan again.

When I got the *Country Wife* job and became a professional actress, I felt again—even more urgently—that I had to do it. The logical person was one of the actors in the play. He had gone to Princeton, had blue eyes, and wore loafers. We had gone out a lot during the summer and smooched a bit, but our relationship did not seem to be moving forward (horizontally) the way I thought it should. He never made me feel that he found me especially pretty or sexy, but I thought that was because he was shy, or maybe because he knew a lot of actresses and had become blasé. He did seem to like me, though, and he laughed at the things I said.

Finally, near the end of August, we did it. Or I think we did it. When whatever-it-was was over, I said three words— three words, I found out later, which should never be said: "Was that it?"

By the end of the summer, he and the male lead were lovers.

It was different with my beefy Western acting classmate. This time something happened. I suppose that's why it surprised me that it wasn't nicer.

CHAPTER
2

Summer came, and with it, mercifully, a job at last. I landed a part in a "strawhat circuit" tour of an old chestnut called *Dulcy*, starring Dody Goodman, who had just made her mark by acting dumb on the *Tonight* show. (This was the fifties, remember, when acting dumb was the only way a woman could get a laugh.) I had a featured role—that of the moronic ingenue, Angela. But never mind; a featured role in a "star package," as it was called, was a young actor's triumph. It meant ten weeks—one week in each place—playing the best summer theaters in New England, all of which seemed especially nifty when one considered the alternatives: enduring a steamy summer in the city with no work; or laboring in a stationary summer stock company, where, for no money, no glory, and no end of work, you do as many plays as there are weeks, performing one at night and rehearsing the upcoming one all day.

Some actors saw summer stock as great experience, but Meisner had warned us away from it with the same tone of voice my mother used about hot dogs and Twinkies. It was Meisner's view that stock encouraged bad habits—that the pressure of continuously having to learn so many lines led, inevitably, to glibness and superficiality. Years later, I would hear the same warning about daily newspaper writing. The warnings had some merit, I think, in both fields, but they gave the false impression that written works of length, like books, were necessarily more substantial than shorter ones. Even sillier was the notion that artistic invigoration would automatically be forthcoming just because you were doing one play per summer rather than one each week—which is what you'd do in a stationary summer stock company.

Dulcy disproved this theory grandly. The play itself was crap; the only reason for reviving it, aside from the general assumption that summer audiences *want* crap, was that the producers—the distinguished Theatre Guild, no less— thought it would be a good vehicle for Dody, whose dumb act, even then, was one of the more amusing ones. But the lines in the play weren't nearly as good as the ones Dody had made up herself on the *Tonight* show. Nor, on the *Tonight* show, did she have to deal with a leading man who, though a darling, was a drunk and, with astonishing regularity, talked to himself onstage. (The only thing worse than being on a stage with an actor who forgets his lines is being on stage with an actor who makes lines up.) And that wasn't all. Often, during an embrace, he'd forget to stop and poor Dody would wind up supporting one hundred and eighty-five pounds of dead weight; at which point she'd separate herself from him and prop him up, where he would or wouldn't stay.

None of this helped the play's tempo.

As for my role of the simpering moron, Angela: even more than what she had to say, I hated what she (I) had to wear— frilly print frocks, styled to look like the twenties, which is to say, they got smallest (in the seat) where I got biggest.

Class hadn't prepared me for these difficulties. Nor had it prepared me for the director, a sharpie from the West Coast, who wore shiny white pants and shiny white shoes, and did not wear several gold necklaces on his hairy chest, *only*, I am sure, because men weren't doing that yet, even in Los Angeles. The dress I could deal with. I simply wore a satin-covered vise known as a girdle, which impaired both my breathing and my ability to walk. But I learned to breathe higher, and fortunately baby steps were in character. I might even have learned to handle Angela's insipid dialogue, because Class had taught me that words didn't matter, only creative moments. But Class didn't teach me what to do when the directorfromtheWestCoast made it very clear that, as far as he was concerned, creative moments sucked and he wanted lines said the way they were written and he wanted them said loud and said fast. Nor, most important of all, did Class teach me that when they're paying you, you do it their way.

In the midst of my suffering, God sent Leo Bloom. Leo Bloom, who was thin and dark-haired and long-nosed and *very* pale—as if he hadn't been outside for twenty years—had the sort of goofy, self-effacing sweet nature ill-natured people step on. He had a lovely sense of humor, except about one thing: comedy. To him, comedy was serious. His role in the play was that of Vincent Leach, the unctuous movie director who woos baby Angela. Like me, Leo Bloom had been to Class and shared my need for Creative Moments. In no time, we became co-conspirators. Late at night, after rehearsals were over, we'd meet, in my room usually, and conduct our own rehearsals. The company got wind of our meetings and assumed we were having an affair, not imagining that we were up to something far wickeder than sex—namely, subverting the director's orders and working out our own "business" for our scenes together. Each morning at rehearsals, then, our task would be to insert into our performances what we had secretly re-hearsed the night before. If the change was minor—an intonation or a gesture—we'd get away with it.

What we did to our proposal scene, however, was not

considered minor. During our illicit rehearsal the night before, Leo came up with what struck us both as a frightfully amusing switch. We had contrived our moments so that, on Leo's line, "Will you marry me?" Leo was standing and I was on my knees. It took some doing to get down there—the only way I could make a successful landing in that blasted dress was to keep my knees together as I lowered myself, which hurt on impact—but we felt it was worth it.

The director had another view, which was apparent the moment my knees hit the floor. "WHAT ARE YOU DOING?" he screamed. Then, as if we hadn't heard, "WHAT ARE YOU DOING?" again.

Leo mistook this for a question and ventured to answer. "W-w-we thought it might be funnier if—" was as far as he got.

"GODDAMMIT, I DON'T CARE WHAT YOU THINK! YOU'RE NOT BEING PAID TO THINK, GODDAMMIT. I DECIDE WHAT'S FUNNY AROUND HERE, GODDAMMIT." And so forth. Meanwhile, I was concentrating on trying to get from my knees to my feet without ripping the dress (we had neglected to work that part out) while the rest of the cast stood there, sighing and saying things under their breath, like "Jesus."

At times like these, Leo got most of the blame. I was the girl, after all, and moreover, the Ingenue. I suppose they thought I was the innocent dupe and Leo, the mad Svengali. Gradually that changed. By the end of the summer, everyone hated us both. Looking back, I don't blame them. After all, the play was in the Westport Country Playhouse; the cast was in the Westport Country Playhouse; and Leo Bloom and Betty Rollin were in the Moscow Art Theater.

As for the audience, to us the audience was bumps in the darkness. We were conscious of the people out there, but mainly we were conscious of ourselves. In those early days on the stage, as a result of Class, I never really thought of acting as performing, as something you do for an audience. I thought of it, rather, as something that happened between myself and the other people on stage whose faces I could see. That was bad and good. It was bad because it made us self-indulgent. It was good because it means we didn't show off on stage. We acted. And when the acting worked, it rang true, like something that was really happening between people. Then, that audience whom we didn't care much about pleasing got pleased, in spite of us.

Bruised by that summer's reality (but not yet enlightened by it), I returned to Class in the fall. Now that I was aware of the artistic wasteland in the outside world, I was more determined than ever to hone my skills.

So I honed. I didn't work. But oh, how I honed. And how I auditioned. Once I even sang. I sang: "Give me some men who are stout-hearted men . . ." Since my voice was lousy, Leo said I should try to sing something to make them notice me.

They noticed me.

But they did not hire me. No one hired me.

My visits to the Astor phone booths both increased and became longer in duration. In the old days (last year), I'd have my cry and get up. Now, sometimes I'd linger after my eyes had dried and think, what am I doing here? How did this happen to me? *What* is happening to me? How did I get caught up in an experiment where a bell keeps ringing, but there's hardly ever any food? Why do I keep entering—and losing—all of these contests when I'm not all that sure I want the prize?

But if I don't want this, what do I want? That's the question that usually got me moving—up out of the phone booth, then down into the Broadway subway, and finally home. Home, this year, was a dark but rather grand three-bedroom apartment in an old mansion on West End Avenue, which I shared with two other girls from college—Carol Rossen, another would-be actress like me, except unlike me, she had a film director for a father, which, as they say, didn't hurt; and Joanna Simon, who was five feet ten, abundantly blond, and glamorous even in the morning, at which time, in lieu of fried eggs, she would open imported tins of mandarin oranges and spoon them into her mouth as if she were feeding someone else.

Joanna was studying to be an opera singer and practiced at home on an upright piano, which one of her boyfriends had painted rose to match the flowers on her bedspread. Joanna had the biggest bedroom, because her father was the richest, Carol's was next, and I had Cinderella's broom closet, which was fine with me because I only had to pay fifty dollars a month, while Joanna and Carol divvied up the remaining two hundred. Joanna's mother threw in the furniture as well— lovely discards from their country house—and my mother threw in a bed, curtains and lamp and a chair for my room; so all I had to buy was a chest of drawers, which I did at the Salvation Army for twelve dollars.

The way I managed to maintain my non-career in those days without either buckling under or, God forbid, learning shorthand, was by having mastered a few key survival tricks. Like setting myself up on West End Avenue, where I could live like a person with a salary—or a rich father—when, in fact, I had neither. Or better yet, the trick of not exactly living anywhere.

Except for West End Avenue, most of the other places I parked myself from the end of college until 1964 were sublets, like the one I had had the previous year on Forty-fourth Street—furnished apartments vacated for a few months or more, usually by an actor on tour. Or sometimes somebody-from-college's roommate would get married and leave behind a single bed onto which I and the single-bed sheets my mother had given me would speedily move.

Most of the subletters were not out for profit. All they wanted was someone who would water the philodendron and refrain from grinding cigarettes into the carpet. So I never paid much rent, never had to buy furniture, and never had to sign a lease and commit to long-term payments, which, given the financial instability of the life I had chosen and was by now determined to maintain, would not have been possible. And if one sublet wound up before the next began, I could always crash at my parents' house, thirty minutes up the highway in Yonkers—a last resort and one I seldom used—but knowing I had a safety net made it easier to keep jumping.

Although civic enlightenment did not top my list of priorities in those days, moving from place to place the way I did turned out to be a fine way to get to know New York. Altogether, I must have holed up in about twenty apartments in about fifteen or so neighborhoods. Some were more unlikely than others: a ratty but sweet garden apartment on East Eighteenth Street with cockroaches inside and birds outside; a stuffy studio apartment that smelled funny with a Murphy bed in Tudor City; and a wall-to-wall-carpeted Park Avenue apartment with shiny wood tables, sterling silver flatware, and an antique writing desk, which belonged to a newly divorced Sarah Lawrence chum who had taken herself and her two children off to her mother's house in New Jersey for two months.

Of course a body needs more than shelter. A body needs food. For that, one had men. So another trick was to be pretty enough so that, even though you had not passed the emotional age of twelve, men liked you and asked you for dates and paid for your veal at Italian restaurants. (In 1958 men, except for actors, paid, thank goodness.) Okay, sometimes you had to kiss them at the end of the evening, even if you didn't want to. But you did not have to go to bed with them. (You didn't have to do that until the late *sixties*.)

Probably the key factor in the maintenance of such a life is to be an only child, so that your parents are hard put to write you off, even though they hate your elevator and your life, the worst of which (sleeping with actors) they don't even know about. So they bring you steaks with the fat cut off wrapped in waxed paper. And they bring you glass jars with cooked fruit ("How do you know what it tastes like until you try it?") and vitamin pills and (single) bed sheets, and an occasional article of clothing "picked up" at Saks. And your mother brings you the classic Jewish-mother-double-message: (1) You are making us miserable, and (2) You are the best and can do anything. Which on the one hand makes you crazy, but on the other makes you confident and strong, and helps you to dare (it's 1958, remember) not to be a secretary.

Of course, with a mother like mine, it was easy to dare not to be a secretary. It was easy to do exactly what I was doing because, in a way, in *her* way, my mother had done the same thing.

My mother was one of four children, born on the lower East Side of New York to a despotic orthodox rabbi and a softhearted but strong-headed orphaned-in-childhood mother, both from Russia, neither of whom on principle (his) ever learned a word—well, maybe a word—of English. Religion and education were the two things that mattered in my mother's childhood home. Religion was a duty; education, a reward. My grandmother's idea of giving to her children was to educate them, daughters included, however loony that struck her husband, who thought education for daughters was all right up to a point—but not so that it interfered with the main business of finding husbands. My mother's sisters agreed and found husbands while still in their teens. But my mother—perhaps because she was her mother's favorite and made to feel special—went for more education, even at the risk of turning off the traditional males in the Jewish ghetto who valued conformity more than daring. So she ironed her middy blouse, smoothed her navy blue skirt, pulled her cloche hat down over her ears, and ventured out of the neighborhood to exotic Brooklyn and its Maxwell Teacher's College. She got a degree, a license to teach (first she had to take a special education class to get rid of her Jewish lilt and dentalized t's), and became a professional woman, the first in her family.

My mother first saw my father one evening at a friend's house. He was playing the balalaika and singing a Russian folk song and she fell for him on the spot. Like her parents, he, too, had emigrated from Russia. It was an odd match: he was the prettier, she the smarter. My mother's mother wasn't thrilled. Her father cared only that he knew Hebrew and had studied the Talmud. They married and had me and tried to have more children and couldn't. My father went to work in his brother's hardware store. My mother put teaching aside and threw herself into the wife/mother routine, riveting her attention on my father, me, and the succession of little houses we lived in—each one slightly bigger than the last, all in Yonkers, which my mother thought was the country.

My mother and father were devoted to each other's well-being, but agreed on practically nothing. That's because my father's view of life was: Enough; and my mother's view was: Never Enough. My mother always won.

It was not that my mother wanted things; nor, in fact, that she wanted anything (directly) for herself. Rather, she wanted what her mother had wanted: the best possible life for her children, as she saw it. That she wound up having only one child meant that all of her maternal energy—which in my mother's case was enough to power a jet liner—was harnessed, instead, into pulling one small model in balsa wood: me.

Education remained the destination, but my mother took it a step further: she wanted the *best* education. Whatever that was. My mother had no idea, but she figured it would probably cost money; so she began to save. When she had more than a small pile, she invested it in property, although I can't imagine how she knew how to do that. Whenever she explains it, she sounds like a criminal. "I wanted money," she says with a shrug, "so I got it." I'm sure it wasn't a fortune, but since my father had by then a fairly successful wholesale rubber business, all the money my mother made was extra; in other words, for fueling her only child.

When she guessed that she had gathered enough money, my mother went downtown to the Child Study Association, a sort of advisory board, where as she tells it, "for five dollars" she got a list of "what the lady said were the best private schools." Since the Fieldston Ethical Cultural School was on the top of the list, it was there, naturally, that I would have to go. I thought the place sounded yukky (or whatever the word for yukky was in the late forties) but my mother said that if I didn't like it, I didn't have to stay. That seemed reasonable to me, so we made a deal, neither of us paying too much attention to the fact that I had not yet been admitted to Fieldston, and that it took more than the price of tuition to get into such a place, yukky or not. Like you had to take an entrance examination, which was supposed to be a killer. And, although officially it didn't matter whom you knew, knowing someone didn't, as my mother pointed out, hurt.

The first part was easy. Using a sixth- and seventh-grade syllabus she got from the Board of Education, my mother simply resumed her teaching career with me as the sole pupil, and grilled me two hours a day, five days a week for a year, until I could have made Harvard. The second part wasn't so easy. We were not what anyone would call a family with connections. But my mother's attitude about connections was the same as her attitude about money: if you didn't have it and you needed it, you got it.

First, she decided on the kind of connection she wanted to have. Since Fieldston was run by the Ethical Culture Society (my mother didn't know what that was, but she thought it sounded nice), she figured she would nail the person who ran it. She had only to get his name—Algernon Black—for him to become, as they say in the Mafia, a marked man.

Within weeks my mother had unearthed a friend whose physician was also the physician of you'll never guess who. My mother went to work immediately and invented an ailment. Then she made an appointment with the doctor. She wound up a week later in Algernon Black's living room, giving what I'm sure was one of her finest solo performances.

I got into Fieldston. Because of Algernon Black? In spite of Algernon Black? Since I did very well on the exam, perhaps neither. I never knew.

But, ah, never enough. "The best school" was only part of the plan. I had to have Culture, too. My mother wasn't altogether sure what Culture meant in practice, so back she went to the Child Study place and they told her. Culture, said the nice lady, was music lessons or ballet or dramatics or, perhaps, art. My mother paid close attention to everything but the "or's." Within a week, I was grinding away at music, ballet, dramatics, and art.

So as not to interfere with my schoolwork during the week, the cultural infusions were administered on weekends. From my tenth birthday until past my fourteenth, every Saturday morning at nine o'clock—as the other children on our block in Yonkers pulled covers over their heads, played Parcheesi with their siblings, or hopped on their two-wheelers—I downed my juice, eggs, whole wheat toast (no white flour or sugar ever made it inside *our* kitchen door), and ran up the block in my going-to-school clothes with my mother to catch a trolley which took us to a subway which took us to Seventy-second Street and Central Park West. Then together we'd walk, leaning against the wind in winter, to Sixty-seventh Street, where in a small old mansion the day's peregrinations began.

First, ballet class, which consisted of me, two other spindly-legged girls of about ten and twelve, and a teacher, who was a Christian Scientist and knew not from her pain nor, more to the point, from ours. After an hour of that, it was hurry-get-dressed and limp across the hall to dramatics class, where everyone learned to say *Tyewsday* and *tomahto* (which was fine as long as you never set foot in the Midwest); and then rush-rush down the street to the corner drugstore for lunch. As long as there would be no direct benefit to my mind or body, my mother saw no point in spending money on fancy restaurants. I always ate the same thing at the drugstore, an American cheese sandwich. That way, I could say "the usual" to the man behind the counter. Which I thought was pretty neat (until I turned twelve and decided saying "the usual" was pretty dumb). Then quick-wipe-your-mouth-drink-your-milk, and tear back up to Seventy-second Street, tumble down the stairs, catch a local train to West Fourth Street, run over to Washington Square, where I spent the rest of the afternoon at a place called The Clinic for Gifted Children, painting fruit.

On the way home, the subway usually got crowded and we'd have to stand. My mother would hang onto the strap and I'd hang onto her. Then the grammar lessons would begin.

In the late 1940s the New York subway in no way resembled the filthy, dangerous, elongated hole in the ground it is today. But even in those days, it was a less than congenial place to teach a child English grammar. The train would rattle and roar and my mother would bend down and shout in my ear, "What's 'will make you strong'?" referring to the advertisement above the window which read, "Wheaties will make you strong."

"A predicate?" I'd say, trying not to lose my balance as the train lurched.

"WHAT?" she'd yell.

"A PREDICATE!" I'd scream.

"AND WHAT'S 'WILL MAKE'?" she'd press on, ignoring the looks from the other passengers.

"A COMPOUND VERB."

"VERY GOOD. AND WHAT'S 'STRONG'?"

"PREDICATE ADJECTIVE."... And so it went until the last stop, where we'd catch the trolley at Van Cortland Park back to Yonkers. In the trolley we did spelling.

Sundays were a snap. On Sundays all I had was a piano lesson.

Incredibly, except maybe for piano practice, I thought this weekly scourge was fun. My mother told me it was fun and I had no reason to doubt it. I can't even say I felt pressured. Perhaps that's because, although I was pushed to "do," I was not pushed to "succeed" or to "win." The Little League syndrome was conspicuously absent. I ran, but I didn't race. No comparisons were made between me and other children. And in place of criticism, I got praise, abundant continual praise. My mother knew better than most other mothers I've known—and employers I've had—that what keeps people moving is to think they're moving well. After dancing class the muscles in my calves and the tops of my thighs hurt so much I'd have to clutch the rail in order to get down the subway stairs, but as I clutched, my mother would chirp about the improvement in my barre work, and how much steadier were my tour jetés. She'd find nuances in my dramatic school performances and proclaim them "sensitive" (a word she'd heard the teacher use). And she'd take my (dreadful) little watercolors and hang them, not on the refrigerator door, but in the living room, over the piano.

I wasn't blind. I knew from watching other kids that I was nothing special. But my mother's insistence that I was special made me feel that I could be.

My mother, I hope I've made clear, was no stage mother, no seeker of vicarious glamour gained through the performing antics of her only child. Oh, she'd lean on me now and then to play "Für Elise" on the piano when we had company, but I know she had no commerce in mind. I truly think it never entered her head that one day I might become a professional performer. When, in fact, on one occasion a "talent scout" came sniffing around the drama school and told the teacher, who passed the word on to my mother, that he was interested in me for a Broadway show, my mother drew herself up and told the teacher that if I so much as found out about the offer (I didn't until years later) she would withdraw me from the school. My mother turned up her nose at anything that even smelled of show business. When, on another occasion, a kid from Yonkers urged me to join her tap-dancing class, my mother investigated the class and pronounced it out of the question. She didn't know *what* to make of a bunch of children making such a commotion with their feet, but she knew it wasn't Culture.

I can't really call my mother an early feminist. Had *Ms. Magazine* existed in 1949, I doubt that she would have made their Mother of the Year. The arts as a field of study, after all, have always been more pink than blue. But my mother wouldn't have won any prizes from *Family Circle*, either. To be *their* version of perfect, she would've had to have dragged me to sewing and cooking classes, too, along with the painting and music; and there was none of that.

Nor did I get the feeling, ever, of being culturally fattened up in order someday to get a better husband, which in those days would have been considered not only appropriate but wise. Instead I sensed—and perhaps for a girl-child growing up in the forties and fifties, this was the most important thing about it—that the whole routine, however naive and over-done, had no other purpose than my own betterment. The clear message my mother sent me as a child was that even though I was a girl, I counted as a person, and that my growth was important for its own sake.

So my mother was both usual and unusual. This country is full of immigrant and first-generation mothers who have sacrificed, scrimped, saved, pushed, and wheedled for their— sons. Now and then I've wondered, had I had a brother, whether my mother's focus would have shifted. . . . Or did she ever feel that her energy would have been better spent if *I* had been a boy? No to both, she says, and reminds me that she had a brother, and of her own mother's attitude toward her.

I think it's a pretty good answer. Anyway, I believe it.

CHAPTER
3

With summer came my annual job. It was very nearly a replay of the summer before: another summer package, another old chestnut, *Red Letter Day*, and another star. Except, of course, Gloria Swanson was hardly just "another star." I remember our first meeting: she fixed those astounding eyes on me, raised that remarkable chin, moved the narrow vermilion mouth slightly to one side, and informed me that she would be wearing red in the play and suggested, in a way that sounded like more than a suggestion, that I wear brown or dark green. That turned out to be our longest conversation, and also, except for the American cheese episode, the most emotional.

For a rehearsal snack—an admittedly inelegant one—I used to buy packages of sliced Kraft American cheese, harking back, I suppose, to my drugstore lunches with my mother. As the day wore on, I'd open the package and peel off one slice, then another, and so forth, in lieu of—ironically, I thought of it as a healthy choice—chocolate bars or potato chips. One day, simply to be polite, I offered a slice of cheese to Miss Swanson. At first she stared at it. I think she was truly stunned. "Processed cheese!" she hissed, and then backed off as if I had offered her a slice of raw toad. How was I to know that even before the tour began, she had arranged to have organically grown grapefruit flown from California to each town (her chauffeur would drop her off, then hit the post office) timed for her arrival?

I believe she shared her grapefruit occasionally with a favored member of the company—her leading man, for one—Buddy Rogers, now Mary Pickford's widower, a sweet man with an astonishingly large wardrobe. (I think the young actor who played Miss Swanson's youngest son got a few grapefruit, too. But that could have been rumor.)

The role I played, that of Miss Swanson's daughter-in-law, married to her eldest son in the play, was not too dissimilar from the moron, Angela, but she was slightly older, and married; so instead of having to act a goony virgin, I played a somewhat less goony young-married.

The director, too, was different from *Dulcy*'s, but no more endearing. No sleazy hotshot from the West Coast he, but an effete Easterner, who was unctuous around Swanson and snooty around me.

This time God did not send Leo Bloom. He did better. He sent, instead, a handsome prince....Well, not a prince, exactly; but he was handsome and blond, and played the role of my husband, so the romance had a bona fide storybook contour. Best of all, he was as stuck on me as I was (immediately after our first stage kiss) on him.

I'm not saying a gong went off in my head. I had no this-is-it seizure. More like this-is-it-for-now. Which surprised me. I thought falling for someone, by definition, meant wanting to marry the person. With Greg, I *wanted* to want to marry this person. But I didn't somehow. Too goy maybe, too handsome, too lightweight, I don't know. Anyway, I tried not to think about what I didn't feel and focus on what I did.

Which was plenty.

We smooched onstage, we smooched offstage. We sneaked in and out of each other's motel room and didn't rehearse once. Art went out the window. When the summer ended, he told me I would move into his apartment in New York. I said yes of course, even though it wasn't a question.

Now that I think about it, I probably said yes *because* it wasn't a question.

J oanna's sister, Lucy Simon, moved into my room on West End Avenue and paid my fifty dollars and received instructions about what to do when my mother called: (1) Act natural. (2) Say I'm at an audition, or having dinner with a friend, depending on the time of day. (3) Hang up and, immediately upon hearing the dial tone, dial Greg's number. I'd then bolt outside and call my mother back from a pay phone. The idea behind the pay phone was, simply, to make the lie smaller. "I've been at an audition," I'd say, "and I just called home for messages and they said you called." That way, if my mother then said "Where are you?"—which she almost never did, because I think she suspected something, but didn't really want to know about it—I could say, "I'm in a phone booth" and at least *that* part would be true. I also tried to avoid all of this by calling her a lot, which worked, more or less.

Meanwhile, living with Greg didn't feel as wicked as I thought it should. I had barely unpacked when he took me by the hand and introduced me to all the neighbors on the floor, Irish and Italians mostly, with packs of children, each of whom Greg knew by name—even which kids belonged to which apartment. With each introduction I'd feel my skin go hot from embarrassment. I knew these people were Catholic and thought they'd surely hate me for my loose ways (the fifties, remember). But they greeted me as if I were a bride—

31

shyly but warmly. I knew why. They loved Greg, and anything he did was all right.

He introduced me to the butcher, too. He dragged me into his shop on Second Avenue one hot September afternoon and said, "This is my woman." I looked at my toes sticking out of my sandals and felt all of the blood in my body rush to my face. I certainly didn't feel like a "woman" and I knew perfectly well that the butcher didn't think I was, either. Besides, it was cheaper to buy meat at the supermarket. Why did he have to do this? Why did he have to keep playing these down-home scenes? We were a couple of out-of-work actors living together. Why couldn't he let it go at that?

But he couldn't. He kept wanting us to be respectable. And *he* wanted to be respectable. The way he conducted his professional life, for example, as if it were normal. He got up at seven-thirty in the morning. I didn't know anyone who got up at seven-thirty in the morning except my father. But what your parents do doesn't count; and, even if it did, my father had somewhere to go—work—so he had a reason to get up at that hour.

For the first week or so after moving in, I lurched out of bed after him, because I thought a wife, even a pseudo-wife, was supposed to fix breakfast for her husband. I quit when I noticed that he seemed to like fixing his own breakfast. After his shower, during which he actually sang tenor arias, he would shave; then, in his pants and nothing else and carrying his shoes and socks, he'd walk into the kitchen whistling, pull things out of the refrigerator, sit down at the makeshift kitchen table—a wide shelf that folded out from the wall—and eat, putting on his shoes and socks between mouthfuls. Then, suddenly, he was dressed, sometimes in a suit, always a tie, and he'd grab his book of photographs and résumés from its place on the bottom of the bookshelf, give me one of those smack kisses that Dagwood used to give Blondie, and he was gone.

Anyone watching would think he had somewhere to go.

Sometimes I'd linger in the kitchen with the smell of toast and after-shave mingling oddly in the air, and try to imagine where he *did* go and what he was doing. Technically, I knew. He was "making rounds," as they were called—which amounted to unsolicited personal appearances at the offices of agents and producers in order to remind them of your existence, so that *if* a part came along that you were "right" for, maybe, just maybe, they'd think of you. Or maybe they'd see your glossy photograph, in which you have tried to look like someone someone would want, among the tens or hundreds left in the "In" box, and on the basis of Bruno of Hollywood's rendition of your face, consider you for a part.

So I knew what he was doing. What I didn't know—and continued not to know even after he'd tell me about his day, which he always did—was what his day did to him. As long as I knew Greg, he never spoke about how he felt going out there, all clean and dressed up and kindly disposed toward the world, winding up, as I knew he must have, with the remains of his pride and dignity hanging from his person like the carcass of a dog roped to the back fender of a car. How did he feel, for example, as he offered himself for sale to the receptionist? Because only occasionally, when one made rounds, did one get to see a real live producer or agent. Some actors considered it a morning well spent if an agent or producer walked through the reception area on his or her way to the bathroom, in which case one could say a bright "Hi!" Or maybe even get in one's name.

It was a long, long time after we broke up before I began to understand that the reason Greg never talked about all of this was that if he did, he might not be able to continue doing it.

And he was committed to doing it. That was part of his character. He had decided to be an actor, and he was determined to do whatever he had to do to act. But it was clear that no one had prepared him, any more than they had prepared me, for the central perversity: that the primary requisite of being an actor was learning to adjust to not acting. And he could not adjust to that. . . . Nor was Class a solution for him, the way it was for me. He needed to work to get paid. He needed to work and get paid like a man.

Yet he wasn't miserable. Not facing any of this helped. So did his nine-year-old freckled brother, Freddie. Every day after rounds, he'd pick up Freddie after school and take him to a gym. I never knew exactly what they did at the gym, but whatever it was, it did the trick. By the time he came home, he had regained whatever the rest of the day took from him. He had his shine back. It was, as I think of it now, an odd pattern: castration in the morning; body-building in the afternoon.

He also built *things*. He virtually rebuilt his apartment, which had a lot of rooms—about five—all so small that together they would have fitted inside the living room on West End Avenue. For each room he made shelves, bookcases, even furniture, like the bed—a great big thing, which took up almost the entire bedroom, so that in order to make it, you had to lie on it.

For my part, I tried, at least, to be a good housekeeper. I was better at it than I thought I'd be. I learned hospital corners, I learned how to take a stove apart and how to keep white clothing white; I learned a lot. But one thing I did not learn was how to gracefully coexist with our uninvited boarders, the Second Avenue cockroaches.

We bought poison. We bought more poison. We practiced fastidiousness of an order I wouldn't have thought possible of myself or anyone who ingested food. Nothing worked. One evening we came home from the movies and I went into the kitchen to make a cup of tea and turned the light on, and there was such a sudden, massive, repulsive scattering of cockroaches that I burst into tears.

"What are you crying for?" Greg said, sounding cross. "They're only bugs."

"Only bugs!" I screamed. "They're not 'only bugs.' They're disgusting, horrible, awf—"

But he went into the bedroom and slammed the door.

"What's the matter with you?" I shouted at the door. No answer.

I sat down on the living-room sofa and picked at the frayed arm with my fingernail. I've done it again, I thought. I seemed always to be hurting his feelings, lately, without meaning to. Now I've insulted his cockroaches. No, *our* cockroaches . . . or are they? They are if it's our apartment. Greg wants it to be our apartment, I thought. He wants it to be our everything. He acts as if it is. And so do I, in a way. But I don't feel it. Inside, I don't want it to be that way. . . . And it's not the cockroaches and it's not the apartment. Actually, it's a nice apartment; he made it nice. The thought of how hard he worked on the apartment suddenly made my eyes fill up. . . . The trouble is, I thought, I have feelings for Greg, but I don't love him. I sat up straight. It was awful to say that even to myself. Maybe I'm wrong, I thought. I don't even know for sure what love is. Maybe when you live with someone and see them every day you can't love them. I've heard people say it turns into a different kind of love. But I didn't remember feeling the first kind. . . except when we kissed the first few times in the play. But that's not love. Is it? I don't really want to know the answer. Because whatever it is, it will be bad. If it's not love that I feel for Greg, then that's bad, because then I shouldn't stay here. And if it *is* love, that's bad, too. Because it's not the way I want love to be.

CHAPTER
4

The next day I went out looking for work. An actress friend had just made a pile of money doing a "voice-over" (that's when you're heard, but not seen) for a commercial, and had generously offered to send me to see her agent. "How young can you sound?" said the agent, looking at me through the smoke of her cigarette and above her bifocals. "Two?" I said.

The following week I found myself in a sound studio in front of a microphone, in the employ of a textile company, which had made an animated film about itself. The movie had five characters, and I had been hired to read three: Dacron, age seven; Nylon, age five; and Polyester, age two. Seven hours of baby talk nearly destroyed my larynx. But when I got home that night, I felt wonderful. This was the start, I was sure, of a whole new career.

"If I can be Dacron," I said to Greg, slapping the dinner table, "I can be Minnie Mouse!"—not realizing, of course, that the Disney characters had long been bagged by a flotilla of regulars on the West Coast.

A few weeks later, when it sank in that my future as a mouse seemed less than inevitable, I sat down on a small bench Greg had built next to the telephone and took stock the way I used to in the Astor phone booth; except these days I wasn't crying.

Who *needs* this? I thought. Who needs to act? I don't even need to make money. Lucy pays my rent uptown. Greg pays the $67.50 it costs to live here. Greg doesn't even like me to buy any of our food. Greg wants me to be a housewife. Well, why not, I thought. If I really throw myself into it, I won't even notice the damn cockroaches.

I began reading cookbooks. I focused on spaghetti recipes. Spaghetti with things. Spaghetti with meatballs. Spaghetti with (my mother needn't ever know) bacon. Spaghetti with green peas. Spaghetti with chicken. Spaghetti with spaghetti.

Now that I was a housewife, we entertained. That is, we shared our spaghetti. Leo came over a couple of times. That didn't work. Greg thought Leo talked too much and Leo thought Greg was White Bread. Neither of them said that, but they didn't have to. It made me sad, because Leo was like my brother. And it bothered me that Greg and I seemed to be so separate from the rest of my life. He didn't like my Sarah Lawrence friends, either—or maybe it was their boyfriends, most of whom were in law school, that he didn't like. They made him gloomy. And he felt the girls on West End Avenue looked down on him, which they sort of did. They thought of him as a chorus boy, a dumb blond. Gradually, I stopped seeing them.

I had one other friend, a psychiatric intern at Bellevue, whom instinctively I kept away from Greg. Richard was thin and serious and very wise, or at least I thought so. He was always giving me advice, which I usually took. Sometimes it was about a book he thought I should read or a film—Ingmar Bergman, usually—he thought I should see. And sometimes he practiced psychiatry on me. He was the first person who suggested that even if my mother found out I was living with an actor in a sixth-floor walk-up apartment in the East Twenties, instead of where she thought I was—on West End Avenue with two other Sarah Lawrence girls—my life would not be over. What could she do about it? he'd say. Have me arrested? Beat me? None of that made me less afraid, but it was reassuring to know that I wasn't supposed to be afraid of my mother and that someday, maybe, I wouldn't be.

Having Richard for a friend was like having one's own private genie. He'd come out of his bottle, say something smart, and vanish. Years later, when I began to see a psychoanalyst (Richard later became one himself), he vanished altogether. I liked to think it was because he was coming out of other people's bottles, but I never knew. As for Richard and Leo, they, too, like Greg and Leo, were fish and fowl. There was no hostility; just indifference. My mother met Richard once and liked him. She couldn't understand why I didn't marry him. She tolerated Leo. She never met Greg.

The challenge of learning newer, greater, cheaper spaghetti dishes began, finally, to pall. Moreover, the cockroaches had won the war. I knew it, they knew it. And I was sure they knew I knew it.

I began to steel myself to make acting rounds when, altogether unexpectedly, a very different sort of job came along. The uncle of a Sarah Lawrence chum, who was a writer, knew another writer, who was looking for someone to do research. I told my friend I didn't know how to do research, but she said if I could read, I could do research, and the pay was good—four dollars an hour. I said okay. It wasn't acting; it wasn't even Minnie Mouse; but it wasn't spaghetti, either.

The writer's name was Morton Hunt and he lived in a huge—or so it seemed to me—apartment on Central Park

West with his family and a lot of bookshelves packed with books. I told him I hadn't *exactly* done any research before, but I was sure I could do it and he said he was sure I could, too. Everything was fine until he told me the name of the book he wanted me to research: *The Natural History of Love.* "Don't worry," he laughed, noticing that I had paled. "It's sociology. All you have to do is read about past customs in library books and make notes."

My, he was kind. And, even more important, he made himself clear about what he wanted and where it could be found. He was the first, and happily not the last, of the employers I've had who were natural teachers. "As you read, pay attention to what grabs you," he told me once, having asked me to skim some material for him. "Chances are, if it grabs you, it'll grab other people, too. Same goes when you interview someone."

The other nice part about learning from employers was that, unlike school, they pay *you*. As a result, I found I learned better. I also started having a good time. I liked the idea of going to a library with a funded mission. And the New York Public Library itself was wonderful. Just walking in that place, up the wide, white stone steps, past the stone lions and inside the mammoth doors into the marble-floored, echoing rotunda, did for me probably what Greg's gym did for him. No one invited me to the library, but I felt invited. I had something to do here and it was something I *could* do—by myself. No agents, no pushing, no selling. Just me and my (apparently still intact) brain. And the more I got to know my way around—where to find what; how to use the card catalogue; how to get help when I needed it, instead of stammering incoherently as I did the first day—the better I felt.

Then it was over. I delivered the last batch of notes to Morton Hunt and he handed me a check. "I'll call you up when I get going on another project," he said, sensing my sadness. "Oh, great!" I said, trying to hide it.

Instead of going home, I called Richard. He was on a break, but it was almost over, so we decided to meet in the hospital cafeteria. "I feel awful," I said.

"What about?"

"I finished that research job and now I have to be an unemployed actress again."

"Why?"

"What do you mean why?" I said. "What else am I supposed to do?"

"Do your own book."

"Don't be dumb. How am I supposed to do that?"

"Think something up." He stirred his coffee. I took a swallow of mine and burned the roof of my mouth.

"You're crazy ... I can't do a book. You have to be a writer to do a book.... What kind of a book?"

"Well, it's only a thought, but I've been reading this book about sex in history — not so different from the subject you've been researching, I think. Anyway, one section of the book is about marriage vows. Some of them are incredible. And there's gotta be more where they came from ..."

I took another sip of coffee — it was cooler now — and stared at him. "You mean I could maybe collect — a collection of marriage vows?"

"Yeah, why not?" He smiled his genie smile.

"Of course, it's *totally* ridiculous," I said, looking at him hard. "How many marriage vows were there in this book?"

"About six."

"Six. How do I know I could find more?"

"You don't know. Until you look."

"Even if I could find them," I said slowly, "what makes you think anyone would want to publish a collection of marriage vows?"

"Maybe nobody will. But you won't know until you try."

I said not one word to Greg or to Leo or to anyone. But the next morning I got up early and as soon as Greg had left headed uptown for the library. I ran up the same stone steps I had been walking up for weeks, then up the stairway inside, to the second floor and into the main room. I faced the card catalogue, caught my breath and headed straight for the M's. There it was: "Marriage: Customs and Vows." I started ordering books.

By the end of the afternoon, there were four candidates: a Quaker vow from 1690 which began, "Friends, in the fear of the Lord and in the presence of you his people I take this my friend...to be my wife..."; an old Mohammedan marriage vow in which the groom says, "Give thyself in marriage to me for 1000 [coins of some sort]. Bride: I will not do so except for 2000 ..."; old English vows in a marriage by proxy; and a Chinese Communist vow in which both bride and groom promise "to love ... live in harmony ... and to strive jointly ... for the building up of a new society."

Still, I told no one. The next day, after Greg left, I hit the Yellow Pages. Under Churches, I found Baha'i. I dialed the number. A faint voice answered. I asked for "the—uh—priest, please."

Another, still fainter, voice came on the phone. "Yes?"

"Hello," I said cheerily, "I'm collecting marriage vows for a book and I've got some lovely old ones and I thought it would be nice to—uh—include a modern one from the Baha'i religion."

"Of course," said the voice, as if it were the eighth request he'd had that day. "What would you like to know?"

"Well, what—what exactly *is* your marriage vow?" I said. No answer, so I went on. "You know, what is it exactly that people of your religion say—on the threshold—before they—do it?"

41

"Oh yes, I see," he said. "May we send you the information you require by mail?"

"Of *course*," I said, trying not to sound inappropriately excited.

It came three days later in a long, thick envelope addressed to Mrs. Betty Rolling. There was so much material on the church itself, it took a few seconds before I saw the attached typewritten note: "Baha'i Marriage Ceremony," it said. Then: "The Speaker addresses bride and groom: The hearts of man and wife must be spacious as the universe; their ideas luminous, their thoughts lofty; and both must dedicate their knowledge, their bodies and their spirits. . . . Do you accept the Will of God? The bride and groom answer, Verily we accept the Will of God."

I began to count on my fingers: four from the library, this one makes five, plus maybe five from Richard's book, that's ten. . . . This is going to work, I thought. This is going to work.

Greg got a commercial! Spaghetti and steak! A place to go in the morning three days in a row! He was thrilled. I was thrilled. Leo was thrilled. I forget the product, but whatever it was, we revered it. When he finished shooting, Greg suggested I try to get a commercial, too. "Do you think I could?" I said, while "what would Sandy Meisner think?" was what I thought. But I knew what Sandy Meisner thought was no longer the issue. Like it or not, I had become a citizen of the Real World. And in the Real World, as I had begun to learn, you take what you can get.

But the laugh was on me. The princess descended from her high horse, and her little foot landed in a little pile of manure. Nobody wanted me to sell their toothpaste—or anything else. I—Greg and I both—had overlooked that we were different species. Greg was straight-nosed and square-jawed, blond and gentile. In 1960, he was whom American industry wanted selling its products. There was, to be sure, a female version of Greg whom American industry wanted selling its "female" products (i.e., things that cleaned other things). With my dark hair and eyes and less than pale complexion, I wasn't it. Nor was I dark *enough* to fit into the exotic category. "Forget it, honey," an agent told me once when I asked him to send me up for a Ronzoni commercial. "You gotta be an ethnic for this one, and you ain't no ethnic!" I felt sorry for myself until a black actress I knew reminded me that if you were black, you were not considered in any of the above categories. You were simply not considered.

Like me, Leo also fell between the ethnic cracks on Madison Avenue. Like me, he wasn't scoring on Broadway, either. But at least I kept trying—not as diligently as Greg, but I did force myself to make rounds at least once a week. Leo's problem was that doing rounds literally gave him indigestion. He'd walk into one of those producer's or agent's reception areas, take one look at the "In" box piled high with eight-by-ten glossies into which he was expected to drop his, and his entire gastric system would stage a revolution. He felt better about it when he got his chest X rays reproduced and began dropping *them* in along with his résumés. And eventually he took another tack, which helped his stomach but not his career. He began writing letters, like this one, which went to a casting director of a theatrical packaging company:

Washington's Birthday, 1960

Dear Miss Terry,

I am writing you from the top of the Empire State Building. I have enough food for ninety-seven hours. If I don't hear from you within that time ... I shall jump. And it will be all your fault. I am sorry I must resort to such drastic measures to get a job out of you; you are such a nice person. But as you know, this can be a nasty business. It is no use calling the police as I am disguised . . . Remember, my future is in your hands. This is a great opportunity for you.

Don't mess it up.

Yours,
Leo Bloom

Another letter followed:

Dear Miss Terry,

I am writing to you from a flagpole off the eighty-third floor of the Empire State Building. I thought I would give you another chance, so I grabbed it on my way down. I have one hand free, and so I am able to type . . .

I began to worry about Leo. The letters were harmless, but gradually he seemed to forget their purpose: namely, to get him jobs (which they weren't). Instead, he got carried away writing the letters themselves. Lately, whenever I'd call him on the telephone, he'd say, "Oh, hi—listen, I'm in the middle of a letter. Can I call you back?" And then two days would go by before he did. Once he called to say that Garson Kanin actually had written him back.

"Great!" I said. "Is he putting you in his play?"

"I don't think so," said Leo, in a way that made me feel vulgar for asking. "It's a terrific letter, though. Wanna hear it?"

Meanwhile, I had decided to cool it somewhat on the marriage-vow front. I'd keep it alive, but I would not let myself get hopeful about it. In the three years out of college, I had sent up enough kites and watched them tear on enough branches.

"I just don't feel like having a big letdown," I said to

Richard at the hospital one day, "over a bunch of dumb marriage vows."

"Does that mean you're giving up?"

"Of *course* not," I said. "It just means I'm not going to get all worked up about it. And I'm not going to daydream about happy endings!"

So I pushed on—guardedly.

Then I got lucky. One of my "roommates" in the apartment on West End Avenue—Joanna—had a boyfriend who worked at Doubleday. He was a very tall, serious, young editor, named Bob, and he liked the idea, which I almost didn't catch because he sounded so sober when he said so. He also used words I didn't understand.

"Make a dummy," he said, which, I found out later, meant a presentation. "It wouldn't hurt to have a few illustrations."

"You mean—pictures?" I said meekly.

"I mean drawings," he said. "Find an artist."

Find an artist. Thanks a lot. But wait . . . there was that girl a couple of classes ahead of me at school . . . what was her name? She had illustrated some children's books . . . and she wrote, too . . . one of those people who was good at everything . . . Sheila something—Sheila Greenwald, that was it. I called Sheila Greenwald. She loved the idea. She drew funny pictures. I typed. We made a dummy. We put it in a new manila envelope I bought at Woolworth's. I took it to the reception desk at Doubleday, and laid it down carefully. The lady there assured me that Bob would get it. Then I went back into the subway, and home. And waited. And waited. After three days I called Joanna. Had Bob mentioned anything to her? He hadn't. I hung up the phone and got mad at myself for caring. It was exactly what I had promised myself I wouldn't do.

The call came late in the afternoon on the following day.

Greg's commercial was long over, and he had just come back from his routine at the gym. He was sitting in a chair, unlacing his sneakers and pulling them off when the phone rang. I was on my way into the kitchen to start dinner, but I bolted at the first ring and got to the receiver on the second.

It was a short conversation, less than a minute. Bob said he didn't have the details yet, but he did want to let me know that Doubleday wanted to publish the book. I put the receiver down and stared at Greg. "They're going to do it," I said in a voice that didn't sound like mine. "They're going to publish the book."

For a few seconds there was an odd silence. Neither of us spoke and neither of us moved. Then a very strange thing happened. Greg placed his shoes under the table where he was sitting, put his arm on the table, lowered his head onto his arm, and started to cry.

I was stunned. Really stunned. "Wh-why are you crying?" I whispered. He picked up his head and looked at me. His eyes were red and his face was wet.

"You're going to leave me," he said in a terrible, cracked voice. I looked at him hard.

"That's a—crazy—thing to say."

But I knew that it wasn't.

Two months later, I left. The book was, undeniably, a cause. Not because getting it published made me uppity. It didn't do that, and I don't think Greg thought it did. First of all, there was nothing to get uppity about. It wasn't as if I had written a real book—or even that I had dreamed one up. Richard had done that. And if my friend's current boyfriend hadn't had a job in publishing, I wouldn't have known how to sell it, either. So getting the book published did not make me feel like hot stuff. But it did make me feel good. Very good. It did provide me with a small but very potent shot of success at a moment when I longed for it, even more than I knew. I would have preferred a theatrical success. But psychologically, this did the trick. A win is a win.

The fifteen-hundred-dollar advance also provided me with paid employment for a while. (In those days, with or without Greg, I could live on a few hundred dollars a month, including rent and movies on Forty-second Street, without even feeling deprived.)

Unlike doing research for other people, doing research for myself also meant that for the first time in my life I was the boss. And the fact that I was also the employee did nothing to diminish that. Being the boss of myself put at least a temporary end to the Eighth-Avenue-doorway-here-I-am-doesn't-anybody-want-me syndrome. Being the boss made me feel like the parent instead of the child. It made me feel powerful. And happy. And, ultimately, it made me feel lonely, because I couldn't share the happiness with Greg. I didn't blame Greg for this. I understood, even though at the time I probably couldn't have explained it, that I couldn't expect Greg to share the joys of power and autonomy (however two-bit) when he had none himself. That's asking a lot of a man in any era. In 1960, it was asking for the moon.

There was no conversation about any of this. Conversation wasn't necessary. All I had to do, every time the subject of the book came up, was to look at Greg's face. So I tried not to let the subject come up. If I came upon a juicy vow that made me want to click my heels, I clicked them by myself. Or I called Richard. Or Leo.

But it wasn't the same. I remember thinking, it's funny, Greg would have shared my sorrow, had I had any. If something awful had happened to me, he would have been right there. That's what counts, I told myself. But then I started asking myself some questions. I can hide this, I thought, but what if something else good happens to me? Will

I have to hide it, too? Answer: Yes. So, then, the only way this relationship will work, the only way *not* to make this man miserable is for me to be a flop? Answer: Yes. But that sounds nutty. Can it be true? Yes. Oh, sad to say, Yes.

What's the best way to leave someone? Quickly. I knew that much. Best to pull off Band-Aids fast. But do you pull when the person's looking? Or do you sneak it? The latter, I decided, not altogether selflessly.

It was May. Greg had gotten work at a small regional theater in New England. He would be gone two weeks. There was no hurry, but I acted fast anyway. It took only two days—both to pack and write the letter. When I was ready, I watered the plants. Then I called Leo. I told him what I was doing and that I needed help getting my suitcases down the six flights of stairs. He was writing a letter, but he said he could get there in a couple of hours. Fine, I said. And he did.

Going back to West End Avenue was like going back to college. It was gay (old meaning of the word); it was boisterous; it was girlish; it was hot and cold running boyfriends (Joanna once hid one under her bed while we stalled the one who had painted her piano at the door); it was *Wonderful Town* instead of *Waiting for Lefty* and I was ready for a little music. (Good thing, too, since Joanna practiced her singing at home.)

It was odd to be sleeping in that narrow bed again. I didn't mind, though. I felt guilty and sad about Greg and a bigger bed would have made me guiltier and sadder.

Of course, I wasn't *that* guilty or sad. Mostly, I felt astoundingly cheerful.

It was definitely all right to be happy here.

It was also nice—for the first time in eight months—to be able to answer the phone when my mother called.

I *Thee Wed* turned out to be pretty cute—and quite a little hit it was, too. It didn't exactly look like a book, any more than a doll looks like a baby. Really, it turned out to be a fifty-six-page greeting card between hard covers—white, naturally, bound in pink, with a drawing of a bride and groom, flanked by a bunch of chubby cupids.

The publisher sold both first and second serial rights (that meant excerpts appeared in magazines and newspapers both before and after publication) and a respectable number of books were sold as well, about 8,000. I engineered some of the sales myself, in a way that was more outrageous than I knew. It did not occur to me, as I walked into Tiffany & Co., a pack of books under my arm as if they were Fuller Brushes, that it was neither seemly nor legal for an author to peddle her own books on Fifth Avenue. Which is probably why it panned out. I asked to speak to the manager of Tiffany in the Long Island Lockjaw I had selected as the accent which would best advance my purpose, and worked the poor man over until he gave in. Wouldn't it be *divine* to have a little collection of marriage vows right here in the stationery department near the wedding invitations? The setting *couldn't* be more perfect!

Tiffany bought one hundred books.

Next I hit the Plaza, modifying the Lockjaw somewhat, but employing a similar pitch. Wouldn't it be a *lovely* surprise for a honeymooning couple to find the book in their room? *So* much more original than flowers!

Sold to the Plaza: one hundred and fifty books.

Meanwhile, the promotion department began getting bites from the media: *The New York Times* Women's Page (it was still called that then) ran an interview slugged, "COLLEGE GIRLS TURN BRIGHT IDEA INTO BOOK." Not too accurate, but who cared? They even got me on some radio and television shows—among them, *Who* (sic) *Do You Trust?*, hosted by a popular new daytime star, Johnny Carson.

Suddenly, my acting career revived. I ignored the remnants of any feelings of refinement or modesty I once had and brought the book along to appointments with agents, and they sat up and took notice. I began getting sent out on auditions again and I began getting jobs. What had happened was that I had a gimmick, like Leo's letters, like the brass horn of the stripper in *Gypsy*. Some world. But I didn't waste time feeling cynical about it. My days of kidding myself about Art had passed like rainfall into a sewer. I wanted to work as an actress. If a bunch of type between hard covers helped, never mind that it was stupid and unfair. Never mind where it came from, as Meisner would have said about an unexpected flash that made a scene come alive: use it.

CHAPTER
5

God makes such monkeys out of us. Cockily, we gear up for what we assume is in store. We chart our little courses, rig our little boats; then, three miles offshore, wham! And what manner of wham it is depends on whether, on that particular day, He feels like wiping you out or just scaring the hell out of you.

It would be one thing if God were simply a spoilsport. At least, then, you'd be prepared. But He's no more a spoilsport than he is Santa Claus. That much you know by how little attention He pays to who's been naughty and who's been nice. Prayer, for that reason, has always struck me as a strange conceit. "My prayers were answered," you hear people say. Oh, yeah? Why yours and not that woman's next to you whose child has leukemia? What makes you think He paid attention to what you want and not to what she wants? Because you asked nicely?

Oh, there's *some* justice, some reaping of what has been sown. One had some control over one's small patch of dirt. But a capricious God is still in charge of the big computer in the sky.

I know, I'm digressing. I meant merely to sigh about all the energy, tension, and hope one puts into the act of going forward, only to be so frequently and deftly clobbered from the rear. By disease, for example, or for another, by love. The first man I loved (there have been two)—the man who turned me like a top, then infused me with more longing and pain than I knew it was possible to feel—hit my life like a car on a sidewalk.

Even though I wanted to get hit, the chanciness of it made an impression on me. A negative impression. I didn't like knowing that important things could be that chancy. At the time, I remember, it threw me into paroxysms of what-ifs. What if I hadn't been home when he came by the first time? What if his flight hadn't happened to come through New York, in which case he wouldn't have come by at all? What if I had looked awful when he first saw me—and, therefore, he surely would not have wanted to see me again? What if I had still been living with Greg? What if everything.

There were no violins when I met Daniel Moore. More like a low drum roll. It was a cool summer evening. I was living in one of those charming-if-you-squint sublet apartments—a studio walk-up in the East Eighties. An actress I knew, and didn't even like much, came by with her boyfriend, who had a crew cut and whom I had always found awfully rah-rah, and his friend from California—Dan. He was a law student, she had told me on the phone, in town for a few days to raise money for a project (?) and how would I like to join them for dinner? Love to, I said. Why not, I thought.

Something about him threw me right away. He didn't fit in a category. He was large and western and had a lot of straight white teeth like the son of the movie star in my acting class; but his eyes were small and intelligent, like Richard's, and his fingers were narrow and bony, like an old person's. He laughed a lot, but when he wasn't laughing he looked almost alarmingly somber. He seemed more worldly than the rest of us, but he drank beer and sat with his legs wide apart like a college boy. "That's okay," he said, stopping me as I went into the kitchen for a glass, signaling that he preferred to drink beer from the can. But it wasn't a macho routine. This was not a man who did things for effect.

He didn't seem to want to talk about himself. In my world, that was noticeable. His friend Brian wanted to talk about him, though, and did in a tone which struck me as odd. During the next few months I heard that tone so often when people spoke about Dan that, although the precise word eluded me, I knew where it fit: halfway between respectful and reverent.

"Lemme *tell* you what this guy is doing," said Brian, leaning forward with his elbows on his knees. "He's gonna *save* the Indians of this country and he's doing it, *himself*—raising *private money*—none of this government handout stuff. *Private* money."

Having never seen a conservative Republican close up, I didn't catch the significance of "private money" right away. But from the way Brian said it, I knew it must be good. "It's *virtually* in the bag," Brian went on, taking a swig of beer and looking over at Dan. "Isn't that right, Moore?"

"Well," said Dan, blushing, "let's say we're at the starting line. With another few hundred thousand, we might be able to get something going—in the Southwest at least." Big, shy grin plus flash of big, white teeth.

"Wait a minute," I said. "I'm confused. I thought you were in law school."

Brian slapped his thigh. "He's in law school, *too*," he shouted before Dan had a chance to answer. "He's doin' this on the goddam *side*. I'm telling you, Moore, someday you're gonna be president of the goddam *country*."

"I don't remember hiring you as my campaign manager," said Dan, laughing uncomfortably. Then to me: "Got any more beer?"

"Oh, *sure*," I said, springing up, as if by electrical charge. "Sure no glass?"

"Sure."

We went to dinner at a checkered-tablecloth place in the neighborhood. Brian calmed down (with some urging from his girlfriend) and I got Dan to talk about his project himself. The idea had crystallized, he said, during a field trip he had been on in college, which took him to some Indian reservations in New Mexico and Arizona. He had never seen anything like the poverty there—not enough water, he said, and people sending their children far away to federal boarding schools because that was the only way they'd get three meals. He knew perfectly well, he said, that he couldn't make a real change in people's lives (I was transfixed; imagine even thinking about such things), but he thought there must be a way "to get some young people down there to help—to do *something*. No handouts, you understand, just helping people to—help themselves.... So," he went on, since I seemed to be neither speaking nor breathing, "I started to raise a little money."

"Just like that?" I said, having finally relocated my larynx.

He took another bite of his hamburger, at which point I realized I hadn't even started mine. "Well," he said with a shrug, "I know a few people." I can't remember what led up to it, but he dropped one other stunning piece of information that evening. He said he was a Christian Scientist. I should have known how smitten I was by the way I received the news—as if it were fascinating and reasonable, instead of fascinating and loony, which, until that moment, was how Christian Science had always struck me.

Brian and my actress friend were, by now, launched in

their own conversation about (what else?) some audition she had screwed up. Dan ordered another beer. I began to try to eat. The beer came. Dan took a sip and looked at me over the rim. "Brian tells me you're an actress and that you wrote a book."

"Oh, no," I said, shaking my head and swallowing the hamburger too fast, so that it made me cough. "It's just a collection of (cough) marriage vows. It's only fifty-six pages. It's hardly a book at all....It's just that if you have something between hard covers, all of a sudden you're Hemingway!...I mean I can't even (cough) write!"

"What about acting?" he said quietly.

"Oh, I do that now and then. But it's pretty difficult. I mean, there's a lot of competition."

What would a guy like this want with me? Then a second thought, which hit me like a cramp: if, at that moment, he had asked me to leave the entire contents of my life on the red plastic seat next to us in the restaurant and go off with him— anywhere—I would have.

It was many months before he did ask me to do that. By the time he did, I had almost nothing to leave.

After that first date there was an immediate second, then a third, and fourth. Mostly we talked. We'd go to a cheap restaurant, he'd eat a lot, I'd try to eat a little, we'd talk and then he'd take me home and he'd sit on the sofa and I'd sit on the armchair next to the sofa, and he'd drink beer and I'd sip club soda and we'd talk more. About his work more than anything, but also about his family, friends, and, when I questioned him about them, his past girlfriends, who all sounded cute, blond, and *good*. I guess I talked about those same things in my life—carefully leaving out anything that I thought made me sound less than wonderful, without really being sure what his version of wonderful was. I talked about acting as if it were all pretty exciting and told the *I Thee Wed* story with embellishments, which made him laugh. I tried to sound happy. In a way it felt like an audition. In a way, hell. It *was* an audition.

When it got to be after midnight, he'd get up and I'd get up and we'd kiss, whereupon my body would lose its bone and muscle and turn to sinew and string.

Yet he did not, I noticed, nudge me into the bedroom. I hoped it was his religion or something, and not that he didn't want to.

And then, unexpectedly, on one of those dates, he wanted to.

Then, like a phantom, he was gone—back to California, and to law school.

We continued to talk in letters. I had never had such conversations on paper before. About life. About Indians. I went to the library and looked them up, and tried to memorize names of tribes: Pima-Maricopa, Mohave-Apache, Papago ... We were silly sometimes, too. Dan even wrote jokes. Generally, I hated jokes and his were pretty corny, but I found them hilarious.

Gradually, he began to say things in his letters about my coming out there. They weren't romantic things, exactly, more like: "I did this interesting thing or spoke to this interesting person and you would have found it or him interesting, too, and it's too bad you're not here, but maybe we can change that ..."

Just say the word, I thought, just say the word.

Finally, he did. "It would be great if you could come out here. You could help with the project and we could have fun, too. I can't pay for your air ticket, but you can stay with me here and ..."

Goodbye, West End Avenue! Goodbye, skinny bed! Goodbye, Joanna's mandarin oranges! Goodbye, Broadway subway! Goodbye, Broadway! Goodbye, Leo, Mother—I'm—uh—going to California to try to get work in—uh—television. Goodbye!

Dan had a furnished apartment on the top floor of a dilapidated three-story shingle house. The furniture was strictly flophouse—unmatched upholstered once-plump chairs and sofas with faded rose slipcovers, hanging from them like shawls on old women. The biggest, brightest room was the kitchen, which, inexplicably, had been painted fire-engine red.

I did most of my stenciling on a white Formica table near the window. I stenciled maps for fund-raising brochures of areas in the country most densely populated by Indians. I was good at it. I had a steady hand. All those Saturday afternoons of my childhood propped up in front of easels must have helped.

I loved helping Dan. Of course, I never felt I did enough. Whenever I said that, he contradicted me. He said I helped a lot. He said that I especially helped him "make decisions about people." I felt wonderful when he said that. He even complimented me on all my spaghetti recipes. Although, by now, a lot of money was coming in for the Project, Dan wanted us to live on as little as we could.

I never questioned Dan. Nor did I criticize him, any more than I would have criticized a director for whom I was reading a part in a play.

And never had I wanted a part the way I wanted this one.

Sometimes we'd go out and meet friends for a Chinese dinner in San Francisco. We'd climb on Dan's motor scooter and shoot over the Oakland Bridge. I'd wrap my arms around his middle and put the side of my head against his back and we'd fly. I didn't feel happy, exactly—after all, I didn't have the part yet—but it felt good just to want it as much as I did, to be so sure. I had never before been so sure about what I wanted. It was exhilarating—and frightening, too.

I was pretty sure Dan liked to go to bed with me. But I began to sense it embarrassed him to have me living with him—not that he said anything to make me feel that way. Well, once he did say something, sort of. There were some "dedicated young Christians"—Project volunteers—who, Dan explained to me carefully one day, were somewhat "surprised" to learn I was living in his apartment. The day before, one of them had asked me where I was staying in Berkeley. It was a question I didn't expect, but one I certainly did not mind answering.

"Here, of course," I said merrily. "With Dan."

That did it.

Not that I gave one hoot about the Dedicated Christians. Most of them, as far as I could see, had bad skins and skinny upper arms and I never thought it was an accident that they did most of their hanging around at mealtimes. But they were the disciples and I was Mary Magdalene and we all knew who had the bigger claim to Right.

I could have moved into another apartment in Berkeley, but where would the rent money have come from?

It would be best, we decided, if I went to Los Angeles—at least for a while. In Los Angeles, I could probably find work as an actress—or so we hoped—and it was close enough to Berkeley for an occasional weekend visit.

That I felt miserable about leaving Berkeley mattered not at all, not even to me. Misery and pleasure weren't important then. It was important only to please Dan. I didn't always know what would please him. But when I did know, action followed. In November I went to Los Angeles.

To my surprise, I rather liked Los Angeles. I liked the looming palm trees on Sunset Boulevard, and the clear, dry heat in January seemed magical. I also managed to find one of those perfect, quirky living arrangements, with a blond tap dancer named Moira, whose husband had just left her with a broken heart, a baby, and a house in the Hollywood Hills. Through an actor friend in New York, I found out that she had been looking for a roommate, both for rent money and for somebody to talk to.

Poor Moira. When I moved in, she was still bleeding. "Honey," she'd say, and her sky-blue eyes would fill up and spill over, "I don't know what I did to that man to make him want to leave me and Mary Alice." (She hadn't done a thing. He had simply found another blond tap dancer.) By accident, we saw them together on Easter Sunday at a table near the window at The House of Pancakes. Moira started to cry while we were still behind the rope, waiting for a table, and then the baby began to act up and knocked a jar of syrup off a passing tray. So we went home and ate Easter eggs.

I loved Moira. I had never known anyone like her. She was beautiful and good and kept wanting to think the best of everyone, no matter what they did to her. (Unfortunately, she was a born patsy and they did plenty.) I think she loved me, too. She also respected me—to a degree that became embarrassing—because I had gone to college. She thought that made me smart. Naturally, I'd tell her how silly that was. She wouldn't listen. She was rooted to the idea that everything she wasn't was better than everything she was. Moira never quite understood what Dan was up to with the Indians, but, as far as she was concerned, since he went to law school he had to be a genius.

It was a hard time for her, and although I didn't think of it that way then, it was a hard time for me, too. But it would have been a lot harder for both of us if we didn't have each other. At home and away from home, the moral is, a girl needs girlfriends. I still do. We just don't call it that anymore.

As for getting work as an actress, my timing, by accident, was on the money. There were loads of parts in television sit-coms and, although there have always been several hundred actors in Hollywood available to fill any one part at any time, there was a certain cachet, still, to being from New York. The migration of New York actors who left their dark apartments and arrived (squinting) on the West Coast had begun, but it had not yet peaked. Many were still skeptical of what lay out there: "California offers entirely new and even greater opportunities for unemployment!" the joke went. So, many actors lingered in New York.

Which meant I beat the crowd. It seemed, however, my type had changed. In Hollywood I was not an ingenue. Ingenues in Hollywood were blond eighteen-year-olds from Fresno and Terre Haute. Also, I could speak. That made me "offbeat," a "character ingenue," which was just as well, since most plays had only one "ingenue-ingenue"; whereas there were usually at least two or three "character ingenues" and/or just plain "characters." Later on, after I said something funny once at the William Morris Agency, I became a "comic character ingenue."

William Morris, meanwhile, the most powerful and august representatives of performing flesh in America, had signed me to a (three?- ten?-year—that was before I knew you were supposed to read them) contract. I loved William Morris. I loved the carpets. And I loved how—except for the agents— big everything was. The armchairs were big, the table lamps were big (if you were to hug one, your fingertips would have barely touched), the deals were big, and everyone was big on saying how big everything was. Everything big tended also to be beige, except the plants, which were brilliant green and had wide, fat leaves.

I wrote about all of this in long letters to Leo, who had viewed the entire California pilgrimage with misgivings. First, he didn't believe in airplanes; he couldn't understand why a reasonable person would get on one voluntarily. And second, he couldn't believe I would follow someone across the country whom I hardly knew "to work on some cockamamie project, which is not the reason you're going anyway and I know that and so do you!"

"I admit it!" I roared back. "I love him!"

"How the hell do you know about love all of a sudden? How do you know he won't . . ."

But I never let him finish. "I know him," I said with a convert's smile.

I did a "pilot" and signed, as is the custom, a seven-year contract to do a television series. It never sold, thank God. If it had, I've often thought, I might still be out there, playing "character" octogenarians.

When I landed the part on the pilot, the small, hairy chest of my agent at William Morris expanded visibly. He didn't know that it would bomb; nor did I. I had a featured role, that of the lead character's best friend. The lead character was a magazine editor, crusty but lovable, played by Audrey Meadows. I don't remember much about Audrey Meadows except that she had thin legs and that the top of her agent's head came to her collarbone; also that he walked everywhere she walked, behind her, holding her pocketbook.

I don't remember much about my role, either, except that it required me to do and say a lot of cute things that were not believable. But never mind. It led to great things—like a featured role in an episode of *Dobie Gillis*. The action took place on a ship and, as we said the cute unbelievable things we had to say, we had to sway.

I hadn't known that I would be hitting the big time, so I had lined up a couple of research assignments in Los Angeles for insurance, and now had to do them as well. Not that I minded. The more I had to do, the easier it was not to think about Dan all the time. The research provided brain exercise, too. "Nothing strenuous," I wrote to Leo. "No bar bells, just a little stroll. But, around here a little stroll in the head is a hike anywhere else."

One of the assignments—for a writer who was doing a piece for *Reader's Digest*—required my doing interviews. Except for calling people to get information about this or that, I hadn't really ever done interviews, not personal ones, and what could be more personal—or petrifying—for the likes of me, anyway—than having to ask Pearl Bailey about her marriage to a white man for a piece about interracial marriage? But when I finally got to it, backstage one afternoon in a seedy dressing room of a theater in San Francisco, it was a snap. To my amazement, no matter how impertinent the question (in my view, they were all impertinent), she just waved those extraterrestrial hands of hers around and *answered*—beginning each response with "Honey" this or "Honey" that, as if I were an old girlfriend, and we were sitting around shooting the breeze.

Thanks to my determination never to be a secretary, I had never learned shorthand, so I got a cramp in my fingers trying to write everything down exactly as she said it. Which I did. Something told me the effort would be worth the cramp. Which it was.

As much as anything not having to do with Dan could thrill me in those days, that piece, when it came out several months later, thrilled me. It was the quotes. It's not that they were so remarkable. But the writer had used them just as I had written them down and I had written them down just as she had said them, so they sounded real. They sounded like a person. A *particular* person. A particular person who jumped off the page. It excited me to think I had helped make that happen.

Not that I had the slightest wish to—or expectation that I *could*—do that all by myself. I no more wished to be a writer than I wished to fly on a trapeze. Writers were those men I worked for. They were smart. They knew things. They had files. Once I saw the inside of Morton Hunt's file drawers. I felt like a seven-year-old who had stumbled, by mistake, on a couple having sex. I knew I would *never* be old enough to do that. Nor did I care. In the winter of 1961 I had other things on my mind. One thing, that is, one goal: to get Dan Moore to marry me. All of my professional flutterings—acting and research, plus an occasional sign of life left over from the little marriage-vow book—mattered chiefly because the man I loved thought it was cute. At least I thought he thought so, and I think I was right. My work, then, became a kind of cosmetic, something I slapped on in order to make myself alluring.

It didn't always work. When the Audrey Meadows pilot went on the air, Dan gathered some of his law school buddies—and even a couple of those Capital D Dedicated, Capital C Christians—to watch it in the student union. Afterward, by phone, he assured me that he thought I was very good, but he was surprised my part wasn't bigger. I felt instantly sick. I knew I had let him down.

Underlying all of this was one simple, unspoken assumption that we shared: his work was important. Mine (however cute) was not. Furthermore, because of its nature, mine would never be important. I spent so much time and energy trying to get work, I had never thought about it being unimportant. But now I thought about it, and now I knew it was. I also knew that the only hope for me, if I ever wanted to do anything that mattered (I guess by that I meant Making the World a Better Place) was to be Mrs. Him.

Before Dan came along, I thought Making the World a Better Place was what senators did. Or social workers. Or missionaries. It had never occurred to me, since I was "artistic," that I would or could ever change anything or help anyone. But now I could. Maybe I could actually do something worthwhile, and drop all the nonsense I had been up to so far. I could be Dan's helper; soothe him; tell him about people (remember, he said I was good at that); cook spaghetti. Meanwhile, I pretended to care about my own work—both for cosmetic reasons and because I could see it made him feel less pressured about marrying me. Assuming, of course, that if he felt less pressured about marrying me, he'd marry me.

Oh, we were crafty, we fifties girls. Trapping Jesus facsimiles or trapping the bloke down the block who owns his father's shoe chain—it amounted to the same thing: technique. We knew, we fifties girls, about balance on the high wire. You exist only for him, but not so that he notices. Not so that he thinks you're God-forbid pushing. Be available, but don't be needy. One's acting training came in handy, but everyone was an actress in those days. If you didn't act, a man would see that all that mattered was him, and then, surely, he'd run.

The word marriage had not come up with Dan, but I knew he had to have been thinking about it. "After all, he's a *Republican*," I wrote to Leo. "Republicans get married."

"Anyway, why *wouldn't* he marry me?" I almost shouted at Moira one morning as we sat out on the patio drinking our orange juice.

I had had a bad night. My twenty-fifth birthday had just

passed and I had hoped (without realizing how much I had hoped until now) that Dan would ask me to marry him on my birthday. Instead, when the day came, one of those clever greeting cards arrived in the mail which had a joke about being old. Naturally, I told him I thought it was funny.

"I'm *perfect* for him," I went on, glaring at Moira, who kept fiddling with her juice glass and sighing. "He says I'm a real help to him in his work. . . . He says I'm good with people."

Moira nodded solemnly. "You're even good with Mary Alice. She just loves you. I can tell."

"Moira," I said, without looking at her, "do you think Dan will marry me?"

Moira sighed again and looked at her empty glass. "I don't know, honey. . . I just don't know."

There was still time, I told myself. It looked as though there might be enough money to send the first group of volunteers to a reservation on the Gila River, near Mexico, by the fall. Dan would go then, too. So that would happen in September, probably. It was now March. Still plenty of time for us to get married. Moira had an etiquette book which said it was okay to send wedding invitations as late as a month in advance. Late in April Dan came down to Los Angeles for a weekend. I tried to be cheerful and also to look as good as I could (without looking as if I tried to look good) but when Sunday came and it was almost time for him to go back to Berkeley—dear Moira had packed up Mary Alice and left the house at nine that morning, so that we could be alone—and he still hadn't said anything, I began to sink.

"I think I should go back to New York," I said finally, knowing that, having made the threat, I would now have to carry it out. He didn't say anything right away. He didn't even seem surprised. Then he looked down, and said in a low voice, "I'll be coming to New York this summer for some final fund-raising before I go to New Mexico ..."

I looked at his face, waiting for the rest. But he just got up, straightened his pants, walked over to the window, and looked out. I stared at the back of his neck. The important thing, I thought, was not to cry.

We got to the airport early. It was about four o'clock, and the air had turned suddenly cool. I parked the car in the lot and we walked, without speaking, into the terminal and sat down and stared straight ahead. By now, I had stopped trying to hide how miserable I felt. Dan looked as uncomfortable as I had ever seen him. In a way I was glad, but I was also frightened. Acting this way—that is, *not* acting—was, I knew, a terrible tactic. I knew I'd regret it.

A Mexican family came and sat near us—a couple and three young children. One of them—a little girl—started to scream. The mother yanked the child's hand, which made her scream louder. The father sat down with the other two children and looked in the other direction. Meanwhile, the mother kept jerking the arm of the little girl, who by now was hysterical.

Dan stood up and picked up his bags. "I guess I'll go to the gate now," he said to me. I nodded and, slowly, got up, too. He took my hand and kissed me on the cheek. "We can talk about things in New York, okay?" I nodded again. Then he turned and walked away.

He did what he promised. He did come to New York and we did talk about things. More than that, he said we would get married. It was what I had been waiting to hear, but something about the way he said it made me feel less than wonderful.

The next morning, after he left for some appointments, I decided to feel wonderful, anyway. I called Moira long-distance. "Oh honey, that's just great. I'm so happy for you! I wish I could come to the wedding, and Mary Alice wants to come to the wedding, too, don't you sweetheart?" I could hear the baby gurgling in the background. Suddenly, I missed them both so much, I wanted to cry. Then Moira said, "Honey, when *is* the wedding?"

Unintentional left hook.

"I—I don't know. I mean, we haven't decided that yet." I realized at that moment why the proposal had seemed odd. There was no plan attached to it, not even a mention of a plan. He had said something about thinking it was a good idea to get married and did I think so, too, and I said yes, and then we sort of laughed and kissed and then we—he—had just started to talk about something else, and I didn't want to be pushy....Moira was saying something: "Honey, is there anything wrong?"

"No, no, nothing. Everything's great!" I said.

"You'll let me know when the wedding is, won't you?"

"Of course, I will."

"You sure you're okay?"

"Yes, sure."

I didn't tell anyone else. Joanna was away. I spoke briefly to Richard—he said he was about to get married himself, to a psychologist, he said—all very unexpected. I wished him well and he asked about me, but seemed more interested in professional things than the rest. That was fine, I didn't want to talk about the rest, anyway. I didn't want to talk to Leo about the proposal, either, because he was always so suspicious about anything that had to do with Dan. I wanted to have a definite wedding date first. Same for my parents, who by now knew there was someone from California in my life, but I knew if I told my mother, she just would have asked me all the questions that Moira asked, and more. And what would I say?

Of course, I never had to say.

One morning about a week after the proposal, I left my apartment—late for an appointment—and on the way out noticed something in the mailbox. Dan had left town for a couple of days and was due back the next day, so I knew it couldn't be from him. Therefore, it couldn't be important and would wait until I got back. I returned with a friend—not a close friend, just a friend. We had been shopping together. I had invited her up for tea. She began going up the stairs—another sublet walk-up, but a lovely one in the East Seventies, the nicest I'd had—and as she continued up the stairs, I stopped to open the mailbox. There were a few pieces of junk mail, so I didn't see it right away.

Then I saw it. His handwriting. My name and address.

The inner voice one sometimes hears at such moments told me not to rip the letter open, but to place it among the rest of the mail and carry it upstairs. My friend was at the door when I got there and said something meant to be funny about exercise or age or both. When I didn't react, she looked at me, alert now to the sudden change of climate. I put the key in the lock and opened the door. My heart and my throat were, by now, in the same place. We both went in and put down our packages on the hall table. I held onto the mail. "What's the matter?" said my friend. "Are you sick?" We were still both standing. She looked frightened.

"No, no. I'm all right. But there's a letter in here that I think might upset me a lot"—I held the packet very tightly now—"and if you want to leave, it's okay."

She looked ashen. "Wh-whatever you want," she said. Poor girl, what could she say? I knew it wasn't fair, but I wanted her to stay. I didn't want to be alone with it.

"Sit down," I said, and we both sat. Then, with a kitchen knife, I slit the envelope.

There were no reasons given ("I'm not sure why. But I do know it would not work. I'm sure of it"). Clean and clear. Clear to be kind. I remembered my note to Greg. No blame was placed, except the customary dollop on self ("I shouldn't have let the relationship go this far..."). There was also, near the end of the page, something meant to be humorous; it had to do with how I would fare in a teepee. But by that time, I began to have trouble breathing. "I need air," I said to my friend, who had turned to stone. I walked to the window, pushed it up, held onto the sill, and breathed as deeply as I could. Then I moved back into the chair and read the letter again. Slowly this time, I bent over it, with my hand on my mouth. I knew now what had happened: I had failed my audition. It was the audition of my life and I failed it. I did not get the part. And there was, I also knew, no telephone booth in America big enough to get me over this one.

"Oh God," I said in a voice that seemed to come from somewhere other than my throat. "Oh God."

CHAPTER
6

My mother and father drove me in their big Oldsmobile to my uncle's office in Mount Vernon, a few miles east of where my parents lived, in Yonkers. My uncle was a doctor. He gave me pills which, he said, would make the trembling stop. It was all right when I stood, but when I lay down, my legs shook. I'd try to stop the shaking by straightening out my legs and locking my knees. But it was like trying to hold down paper napkins at a picnic. I'd let go just a little, and they'd fold up and start shaking again.

My mother said I should try to eat something. She said it gently and kindly and I appreciated that, even though I couldn't possibly have eaten anything. My father was silent, the way he was, years later, when I got cancer. My father was a Russian immigrant who came to this country and lived happily ever after. He couldn't understand how anything bad could happen in America. He thought what happened to me was a mistake. He wasn't sure whose.

To this day, my mother's teeth lock at the mention of the name, Dan. That's silly, I tell her. I brought it on myself. Besides, I'm not the only one. Everyone in my generation had her Dan Moore. Everyone, that is, who thought she could become a person by affixing herself to another person.

When I lost Dan I felt that I had lost myself, what little self I had. I felt there was no longer a reason to get up and eat and move and do. I felt that since I was unacceptable to the man I loved, I was unacceptable, period—a failure as a person and as a woman. I wanted to die. I lay in bed with my twitchy legs and thought about two things: how I could die without making an effort (I felt too weak and squeamish to investigate methods of suicide), and how to get him back, which, someday, I knew I would. But how? How long would it take? What could I do to make myself a better person, more worthy, so that he would want me?

The two trains of thought were, I realized, contradictory. The second train won out. Still, I was reluctant to abandon the first, altogether. I knew I wasn't going to kill myself, but I liked to think about it. I'd muse about being dead, the way other people might muse about a nice but out-of-reach vacation spot. Months later I flew in a plane, for example, and daydreamed of crashing. I felt guilty about the other passengers; but daydreams are correctable. Midway, I changed mine so that when the plane crashed I would die, but everyone else would be saved.

Sleep was good. When, finally, I was able to sleep, I slept a lot. When I awakened, I'd try to fall back asleep. All of this went on in my parents' house, where I stayed for about a month. Later, my mother told me how weird it was for her, having me back in my childhood room again, sleeping as much as I did when I was three.

Two things got me going, finally: the wish to be a better, "worthier" person (I had a specific plan for that); and the wish to get back to the city in order to be distracted from the hurt, which had grown duller, but not smaller. It was as if a car alarm had gone off in my head and I couldn't find the switch to turn it off.

My parents and I had gotten on very well during the period that I was home. They seemed afraid of me, which was pleasant. I suppose they thought I might go over the edge, so they were careful about what they said to me. They were especially careful after the second day, when my father said something critical about Dan. It was nothing, really—an offhand remark about the Project—but I shot out of my chair, walked out of the room, and slammed the door so hard the paint cracked. After that, neither my father nor my mother ever spoke of him again. My parents were easier to control than my friends, however. Leo called often and never failed to make some kind of negative comment about Dan. When he did, I'd simply hang up. I had been cast out of the Temple, but I was still a believer. To hear such blasphemy from my heathen friends and parents both sickened me and made me feel doubly alone—cast out by Him, and distanced from everyone else. Oh, I would have liked to think Dan was no good, as they said. That would have made it so much easier. But I was stuck with what I saw as a Revealed Truth. He was Good. I was Bad. He was Everything. I was Nothing. My only hope was to get him back; and the only way to do that, I knew, was to work on myself.

When I mentioned my intention at self-purification to Leo, he misunderstood, and, to my astonishment "agreed" that going to a psychiatrist was a great idea.

"That's not what I mean at *all*," I shouted at him. "It's not my childhood that's screwed up. It's my *soul!*"

"But you need help," he countered meekly. "You need to find out why you fell for a guy who gives you the bends, so you won't do it again."

"I don't want help," I snapped. "I don't want to *feel* better. I want to *be* better. And I don't want to change who I 'fall for.'

There's nothing wrong with who I fell for. It's *me* there's something wrong with! Me, me!"

God knows, Leo was a pal, but after a while, even he gave up. For the next year or so, the friendship went into storage. (Lucky for me, when I rejoined the world a year or so later, it was still intact.)

Meanwhile, I had found a Spartan, dark, small new sublet in the West Eighties (sighs from my mother, silence from my father), settled in, and chose the route I would take toward bettering myself: Christian Science. I didn't want anyone to know—especially not Dan. I didn't want it to look as if I were using the religion to get him back. In fact, I wasn't. Not directly. I did feel that the religion would, in some vague celestial way, bring me closer to him. But in my grief I also truly bought the Christian Science message. The notion that my pain wasn't real, and that if I worked at it and "corrected my thinking" I could move into a state where there would be no pain or longing, and that, as a bonus of this move, I would achieve goodness and purity—all of this struck all the right chords. At the same time, I restored to Santa Claus his original powers: somewhere in my small, sad heart I felt sure that if I really became a good girl, I'd wake up one morning and find Dan under my tree.

In lieu of physicians and psychiatrists, Christian Science has practitioners; lay people, trained in the teachings of Mary Baker Eddy, who offer help in the way of talk, prayer, or both. I found that I gravitated toward practitioner ladies, rather than men, and spent my first session with a Mrs. Dawson, who looked the way I had hoped she'd look when I made the appointment on the phone: plain and pretty, her hair (graying) in a bun, her body (slim and unsexy) in a suit. Her voice was low and her composure stunning; yet, almost in spite of herself, she was warm and made "oh" and "ah" sounds of empathy, even though the religion said my grief wasn't real.

We had that first meeting—as well as the subsequent ones—in a small, undecorated cubicle in an office building on Forty-fifth Street, which at first struck me as an odd atmosphere for spiritual enlightenment. But, in a way, I probably felt more comfortable there than I would have in a churchier place where, I think, I would have felt the disapproval of my Jewish ancestors—not to mention my Jewish parents. Later on, I did start going to church, but by then I was too hooked for any kind of disapproval, real or imagined, to have an effect.

Mrs. Dawson did a good deal of reading aloud at those sessions. She kept a well-worn forest-green copy of Mary Baker Eddy's *Science and Health* on her lap at all times, and when something came up that related to something in the book, or sometimes even when it didn't, she'd straighten up in her chair, raise the book to eye level, and read:

> There is but one primal cause. Therefore there can be no effect from any other cause, and there can be no reality in aught which does not proceed from this great and only cause. Sin, sickness, disease and death belong not to the Science of Being. They are the errors . . .

I was buoyed by her certainty. She faced me, *knowing* that both recovery and virtue were at hand. And there was that remark she dropped one day about "how fortunate I was to be gifted." At first, I didn't know what she was talking about. But she immediately went on about my "God-given" creative talents, how grateful I should be that I could express myself as a writer and as an actress. At that point, with my self-contempt in its fullest bloom, the comment coming from anyone else would have been lost on me. But coming from Mrs. Dawson—with God thrown in—it registered. For the first time, it occurred to me to be grateful for something that, also for the first time, it occurred to me might have some value.

These days, I think Christian Science is pretty foolish. And, clearly, that whole business of not going to doctors is worse than foolish. Still, I was a needy stranger in 1961 and 1962, and the church took me in and for that I am everlastingly grateful. One does pay practitioners, but not much. And during that year—by far the bluest of my life—the religion calmed, soothed, and even, on occasion, cheered me. In a matter of weeks it helped me to resume the functions of life. The knot in my stomach loosened and I began to eat and sleep again. My professional self-esteem rose to a level which enabled me to, at least, start thinking about work again. Meanwhile, my bank account had dropped to a level where I *had* to start thinking about work again.

Six weeks, then, after the sky had fallen, I bought a new dress for my new, thin body and presented myself to the New York office of William Morris, where, compared with California, the lamps were smaller, the carpets darker, and the agents smarter and meaner. Having been signed on the other coast, I was treated like a distant and indigent relative— dutifully greeted and summarily disdained. "We need another ingenue like we need indigestion," I could hear them thinking. (In New York my type had changed back again. I was cute again, but no longer smart or funny.)

The agency was contractually obligated, as a lawyer would say, to make some gestures in my behalf. So—in the same spirit as one might send the indigent relative over to see another relative about maybe a job in the stockroom—they did send me on a couple of auditions. It surprised them, I think, when I got the second job I went up for. It surprised me, too. I had felt sort of woozy when I got up on the stage to read. It was dark and there was a funny, dank smell in the theater. And I felt as if I had read with almost no energy. Which is probably what did it. The dopes mistook depression for cool and offered me a contract that afternoon.

The part was something of a plum—the female lead in the road company of *Advise and Consent*, opposite Farley Granger. For me, all of the appeal was in one word: road. Even with Mrs. Dawson, my new religion, and my new resolve, I still felt rotten. Shipping out for eight months sounded as if it might, at least, be distracting. The next best thing, I thought—and immediately felt guilty for even thinking it— to a drug.

The papers were signed and the wardrobe fitted. I had two costumes: a pale blue nightgown with a matching peignoir for my first scene—the closest I ever came in my theatrical career to a state of undress—and a ladies'-lunch–like tan wool dress for the second.

The company gathered at ten sharp one Monday morning in a bare, drafty studio on Broadway for two weeks of rehearsals. We sat on metal bridge chairs and began to read and I began to feel some of the old acting juices flow in spite of myself. Although my role was important, it wasn't large and the character, a senator's wife, was no less insipid than any of the other parts I had ever played: "a warm and attractive girl," the script said, "who has lived a life almost devoid of struggle . . ." But I did have two pivotal scenes, both with Farley, whose training, it turned out, had been similar to mine. Therefore, when he looked at me and said something, he really looked at me and said it, and I really looked at him and said what I had to say, and, as Sandy Meisner would have said, something happened between us. So that was nice.

We did seven months, thirty-four cities—the big cities for a week or more, the smaller ones for a few days or less. We opened on Monday, October 2, 1961, at the Shubert Theater in Cincinnati, and went on to Dayton, Columbus, Cleveland; then South Bend, Evansville, Charleston, Grand Rapids, Detroit, Baltimore, Pittsburgh, Providence, Hartford, Reading, Scranton, Rochester (New York); on to Boston, Wilmington, Buffalo, Toronto—for two weeks, over Christmas and the New Year—Milwaukee (freezing!), Minneapolis (worse!), Chicago, Omaha, Lincoln, Kansas City; Amarillo, Lubbock, and Wichita Falls for one-nighters; then Dallas, San Francisco, Los Angeles, Denver, the Air Force Academy near Denver (where, because of the altitude, oxygen was administered offstage); and finally, May 1962, spring, and the smell of wisteria in St. Louis.

I was right about being distracted. Oh, I continued to hurt, but I got used to it, the way, I suppose, people get used to certain kinds of chronic physical pain. Meanwhile, I had the best kind of nonprescription medicine I could have had: the constant company of a jolly, genial bunch of actors, most of whom were elderly men, who had been through all the vanities and the humiliation and the desperation of their profession; and now, with a seven-month stretch of employment in front of them, wanted simply to have a pleasant trip, the way normal people do, and they did. Some of them brought their wives along, and sometimes we seemed more like a tour group than an acting company. House Jameson, a small, white-haired, feisty, and affectionate man (the original father, by the way, in the old radio series *Henry Aldrich*), did most of the restaurant research, along with his peppy wife, who was, as they say, about sixty going on thirty. Chester Morris and his wife led the way when it came to hotels and shops.

As for the play, we were professionals and we did our

collective best. But there was little interest, almost no conversation, and certainly no passion about the work on stage. Out of some old reflex, I put some effort into my role early on, but that waned. It had nothing to do with the boredom of saying the same lines night after night. In fact, that isn't boring. It's not as if you spend eight hours a day saying the same lines. For most roles, it's only a matter of minutes—a little thing you do for a little while at the end of each day, like walking the dog. Also, even if you experience the audience as bumps in the darkness, you know each night's bumps are new. So that gives you a "first-time feeling," even if it's the eightieth time. On the road, moreover, the theaters keep changing, and that helps, too.

Life on the road, in spite of all the locomotion, had a kind of steadiness to it—and because we were working, and getting paid regularly like regular people in regular jobs, there was a sweet and soothing ordinariness about it as well. We even had a routine, which, roughly, went like this: travel on Sunday afternoon (on Sunday morning I'd go off by myself to a Christian Science church); do publicity interviews with the local press on Monday; open Monday night; then, if the engagement ran a week or longer, we played Wednesday and Saturday matinées; which left Tuesday, Thursday, and Friday for exploring the city. Altogether, it was a fine way to see America—like most of my New York friends, I had been to Paris, but not to Chicago—and I took advantage of it. But, largely, I have Ruth Livingston to thank for that because, by myself, I would probably have made more plans than excursions.

Ruth Livingston was one of two other actresses in the show. Both had small parts. The other woman was my understudy, besides. The two were as different as characters in a fairy tale. Phyllis, the understudy, was pretty and bad-tempered. "Jesus," the wardrobe lady used to mutter, "what a mouth on her." (Actually, the wardrobe lady had quite a mouth on *her*.) Phyllis got pregnant, approximately in Cleveland, and began to show, considerably, in Detroit. That meant by the time she went on for me one night late in the run, in Wichita Falls, her girth dampened, considerably, the effectiveness of the scene in which the senator's wife reacts to allegations of her husband's homosexuality. . . . The producer never knew how lucky he was. If his leading lady didn't happen to be a Christian Science convert, he would have had a pregnant understudy going on many more nights than one. I missed that performance only because I was vomiting so violently (one of House's Tex-Mex finds turned out to be a bummer) I *couldn't* go on. Of course, I knew if I "corrected my thinking" the vomiting would stop, but I couldn't seem to correct it by eight-thirty that night.

Anyway, Ruth, by contrast, was the Good Fairy—not that she was goody-goody, just plain old good—and cheerful— the sort of person who looks on the bright side, not because she thinks she should, but because that's what she really sees. We were roommates on the road and I first got the message about Ruth one night in a hotel in South Bend, Indiana. We had just dropped our bags on the torn linoleum floor of our room, and as I looked around at the skinny beds, the plastic walnut furniture, and peeling birds on the wall, Ruth emerged from the bathroom, her small blue eyes opened wider than a baby's. "Guess what!" she said, clapping her hands together as if she'd just seen the season's first robin. "The Kleenex comes out of the wall!"

Every Tuesday, Thursday, and Friday, the two of us would set out and hit the sights of whatever city we were in. And if there were no sights, we hit whatever there was to hit. We missed nothing—from the most arcane war memorial in Dayton to the likes of Henry Ford's Greenfield Village; from Chinatown in San Francisco to the Gardner Museum in

Boston, where, of a Sunday afternoon, Mozart could be heard.

In spite of my lingering melancholia—some nights when I went to bed, the pain was as fresh as new grass—those afternoons with Ruth, soaking up America, were a privilege, and I knew it. *Advise and Consent* was probably my biggest acting job, but the value and pleasure of that trip had nothing to do with acting. Still, I had to admit, if not for acting I wouldn't have had the trip or anything like it.

For that reason, when my divorce from acting finally came, it was sad as divorces always are, but it was not bitter.

Quietly, unclimactically, like a good old car going dead in the garage, the tour finished at the end of May 1962. Back in New York, I came upon one of my customary sublets, settled in, hit the unemployment insurance line; and then, without the routine, the job, Ruth, the sights, the restaurants, and the Kleenex coming out of the walls, I got good and depressed.

I don't like being depressed. Who does, but some people are good sports about it. They lie down, smoke something, and wait for it to pass. That would probably do the trick for me if I tried it, but I've always been too fidgety and, instead, tend to do something, *anything* else. Like work. At this juncture I felt like doing something menial, or at least mechanical. But I didn't have mechanical skills, and, besides, I was too much of a snob. So back to William Morris. (Not her again! Isn't she on the road? Back? Already?) Never mind, before too long I landed a not-bad summer stock job in an Agatha Christie play, in which I got to die onstage. But it lasted only a couple of weeks.

When I got back to New York, my summer sublet had run out and I moved in temporarily (how else?) with another actress from the Agatha Christie play—a model who did television commercials, that is, who was *trying* to be an actress. Ginger, who was very pretty and sweet and sad and looked more like a lady than a girl, kept her lingerie in blue satin bags, and received enormous monthly alimony payments which she used, in part, to decorate her apartment—a wall-to-wall carpeted affair on the fourteenth floor of a fancy building on East Fifty-first Street—in a way that made it look as if somebody's parents lived there. At first it felt funny to be living with mahogany and damask and bone china that didn't belong to my mother, but since it didn't belong to my mother, I got to like it. Besides, luxury, I began to notice, was soothing.

The apartment had a third occupant, a Yorkshire terrier named Tid-bit, who weighed less than a small purse. Tid-bit was friendly, but she stank, and her paraphernalia—doggie bed, doggie toys, poop box, et cetera—usurped an alarming amount of floor space. But Tid-bit, it turned out, played a central role in Ginger's life, both as a confidante (she and Ginger conversed incessantly in baby talk) and as a business asset. When Ginger made rounds, Tid-bit accompanied her, a satin ribbon in the same color as her mistress's dress tied in a bow on the top of her head, which pulled her little forehead up, giving her a sort of continually surprised look. Ginger told me she thought Tid-bit helped casting directors remember her, and she was probably right.

Ginger taught me how to fix my nails and sent me to her agent for hand commercials and I promptly got one. (Below the wrists they don't hassle you about ethnic origins.) I squirted blue liquid soap into a pot and made about eighty-five dollars, not counting the possibility of residuals to come. The only bad part was the week before the shooting, during which I experienced a baroque new phobia: Fear of Breaking Nail. Throughout the week I wore gloves both indoors and out, and when Ginger mentioned that water softens nails, I ceased the ingestion of food requiring washing or rinsing. I managed to make it to the shooting before the onset of scurvy, nails perfect *and* squirt perfect. Even achieved small buzz of satisfaction from all of above. Job well done sort of thing—no matter how dumb job. Amazing.

With the hand triumph behind me, I returned to self-improvement. Christian Science, I had decided, wasn't enough. It was time now to branch out and be Good to other people—the way Dan is, I thought, but not out loud. The people I would help had to be strangers. Friends didn't count. I knew that much. So I wrote checks to the United Fund and Amnesty International, volunteered at a center for foreigners who needed practice speaking English, and read to the blind.

At first, everything went along okay; then I began to get the feeling I wasn't doing it right. I kept noticing things I knew I shouldn't notice: a lack of poverty, for example, on the part of some recipients of my beneficence. At the center they paired me up with a Japanese banker (he had a terrible time with my name) whom I liked perfectly well, and I truly think I helped him with his English. But a banker? Silk ties? I suppose I could have quit and worked in a soup kitchen. But I didn't think it was nice to quit once I started. Besides, even if I knew where to find one, I loathed the idea of a soup kitchen. At about the same time I began wondering about the banker, I realized I didn't like some of the blind people, particularly this one woman who was very bossy and made me read everything twice, then criticized how I read it. Of this thought I was so ashamed I barely admitted it to myself. And, of course, I kept right on reading. But I knew I had a long way to go toward goodness.

Meanwhile, I had a new book project going, which I had begun just to keep myself from sinking again. Another book seemed as good a floating object as any.

The idea had come to me while browsing in a bookstore on Madison Avenue one afternoon, having just failed a mouth audition for a lipstick commercial. (I think what happened was that when I puckered I looked silly instead of sexy.) I frequently surveyed novelty and humor sections of bookstores to make sure they had *I Thee Wed* in stock—not that I did a damn thing about it, except to exit sulkily, if they didn't. Anyway, on this particular day, I happened to notice what seemed like an inordinate number of books about children— about cute things they said, letters they wrote from camp, and so on. As I looked them over, it dawned on me that, as a category, mothers were as funny as children and how come there weren't any books about them.

I fell upon a salesman, an efficient-looking young man in round tortoise-shell glasses and a dotted bow tie, who promptly began leafing through *Books in Print*, a giant directory to which everyone with a swell book idea runs to make sure someone else hasn't gotten the same swell idea first. No, he said, there were no funny mother books. (By his tone, I could tell that he didn't think the world was a worse place for their lack.) I noted his view, agreed with it in a way—and let it pass over my head like a puff of cigarette smoke. One thing interested me and one thing alone: did I have a viable idea? Could a publisher sell it to people who read books?

True, I didn't want to do anything too crappy. I was too vain to do that. Besides, it takes a certain kind of skill to do crap, which I didn't happen to have. Even so, I still saw the professional world as divided in half: the half that did good and "made a difference," like Dan, and the half that sold. Like me.

So, so be it. So I would sell funny mothers. I would get up a collection of writings about funny mothers, the way I got up a collection of marriage vows. And if I was lucky, that would feed me until my next idea of how to feed me.

That afternoon I moseyed over to the library and poked through the card catalogue until I got to Humor, and then under Humor, until I found Mothers. Nobody home. No books, that is; plenty of pieces *in* books, however. I skimmed through them and found a load of stuff, most of it cornball, some of it medium cornball, and some of it not cornball at all. In any case, there was enough of the latter to make me think I was on to something. Long story short: Doubleday went for it—with a word of caution from the editor, Sam Vaughan. "Anthologies don't sell," he said straight out, which was—still is—his way. "You gotta *write* some of this book." I looked at him. I would have preferred it if he had told me I had to design the book jacket or set the book in type.

"But Sam," I said, "I'm not a writer. I haven't written anything since college."

"You can write," he said. "You wrote this proposal, didn't you?" He waved a page I had just written outlining the book idea. I felt trapped. I felt the way I did in high school after finding out that chemistry was a required course.

"You don't mean I have to write a *lot* of it, do you?"

"Nah," said Vaughan, who, even today, although he's vice-president of the company, has still not gotten the hang of being lofty. "Look, see how it goes. If it's no good, we'll cut it out. So the book won't sell. So what else is new? Hey, by the way"—now he looked worried—"you can *type*, can't you?"

Very funny. Yeah, I could type. I could also panic. On the way home, I comforted myself with one thought: that maybe if the material I collected was good enough, maybe I wouldn't have to write after all. With only spurts of acting and do-gooding to (not) fill the days, I could now step up the search.

I pulled the best cartoons on the subject from the place which has the best cartoons on any subject, *The New Yorker*. I also got a good haul one morning at *Mad Magazine*, which turned out to be more like a fraternity house than an editorial office. I had walked in on a hunch, and was greeted by a dozen wild-eyed men in their thirties who, to describe the scene conservatively, did not seem to mind the interruption.

"Lenny, da lady wants funny mudders," said a member of the staff, who turned out to be a lamb with a lout exterior. "So get da lady funny mudders, Lenny, unnerstan?" The truth is, anyone could have walked into that place and gotten anything they wanted as long as they were female and promised not to leave right away. The *Mad* editors virtually turned the place upside down—which took some doing since it was upside down to start with—and handed over every mother they could find.

As a group, the *Mad* mothers were pretty crude. I wound up throwing most of them into a chapter called "Mothers More Gruesome Than Others," which included a tale or two about stage mothers, and, to illustrate the chapter's tone, a poem about a mother-in-law that went:

> He stood on his head by the wild seashore,
>   And danced on his hands a jig;
> In all his emotions, as never before,
>   A wildly hilarious grig.
>
> And why? In that ship just crossing the bay
>   His mother-in-law had sailed
> For a tropical country far away,
>   Where tigers and fever prevailed,
> Et cetera.

Does it sound odd, given my personal doldrums, to have gotten so caught up in such monkeyshines as these? It may, but it shouldn't. The fact is, *many*—maybe even most— people whose business is humor are miserable. And often their misery is not a phase, as mine was, but a permanent condition.

One of the many things I did not learn at Sarah Lawrence—to be fair, I don't think the girls at Radcliffe got this, either—was that misery is not only a fine state of mind for the creation of humor; misery is also one of the best things to be funny *about*. I was too dumb to understand any of that at the time. But it didn't matter. All I knew was that I had done one book, and it had worked, so why not do another? If you make a hole and you get oil, make another hole.

What finally emerged, under the cumbersome title *Mothers Are Funnier Than Children*, was pretty ghastly. True, the chapter called "Mother's Baby Book" wasn't bad—it contained a Mother's Footprint, a prettily decorated chart for Mother's Age, Sex, and Teeth, and a photograph of a middle-aged lady (the photographer's wife finally agreed to do it) lying naked on a bearskin rug; and a friend's aunt, a smart and zany lady name of Ellen Williamson, contributed a few chapters, which classed things up considerably. But as for the rest— "Mothers Who Believe in the Stork, Anyway"; "Mothers Then and Now"; and "Jewish Mothers"—may they, is all I can say now, Rest in Peace. Never has an author been happier to see a book go out of print.

Still, ghastly or not, I got a lot out of doing that book. For one thing, because sneaky Sam Vaughan made me write after all—a couple of short stories here, a couple of jokes there—I found that I *could* write. Well, that *maybe* I could write.

I learned something else, too. I learned it was possible to have a marvelous time working, even though the rest of your life is in the pits. I remember the exact day I learned that, too. I was sitting cross-legged on my living-room floor with the illustrator—a large, handsome, hairy Mexican from *Mad* called Sergio who was (unfortunately) a "newlyweed," by which he meant nothing horticultural, but rather that he had recently married. We needed to find a place in the book for a bunch of one-liners I had collected, when after a day of turning our wheels, the notion of Mom Bombs suddenly hit; they would be inserts, we decided, which would appear here and there between chapters, and, even as we spoke, Sergio set about drawing an extremely cheerful lady with a round bottom and a fuse (get it?), and I clapped my hands and I remember feeling joy, inexplicably high, flamboyant joy.

Sometimes I'd keep on feeling good even after Sergio had left. This surprised me. Then I remembered what my acting teacher, Sandy Meisner, used to say about getting an emotion going when it wasn't there. Start an action, he used to say, and the feeling will come. If you're supposed to feel good in the scene and you don't, start jumping up and down, and then see if you don't start feeling good. You don't always, he'd say, but you do sometimes; and, in any case, it beats standing still.

I had had one letter from Dan during the *Advise and Consent* tour, and one upon returning home. Both were bright and cold. I got the message. Which didn't mean I gave up. But I began to think I might eventually have to. Eventually. Meanwhile, I began to go out with a few men I met at the Christian Science church. That didn't work. I couldn't stand any of them, even the ones I liked. For one thing, they all looked as if they slept in their ties. By 9:30, I'd start to feel exhausted, and with Christian Scientists you couldn't even pretend to be sick. So I quit. I didn't really want to go out with men, anyway. I just thought I should.

I still had Leo, thank God. Although he was beginning to have trouble adjusting to my frequent change of residences. He seemed particularly uncomfortable at Ginger's, even though Ginger tried as hard as she could to make him feel welcome. She liked Leo. She thought he was "very intelligent." But Leo would step into the carpeted foyer and look up at the crystal chandelier expecting it, I could tell from his

look, to fall on his head, and he'd growl, "Let's go out to eat."
So we'd hit one of those places on Forty-second Street where
they cooked the meat in the window (my mother never knew)
and go to a double feature. Or, sometimes, we'd get dressed
up and "second-act" a play. That meant sneaking in with the
crowd during intermission. Except, of course, you didn't
sneak. You breezed in, grabbed a program as soon as you
could, and tried to spot an unoccupied seat; whereupon you
would place your bottom, with an air of confidence, in it.

In the fall of that year—1962—something wonderful
happened to Leo. Two somethings, in fact, both at once: he
got a job *and* a girlfriend. The girlfriend was a blond, doe-eyed
model named Janice, who seemed a little spacy but sweet,
and, clearly, she adored Leo. The job was a Broadway show
called *Come on Strong* with Van Johnson, in which Leo played
a janitor, an Arab, and a fat waiter. The Arab was the best, I
thought, because he did a lot of crazy things with his
eyebrows. My parents and Janice and I went to the opening.
We were all so excited we failed to notice that the show was a
turkey. Unfortunately, the critics didn't fail to notice. It
closed in a week.

Leo and I began to talk again. Once more, he broached the
subject of psychoanalysis, which he had begun himself. He
must have seen that I was almost ready.

CHAPTER
7

I can see as well as anyone the satiric riches which psychoanalysis so generously offers. Every aspect of the treatment—from the patient's prone position to the doctor's taciturnity—glistens with comic possibility. And among those who are unamused, none can prove that psychoanalysis works. One can only say what a believer *can* only say: it worked for me. And what does that mean? Speaking for myself, it means this: when I began the treatment I felt rotten, confused, insecure, and lonely. When I finished I felt happy, enlightened, confident, and loved.

No doubt events and conditions other than the treatment contributed to this conversion—getting older, for example. But I'm pretty sure getting older, by itself, wouldn't have done it for me. Nor would some of the more popular alternatives: e.g., alcohol, astrology, est, avoidance, and/or nothing.

I have also found psychoanalysis professionally useful. As I began to see the difference between what was going on in my own head from what was really going on, I began to see that difference in other people, too—and in other situations.

That's not a bad knack for anyone to have. But for journalists and writers it's especially handy.

Needless to say, plenty of journalists, writers, and other people know what's up without the benefit of psychoanalysis. And, conversely, many analysands are the same fools post-treatment that they were before. There is no syllogism here. Again, this writer can only speak for this writer. Psychoanalysis helped me write—and that goes for everything from articles about movie stars in *Look* magazine to an autobiographical book about what it was like to have breast cancer. I might have written that book anyway, but without psychoanalysis, I think I would have written it phonier.

I didn't begin treatment until the winter of 1963. It took until then for me to face the fact that thinking good Christian Science thoughts was not doing the trick.

Oh, I had made some progress in my life. By now I knew, and even accepted, that I would not get Dan back. I had advanced professionally, and now and then I had a good time socially. I *should* have been out of my doldrums. But I wasn't. So I took the first step. I began to think maybe it's not the situation. I began to think maybe it's me.

The thing is, I wanted to get married. I wanted so badly to love someone and get married and be normal. I wanted to be rescued. I didn't want a career. I wanted a life. The career was a diversion, a nice diversion—I knew that—I knew I should be grateful—I was grateful. I was grateful the way you're grateful if you get a nice room in the hospital.

So why couldn't I find anyone? Why couldn't anyone find me? As much as I had loved Dan, I never really bought that one-man-for-every-woman routine. I knew there had to be someone else. I went out with men. Some of them were okay. But I never seemed to feel anything for anyone. Why?

I must be crazy. I'm not married, I thought, because I'm crazy. Therefore, said Leo—and now I was ready to listen— if you get un-crazy, you'll get married. And how do you get un-crazy? You get your head shrunk. Here's a name, an address, a telephone number, said Leo, pressing a piece of paper into my hand as if it were a tip. I sighed—one of those sighs that starts at the bottom of you and moves up until your lungs swell—and took the paper. And called. And went. And greeted a small, wizened German with a large head and kind eyes, and followed him through a curtain (a curtain? What is he, a gypsy fortune-teller?) and lay down on a black leather couch facing a window out of which I could see Central Park, and began to talk, and continued to talk four, then three, then two times a week for four years.

The funny thing is the joke wasn't on me. Who says in order to get something out of something you have to do it for the right reasons? Besides, the reasons weren't *entirely* off- base. I was right about being too crazy (the fancy word is neurotic) to hitch up with a good man. I was right to think that hitching up with a good man was important. I was wrong to think that hitching up with a good man was all-important. Or that at the end of my analysis I'd get one, like a diploma.

These days, I have a rather Pollyanna view of it all: I'm glad I was crazy. If I hadn't been crazy I would have married young and had children and, I think, not have had a (let's hear it for compensation) career. Not, at least, the one I had. Surely, I wouldn't have given it my all the way I did for about eighteen years, which, it seems to me, was the main reason I got somewhere. In those days, remember, it was pretty much either/or. Anyway, *I* thought it was.

Some women, I know, marry young and have children, never have much of a career, if any, and live happily ever after, anyway. But I don't think I would have. I got to need a career (and derived as much subsequent joy from having one) the way some women need children. A career wasn't *all* I needed. But then, as things turned out, it wasn't all I got.

I'm glad, too, by the way, that I wasn't rich. If I had been rich, I might have done what some of my rich, crazy friends did in those days—analysis in the mornings and pedicures in the afternoons and, in between, vague attempts at poetry and photography. So money—the need for it—kept my career going, too, especially after 1963 when those bills from the head doctor started rolling in. I could have asked my parents for money, but then I would have had to let them in on the fact that their only child was off her nut and I didn't want to do that. Besides, theoretically, the treatment didn't work as well if you didn't pay for it yourself.

I could have opted for a less expensive kind of therapy—"group," for example, or a once-a-week sit-up kind. But, I thought, if I'm going to do it, I should do it right. And "right" to me meant taking the classic route—lying down several times a week and finding one of those old Germans, like the one I had, to lie down at.

Anyway, acting and books were no longer getting me through, financially. The old German charged eighty dollars a week (I didn't know how lucky I was—it costs four times that to be crazy today); since men weren't feeding me much anymore, I also had to buy food; and even though I had moved out of Ginger's by now, into a cheaper apartment which I also shared (with a succession of wandering females whose names I don't remember), I still had *some* rent to pay, not to mention all the other parts of staying alive which require money. Of course, acting paid a person well—when a person had a job. But you could no more count on getting an acting job than you could count on a homer in the bottom of the ninth. As for books, they took too long, even the kind I did.

I considered going the civilian route—trying to get a normal sort of job, as an assistant editor at Doubleday, maybe. But even if I were qualified, the pay was lousy—not only because most assistant editors were women, but because a job, *any* job in publishing, was considered glamorous (implication: she should be paying *us*). Except maybe secretarial jobs. Secretaries did better. But I couldn't be a secretary. I had no skills. Besides, damn it, I didn't want to be a secretary.

I never doubted that sooner or later a Husband would surface and rescue me from all of this. But I had no reason to think he would surface anytime soon.

I also knew, while I waited, I better find something to do which would not only pay me and occupy my time but hold my interest. Writing would hold my interest—if only I could think of a way to make money at it. I didn't have to make a *lot* of money or worry about saving any because when the husband came along, which he surely would, he would surely pay for me and my future. So I had only to worry about today. But "today" had turned out to be expensive. What, the question was, could I write that would take less time than books and pay more? By asking around, I found out: magazine articles.

I didn't know how to write magazine articles any more than I knew how to take shorthand; but I hadn't known how to do books, either. I further reasoned that if I planned to write for magazines, I had better read some. (This deduction is not as obvious as it might sound. Some years later, when I became a magazine editor, I would often receive submissions from people who, clearly, had not read the magazine they hoped to write for. Occasionally, I'd send a mean reply: "Dear Mrs.

Thigpen, In the thirty-six years of its existence, *Look* magazine has never published a poem. It is unlikely that your poem *Bluebird on a Gray Morning* will lead to the policy change that would be required in order for *Look* to publish it. I hope you will not take this personally. Sincerely yours.")

It gave me a pleasant twinge to see the stone lions on their haunches, still, out in front of the library. I moved past them, up the stone steps, through the revolving doors, up the inside stairway, and then, a new turn, into the periodicals room. I figured I'd have my best shot at the ladies' magazines, as they were still called. So I sat down at one of the wide, wood tables with six issues each: *Ladies' Home Journal, McCall's, Good Housekeeping*, plus a few of the minor leaguers. By the end of the afternoon, I had thought up three or four ideas which, based on my perusals, seemed suitable.

I went home and typed up three proposals, similar to those I had submitted for the two books, but shorter—a couple of paragraphs each. Now all I needed was a friend in court, and I knew precisely where to look for one: (where else?) the Sarah Lawrence Mafia. Sure enough, my Cambridge friend, Pat, had a mother, who had a friend, Henry Ehrlich, who was a senior editor at *Look*. *Look* was all wrong for the ideas I had, but a foot in the wrong door was better than none. So I went to see Mr. Ehrlich, hoping, if nothing else, to get a little guidance.

Henry Ehrlich turned out to be a peach. A connection will usually get you an appointment, but it rarely leads to the kind of immediate action that Henry took. In the years that followed, I never got around to asking him why he did it. Perhaps he liked my article ideas. Or perhaps he just liked that I *had* ideas. Anyway, while I was still sitting in his office, bless-his-heart Henry picked up the telephone and called his friend (it always helps if your Pull has Pull) the managing editor of *McCall's*. He used a few nice words about me like "bright" and "imaginative," and an hour or so later, I found myself surrounded by a leather wing chair in the office of *McCall's* managing editor, a plump, remarkably unterrifying middle-aged woman who, without so much as asking to see a single example of my writing (if she had, all would have been lost, since all I had to show were a couple of short stories about funny mothers) gave me the go-ahead to do a piece— one of my own ideas—about women who did television commercials. We made a deal. That is, she told me they would pay $750 and I said fine.

I couldn't do the arithmetic in my head, but as soon as I sat down on the bus going home, I scribbled it on the back of an envelope: $750 divided by 20 equals 37½ analytic sessions. At three times a week, that was . . . (more scribbling) more than three months' worth. Hot diggety. I restrained myself from hugging the other passengers.

Ecstasy lasted the bus ride. Panic hit upon entering the apartment.

What now? I had pulled off the heist. The emeralds were in my hands. But how to fence them? How the hell do you write a magazine article? I sat down at my kitchen table and folded my hands on top of it. I would simply, calmly, plan how to proceed. Simply. Calmly. Proceed.

Help!

A friend of a friend knew a bona fide magazine writer. I called him, pulled a shameless helpless-female act (a woman could still do that in '63 and live with herself), and the next afternoon we were in a coffee shop, me buying, him telling me how to do it. No one can tell you how to do it, but—lucky again—I found in this man someone who, after an hour and a quart of coffee, made me *feel* that I could do it. And there wasn't any male-female stuff, either.

Nerve, need, and a few friends weren't all one needed to move ahead in this world, but, as far as I could tell, they were almost all.

During the next two months, I interviewed every woman in New York who had ever washed anything, wiped anything, served anything, or put anything on her face, on her body, or into her mouth in front of a television camera. My writer friend had left something out of his cram course on magazine writing. When you interview people, he might have said, find out what you need to know for your article, not what they want to tell you (which can easily turn out to be everything that has ever happened to them, including and since their first present from the tooth fairy). But he didn't tell me that. So I emerged from the living room of each detergent queen with enough material for several three-hundred-page biographies. In addition, I interviewed the heads of most New York advertising agencies and their clients. I witnessed the shooting of four commercials. I had amassed sixty pages of notes consisting of about eleven thousand words (for a piece which was supposed to be only fifteen hundred words).

The deadline would strike in exactly twenty-one days. I had to start writing. The next morning, a beauteous one in June, I woke up, washed my face and brushed my teeth in a hurry, made a pot of fresh coffee, tightened the sash on my bathrobe, snapped my typewriter out of its case, carefully placed it on the kitchen table, unwrapped the pack of bond paper I had purchased the day before, retrieved my notes from the floor where they were stacked tidily in manila folders—names of the interviewees written in colored ink on the front—opened the first folder, put the top sheet of paper in the typewriter, looked at it, put my head on the keys, wrapped my arms around its base, and cried.

If I had known then how many times, during the next fifteen years, I would have the same feeling—the I'm-over-my-head-and-this-time-they're-going-to-catch-me feeling—I might have become a receptionist in a carpeted law office and married the first partner in a three-piece suit who asked me. But I didn't know. I thought, if I get through this, it'll be over.

And, after three weeks and six drafts, some loss of body weight, intermittent dehydration, occasional sensations in the chest resembling those of angina pectoris—all the while having achieved new highs in sustained self-doubt—it *was* over.

I bathed, put on something presentable—no small feat, since most of my clothes were either at the cleaner's or needed to be—and twenty-four hours before the due date hand-delivered a perfectly typed sixteen-hundred-word article. My writer friend had told me always to go at least a hundred words over the mark, in order to give the editor something to cut. Why does the editor need to cut? I asked. He looked at me as if to say, nobody's *that* dumb. (But somebody was.) Then, after the delivery, I went home, changed the sheets on the bed, and slept for twelve hours.

They actually bought it. Oh, there were some changes (I would have changed every word, had they wanted me to) and the piece was cut to about thirteen hundred words (I would have been delighted to cut it in half) and finally, in the issue dated October 1963, decorated with scaled-down glossies of four of the women I had interviewed, my piece, "Cinderellas of Commercial TV" (their title), was published in *McCall's*.

I did it. Crime does pay. Don't ask me what crime. I only knew what I had done couldn't be legal. Of course, when I figured it out in terms of the time spent, the take turned out to be about ten cents an hour. But never mind. Surely the second piece would go faster. And I did feel certain there would be a second piece—that if I could pull it off once, I could pull it off again and if this was so, it meant that I had found something I could keep doing which would keep paying—something, moreover, which did not depend on how I looked or sounded or how cute somebody thought I was.

Nor, now that it had all worked out, did writing the piece seem that difficult. (My, when you hold the baby, how the pain of delivery dims.)

"It was *nothing*," I said to Leo one evening as we wound spaghetti around our forks at his house. "Next time," I said, taking a swallow of wine (and my, how a few pages set in type dampens self-doubt), "I think I'll try something harder."

So, in went the next batch of ideas like dollops of dough on a cookie sheet. Of these, *McCall's* said yes to two. I hung up the phone and my feet left the floor. Then I did a little dance. Then I sat down and tried—and failed—to figure out why they chose the two ideas they chose, neither of which I could imagine flanked by recipes for apple cobbler. One of the ideas was Black Muslim women (both Malcolm X and Elijah Muhammad were still alive and preaching reverse racism—that all Caucasians were "white devils"), and the other piece was about the psycho-admitting ward of Bellevue Hospital. My old friend Richard, whom I spoke to now and then, had put me on to that one. He was interning on the midnight-to-eight shift at Bellevue, and had promised, if I wanted to do a piece, that he'd get me a white coat to wear and smuggle me in.

After the telephone go-ahead from *McCall's*, I went in to see the editor who would be overseeing both assignments—a man this time, middle-aged, pleasant, tense—and we had a brief conversation about the tack I planned to take. Since Muslim headquarters were in Chicago, I thought it made sense for me to go there and see what was what. The editor agreed, with a further word about his own expectation of what the Muslim women would be like: wives of Nazis. I sort of doubted that, but didn't say so.

On the Bellevue story, he said fine to my *not* trying to do a definitive evaluation of the place, but rather that I simply spend a night, and report what I see. Then he added a perfunctory word about the sadness and horror of it all. Horror sounded a little strong, from what Richard had told me, but I let that pass, too. Years ago in kindergarten, and more recently on the stage, I had learned not to contradict the grown-ups. Disobey if you must, but no point in flagging the disobedience.

Both pieces flopped. That is, I wrote them; I liked them; *McCall's* didn't. I got a kill fee—that's money most of the big magazines pay for your time (ha!) even when they're not going to publish your article. Actually, *McCall's* kill fee was more than decent—$500 for the two pieces—but whatever they give you, getting paid to go away does not give you that warm feeling, especially if you're the new girl.

Both pieces died for more or less the same reason. The stories I found were not the stories they wanted. When I got to Chicago, I didn't see Nazis and I didn't see wives of Nazis. I saw prideful black people, some of them very angry, living in a society which made it almost impossible for them to have pride. I saw women who wanted to bring up their children so that, in spite of how things were, they would feel good about being black. I knew some Muslims were dangerous, but they had no real power, and to equate them with Nazis would have been not only dumb and trite, but irresponsible. Moreover, the women draped in white—with their straight backs and solemn faces—moved me. And when I visited their Muslim school and saw the efforts they made to teach their kids black history (long before it became a college trend), that, too, impressed and moved me.

But this view did not match or even come close to the story the *McCall's* editor, sitting behind his large oak desk with photographs of his wife and two children framed in silver, had in mind. And, more to the point, he—they—preferred what he had in mind to what I wrote. I argued and, as is the custom, they listened. But of course I lost.

Same with Bellevue. Most of the people who came to Bellevue after midnight, at that time anyway, were drunks, for whom going to Bellevue psycho-admitting was like going to an open call in the theater; only instead of having to sing and dance, you had to act crazy—pretend you didn't know the president's name, or the year. Then, if they liked your audition, you got a hot bath and a clean bed free. (The number of auditioners swelled, Richard told me, during the winter.)

Drunks are not the most talented performers, however, and when a doctor got wise to their act, they'd turn into shamefaced nine-year-olds. "C'mon, Fred," Richard said to one of the regulars, "last week you said the president was Lincoln. This week it's George Washington. Now make up your mind."

There were also some genuine lunatics, and—I hate to say it—some of the lunatics were as comical as the drunks. When, in the middle of the night, two people walk into a room and both of them claim to be God and get into a fight about it, whatever else it is, it's also funny.

I did see a couple of heartbreakers—a very young woman, for example, who couldn't or wouldn't speak or move; and, saddest of all, the relatives—the mothers, fathers, brothers, and sisters who had brought the crazy person in.

The psycho-admitting ward of Bellevue Hospital was no

setting for a situation comedy. But it wasn't a Snake Pit, either. The doctors and nurses seemed at worst mechanical, and at best saintly. For all I knew, it was different upstairs, where patients wound up. Perhaps it was Snake Pitty up in the wards. I doubted it. Anyway, that wasn't the story I had been assigned to write. I was supposed to write about what I saw during one night at the admitting office. And what I saw was a mix of pathos and farce.

Another writer might have seen it differently, just as another writer might have seen the Black Muslim women differently. But, as I took notes and then wrote about Bellevue, it didn't occur to me to write any other story than the one I saw. It didn't occur to me, for example, to write the story the *McCall's* editor saw (and was expecting). Naively, I had thought he would be surprised and delighted that I didn't hand over a predictable, insane-asylum sort of piece. But among most editors, *predictable* is not a dirty word. The dirty word is *UNpredictable*. Editors, by and large, want the story you and they thought you would find when you discussed it cozily over coffee in their offices, not the one you found when you got out in the trenches. To present your editor with an uncontemplated, fascinating new twist to a story—especially if the story has already been scheduled—creates the same effect as a seven-year-old presenting his mother with a spider.

At the beginning, I couldn't understand this. I didn't know that the rigidity did not stem necessarily from the editor's lack of imagination, but more often from his fear of the editor above *him*, from whom the "office concept" of the story might have originally come, and to whom he'd have to answer if the concept changed. Nor did I understand the editors' assumption—probably correct—that the readers, too, had expectations, particularly about subjects like Black Muslims and "insane asylums," and that the readers were also looking, not for enlightenment, but for verification. "Get this idea out of your head," a hotshot editor told me once, "that readers want to learn anything new. All they want is to find out that what they thought all along was right. And if we want to sell magazines, that's what we give them."

M eanwhile, I was twenty-seven years old and what did I know? After the second turndown, the brown paper sack which held my self-confidence had ripped at the bottom and I began to think, maybe he's right. Maybe the story he wants *is* better than the one I've written. But it isn't the story I *saw*, and how can I write about what I didn't see? Never mind morality; even if I wanted to, I didn't know *how* to make things up. Still don't and never have. Even in grade school, when I used to draw—which I did a lot—I could only draw what was in front of my nose, like the tree outside my window.

Never, no matter how I tried, could I draw a make-believe tree. And after a while, it occurred to me that as long as there were trees outside my window, I didn't *have* to make them up.

My magazine-writer friend shrugged, commiserated, and told me to try to sell the pieces somewhere else. So I sent them to *Ladies' Home Journal*. Thanks, but it's not right for us. Ditto from four other magazines. A noncommissioned piece, I found out, is harder to sell than a secondhand dress. Somehow, a finished article smells of rejection—or amateurism—and usually winds up in a file drawer (yours).

By rights, I should have been undone by this sharp and sudden downward turn in my new career. I wasn't. I thought the pieces were good. I had a fine, exhilarating time doing them. I felt that I could write. But the irony was not lost on me: now that I was beginning to think I could do it, my winning streak seemed to be over.

I was beginning to worry about Leo. Not about his private life; that seemed okay. Janice was dear—a touch hypochondriacal perhaps; each menstrual period seemed to bring her closer to eternal rest—but so what? In a nutty way, their nuttiness blended.

It was those letters that worried me. Now he wasn't only writing to theater people, but to dry-cleaners and plumbers, to anyone who got his goat. I understand the need to let off steam and I was all for consumer justice. But to spend *all* of Thursday on a letter to the Swanee Paper Company because the blue border on its paper towels came off on his kitchen wall?

> ... It is incredible that your company neither anticipated this classic use of papers towels, i.e., to remove soil from a surface with a mild cleaner, and compounded a print dye immune to instant running, nor, at the very least, thought it necessary to print a warning on the cellophane wrapper, cautioning the user ...

Or a three-hundred-word letter to Chiffon Margarine, who, it seems, had just switched from rectangular tubs to round ones, rendering useless the rectangular steel dishes Leo—and, presumably, other victims of this perfidy—had recently purchased to fit the rectangular tubs?

> ... I cannot fathom what fickle advertising staff, consensus of industrial designers, apocryphal research, or other arbitrary marketing concept suggested that you would sell more of your product in a round box than a rectangular one ...

"This is crazy, you know," I said, staring him down after dinner one night in my latest sublet, an antiseptic-looking, boxy place in one of those horrible new white brick buildings on Seventy-seventh Street and York Avenue. "If you want to write, why don't you try to write something you can *sell*, for God's sake! Better yet"—Janice had just minced in from the kitchen—"why don't you try to get a *job* writing? You could have a salary like other people. You and Janice could have a *life!*" He looked at me stonily. It was odd for Leo to be so quiet.

"Why don't *you* get a job?" he said finally. I couldn't tell if he was angry or not. "*You're* the one who wants to be a writer. *You're* the one who wants a salary. *I'm* an actor." He was angry. And now so was I.

"Don't give me that lofty, I'm-an-actor-stuff. Big deal, you're an actor. So, I'm an actress. You know as well as I do that ninety percent of it is looking for work, not working! And you hate hustling as much as I do! And what happens when you get a job? It's crap! And you have to act it crappily! So what kind of a life is that?!"

"So get a writing job," he yelled. Janice was in a knot in the corner of the sofa. Any minute she would say, "Leo, don't get so excited!" Leo went on: "Don't keep telling *me* to do what *you* should be doing!"

He was right, of course. I wanted out of acting. I wanted to write. And, besides, analysis was more expensive than Janice. If I were going to stick with it—and, by now, I was certain that I should—I needed steady money. I was also beginning to think it would be nice to live someplace—in my own apartment. I was tired of other people's favorite color schemes and other people's family photographs. I wasn't a grown-up yet, but that didn't keep me from starting to want what a grown-up wants.

W hen, at a party, I first heard about the *Vogue* job, I laughed. Who wouldn't? What could be sillier than a *Vogue* editor, except maybe *me* as a *Vogue* editor. The job, apparently, had nothing to do with fashion. But *Vogue* was *Vogue*, wasn't it? Ladies with hats and all that. Wasn't it?

It wasn't. Without realizing it, until much later, anyway, I was doing the very thing I had gotten angry at *McCall's* for doing—expecting the cliché, swallowing the standard notion of what a place like *Vogue* is supposed to be.

It's just as well that I did. Because if I had known what *Vogue* was *really* like, I might have faltered at the puce-carpeted threshold. This way, I not only sashayed unhesitatingly in, I sashayed in with my nose up. *Vogue*, after all. What a laugh.

My interview for the job followed a letter I had sent to the features editor, Allene Talmey, in which, using a tone I thought cool, I stated my credentials: "two books" (without describing what sort of books they were) and "several magazine articles for *McCall's*" (enclosing the one that was published and omitting the fact that the others were not). When Talmey's secretary called a few days later asking me to come in for an appointment, I knew, so far at least, that the bluff had worked. So I showed up for the interview the following week, feeling halfway there.

Allene Talmey, at our first meeting, did nothing to shake my confidence. Nothing about her person signaled the daily terror she would soon strike to my small, green heart. She was short and sixty or so, slightly rotund, Jewish, and she wore a nice navy blue wool dress and, except for the lack of kisses, she could have been my aunt. She asked fewer questions than I expected—none about the *McCall's* pieces (whew)—and, altogether, the conversation had little fat. Allene Talmey, I learned at that first meeting, said nothing which did not have a point.

The job, she explained, that of associate features editor, was previously held by a girl (her word) named Joan Didion, who had moved to California. The features department, Miss

Talmey continued, speaking in short, perfectly punctuated sentences, included all writing in the magazine which did not have to do with fashion or beauty. That meant feature articles, captions on feature articles written by free-lancers, captions and short features on food or furnishings, and reports on parties or other social events. The associate features editor was one of three (women) who did that writing. Excluded was the "People Are Talking About ..." column, which Miss Talmey wrote herself.

What salary, she asked me without pause, was I expecting? Surprise question. Somehow, I hadn't given the matter of a specific amount of money any thought at all. She stared at me now, her small eyes centered behind the small, round, red frames on her eyeglasses.

"Fourteen thousand," I heard myself say.

"That's too high," she said, again without a pause.

"What salary were you expecting to pay?" I asked.

"Eleven-five," she said.

"That's too low," I said (getting the hang of it now).

Pause.

"Twelve is as high as we can go," she said.

"May I think it over?" I said.

"Of course."

I didn't have the faintest idea what those numbers meant. Every job I had ever had before paid by the hour (research) or day (television) or week (theater) or by a flat fee or advance (books). I had never had nor heard a yearly salary. Later, my mother asked me why I had picked the number fourteen. I didn't know. I might as easily have said nine.

The conversation with my mother took place at dinner that night. I had just told both of my parents about the interview, which, by now, I thought was pretty funny. It didn't strike my parents that way. My mother sort of half-smiled, but mainly she looked startled, as if I had just told her that I had won at pole-vaulting. My father looked horrified. He was sure, by asking for such a fantastic sum, that I had blown it. "It's your first job!" he whispered as if someone might overhear. "You should pay *them!*"

By now, I had figured out what twelve thousand would be a week, and it *was* a lot of money. It was a lot for anyone in those days, and particularly for a "girl," and more particularly for a girl rookie. Still, my father's reaction made me stiffen. "If they didn't think I was worth it," I said, sitting up straight in my chair and placing a large piece of cake in my mouth, "they wouldn't offer it to me."

"How do they know you're worth it?" asked my father. There he had me. I swallowed the cake and wondered myself.

I wondered, too, at how much easier it was to bluff one's way into a job in print than one on the stage. It seemed to have something to do with the level of the job. If I had wanted to be a secretary at *Vogue*, surely they would have made me take a typing test (which I would have failed). For a high position, they had no test. I guess they picked me because they thought I could do the job. But why would they think that?

I never knew why.

CHAPTER
8

Lady editors at *Vogue* did not wear hats. They didn't have to. They were formidable enough without. In 1964 the *Vogue* editors and their like were among the last crop of women who built careers when most women didn't. So, in order to get where they were, they had to have fought to the kill. They had to be, to put it mildly, determined. Or neurotic. Or, like me, both (that is, neurotic, and, in my case, determined by default).

Vogue was tough. The fashion department was tough because it was supposed to be the best—and, under Diana Vreeland, it was. And the features department was tough because fashion, not features, sold the magazine, so the features department could afford to be the best—which, among the women's magazines, under Allene Talmey, *it* probably was. Operative words: Allene Talmey. When she wanted to, Miss Talmey had a special ability to make those who thought they were tough cower. And she wanted to a lot. Those of us who did not think we were tough did not cower; we crumbled. We shriveled. We dissolved. I know Joan Didion only slightly, but we share a unique Pavlovian symptom: to this day should we see or speak to or run into

Allene Talmey—and Joan says the same holds true on coast-to-coast telephone calls—our knees give. And the funny thing is, we both love her.

Throughout my tenure at *Vogue*, mercifully brief though it was, on an average of once or twice a week, something Miss Talmey said—sometimes it was just a look—would lead me to close my office door, lean against it, and cry. It wasn't that Miss Talmey raised her voice, nor even that she got angry. It was simply her way of making everyone who entered her office and stood on the other side of her desk feel like a worm. Say, God forbid, you wrote a convoluted sentence. She would call you into her office (you never knew at those times what you had done, only that it was bad), you would then lower yourself onto the straight-backed polished mahogany chair that faced her desk, hoping, all the while, that your beating heart would not rupture your chest wall. Whereupon she would look at you and, with her eyes fixed on your face, she'd hold up with two fingers—as if it were a soiled bedsheet—this execrable thing you had written. Slowly, she would read the offending sentence, lingering and slightly increasing the volume of her voice, when she got to the (particularly) offensive passage. Then she would place the paper down on her desk and look at you again.

"What is it you are trying to say, dear?" she would ask, pronouncing the word *dear* in the same tone of voice that is normally used for the word *moron*. Then, falteringly, you would say what you were "trying to say." You always knew what would come next, but it had the same sting as a surprise:

"Why didn't you *write* it that way, dear?" Unless you were so stupid as to try to explain, you would then rise, bite your lip (or your hand, whichever was nearer), take your paper back, and, as rapidly as possible, leave the room.

Convolution, however, was not the greatest sin. Writing a cliché was. In that event, the meeting would be shorter and less cordial. Sometimes she would stand behind her desk and, as you entered, spit the cliché at you: "*High as a kite?*" Then, again, louder and slower, letting each syllable drip like slime: "*High—as—a—KITE?*" Then she would thrust the article or caption or whatever it was at you, as if it had been used to wrap a flounder, with a final, deadly: "Change it."

There were two other women writers in the department and two secretaries, clustered in a small suite of offices, which, except for the bright green carpeting (leftovers from the fashion floor), looked like an accounting firm. Each of us dealt with the Talmey situation differently. The secretaries dealt with it by being perfect. The most senior other writer dealt with it by being cool (I never figured out if it was an act or if she had something surgical done to sever her nerve endings). The third woman, who was married to a French diplomat, handled it by being lah-dee-dah. "Really, how *boring* of her," she would say, swishing past me in the small office we shared, having just retrieved one of her pieces from the meat grinder.

Miss Talmey's reactions to pieces were not always delivered in person. Sometimes she wrote down what she thought in the margin and sent it back.

Once I submitted an idea for a piece for the Beautiful People series, which was in full swing then. Almost every issue of the magazine had a spread on the Beautiful People of Rome, the Beautiful People of Tangiers, the Beautiful People of Palm Beach, and so forth. The previous evening I had gone to a dinner party in Brooklyn Heights—a rather fancy section of Brooklyn—at which there were a number of social types who, it seemed to me, made the grade as Beautiful People. So, the next morning, I wrote a memo to Miss Talmey, suggesting *Vogue* do the Beautiful People in Brooklyn. I went to lunch before getting a reply. When I returned, I walked into my office and noticed that the memo had been placed back on my desk. I read the comment in the margin upside down: *"Good, Good!"* I was thrilled—and not too surprised. I *knew* I had a winner—an idea which was in keeping with the concept, yet it had a fresh twist. To think I had actually hesitated before submitting it! I shook my head and smiled to myself. Go with your instincts, I thought, go with your instincts. (I was at the stage where I liked to make lessons out of things.)

Then I walked around to the front of my desk and read the comment right side up. "Good God!" it said.

One reason for Miss Talmey's power over people—aside from the fact that she was the boss, aside from the fact that she knew how, and loved, to terrorize—was that Miss Talmey was always right. Also, she knew everything. She thought we writers should know everything, too. Now and then, probably to make sure that we *knew* that she thought we should know everything, she gave quizzes. The quizzes were not formal. They just felt formal. It wasn't so bad when they were given to the three of us, together. That way, at least, you could usually count on someone else besides yourself making a mistake. To be quizzed alone, however, was excruciating. Usually, a quiz followed a transgression. Once, for example, I spelled the choreographer George Balanchine's name wrong. Miss Talmey *hated* spelling errors. *Vogue* had a "checker" whose job it was to check spelling and punctuation, so there was little danger of an error going uncorrected (only the Lord could save her if she overlooked one) into the magazine; but Miss Talmey held that the writer should *never* depend on the checker and a writer who made a spelling error was simply and inexcusably *sloppy*. In addition to which, an error connoted *ignorance* and even more contemptible than *slop* was *ignorance*.

"How do you spell Balanchine, dear?" I was standing. She was seated at her desk. Her eyes were on the paper.

"D-did I spell it wrong?" I said, trying to keep my voice in a normal range.

"You spelled it B-a-l-*e*. There is only one *e*"—she was looking at me now—"in Mr. Balanchine's name and that is at the end."

"Of course—I—I knew that—I don't know why I—"

"Do you ever go to the ballet, dear?" Oh, God, it was going to be a ballet quiz. But maybe not: "Do you read newspapers, dear?"

"I read the *Times*," I said, confused now.

"Is that all?" she said.

I had no idea where this was leading—only that it was making me feel faint. "S-sometimes I read the *Post*—and, occasionally, *The Wall Street Journal*." (That was a lie. I never read *The Wall Street Journal*.)

"Do you read all sections of the newspaper?" she asked.

"Well, I try to," I said. (Another lie.)

"Who is Willie Mays?" My mouth went dry and my toes curled under in my shoes.

"He's a baseball player, I think."

"You *think?*" said Miss Talmey. "What team does he play for?"

"I'm not sure," I whispered, knowing all was lost.

"He plays for the Giants, dear," she said, pronouncing each word as if I were a lip-reader. "His batting average last year was three fourteen. You should know that. From now on, when you read the newspapers, dear, read every section. *Every* section of *every* newspaper." And then, as she was wont to do sometimes when the beating was over, she moved the corners of her mouth sideways (her version of a smile). "Okay?"

"Yes, Miss Talmey," I said, backing out.

Miss Talmey did have a heart. She just didn't like it to show. I knew that. Even so, it always startled me when it did show.

I had worked at *Vogue* only a few weeks when a problem developed which, I soon realized, I would have to tell her about. The problem was my analysis, which took four hours a week plus travel time, and had begun to cut seriously into my work day. I found myself arriving (sweaty and guilty) late two mornings a week, and leaving (furtive and guilty) early two afternoons. Finally, I couldn't stand it anymore, and on one of the sweaty, guilty mornings I marched, head bowed, into her office and confessed. I could hardly believe it. Before my eyes, she sprouted wings and a halo. "Don't worry, dear," she said with a little wave of her hand, "if you have an analytic appointment, you must be on time. And it certainly doesn't matter if you get here fifteen minutes late." Then, noticing, perhaps, that I had some difficulty making such a personal disclosure, she added, "It's no big deal, dear. Everybody around here has been analyzed." Then she grinned, suddenly, like a small, bad boy. ". . . and those who haven't *ought* to be."

There were other nice moments. Occasionally, there was even praise. That was wonderful—more wonderful afterward, however, than during, because praise was delivered in the same tone of voice as criticism; so often you didn't realize it was praise until it had ended. "Fine piece of work, dear," Miss Talmey would snarl as she swept by your office, on her way to the art department to give someone hell. Fortunately, there was usually someone around to verify. "Fine? . . . Did she say 'fine'?" I'd pounce on her secretary, Fran, or on whoever else might have caught it.

Generally, Miss Talmey liked my full-length pieces, which were mostly reportage. I was good at reportage because it didn't matter that I didn't know much. In fact, it almost helped. In reportage what matters, simply, is (1) noticing things, and (2) noticing them with a fresh eye. God knows, I had a fresh eye. Although come to think of it, with what else would I or anyone else behold an "Eat Happening" (Happenings are art forms related to theater, said the press handout) in a cave in the Bronx? The Eat Piece was my first for *Vogue* and Miss Talmey loved it. That is, she pronounced it "amusing." At *Vogue*, to be "amusing" (not funny—funny was something else) legitimized one's presence on earth.

When I got in trouble, it was usually over a caption or a very short piece. *Vogue* captions tended to be not Boy Walks Iguana or Miss DeWitt Relaxes by the Pool, but rather swift, knowing biographical sketches or short, knowing essays on medical breakthroughs—usually requiring a broad, at-your-fingertips sort of knowing, which, among other things, thanks to all of those artsy-fartsy courses I took at Sarah Lawrence, I did not have. Or, sometimes I had it, but I had it wrong.

Because of Miss Talmey's democratic concept of sin, all errors had equal weight. You could dazzle her with a three-thousand-word article one week, only to wind up in the doghouse the following week because of a grammatical flub in a caption about Brazilian horticulture. Whatever the subject, whatever its length, every piece written for *Vogue* under the command of Allene Talmey had to be stylish, lean, interesting, lively, and, above all, correct. Even if it was about nothing. Or, in a way, *especially* if it was about nothing.

One of the more formidable layouts I ever had to deal with at *Vogue* (thrust at me late one afternoon, natch) consisted of fifty silver cups, photographed by Irving Penn. "Write something snappy about silver, dear," said Miss Talmey, dropping the thing on my desk and sailing on. "About a hundred and fifty words."

I stared at the photostat and died the way I had died a year earlier when I stared at the stack of research on my desk about women who did television commercials. It was your basic oh-God-what-now juncture. Unlike the last time, though, the problem was not a plethora of research but a dearth of it. As I stared, I concentrated on the word *silver*, hoping something would come to mind.

Nothing came to mind.

The clock on my desk said 5:30. People were beginning to leave. I kept staring. Then everyone was gone and the cleaning woman came. I lifted my feet as she vacuumed and kept staring. Finally, for no other reason than the fact that I had to think of something, I thought of something.

Then I rewrote what I had thought of.

Then I rewrote it again. And again. At 8:30 P.M. I pulled it out of the typewriter. The office was still, except for faint blasts of car horns twenty floors below. I pushed my chair away from my desk and read:

It's a brigade of silver cups, polished for inspection, stacked the way we like to see them, and struck by light. With a look that is stubbornly simple, uncompromisingly cool, these silver cups, in ten patterns from seventeenth-, eighteenth-, and twentieth-century designs, work in groups, in twos, or alone. Here, in space-saving shafts at the bar, they are ready for the gamut of drinks—from Martinis to eggnogs. Elsewhere in the house, unstacked, they could just as effectively hold breadsticks, make-up brushes, clusters of anemones, peppermint sticks, vivid Japanese pencils, or miniature parlor palms in small pots.

What bullshit. But never mind. Here was bullshit I could be proud of. I put the paper inside my top desk drawer, covered the typewriter, stood up—not expecting my legs to be as stiff as they were—and walked slowly to the elevator.

Sometimes it surprised me, having heard my insides churn, how breezy and sure I managed to sound on paper. Sometimes I felt as if someone else had written the piece. In a way, someone else had. Although I learned a lot about writing at *Vogue*, I did not find "my own voice" there. But at that stage, I probably didn't have one. In order to have a "voice," you have to have a self; and between Miss Talmey and Dr. Shrink (not his real name) anything that might have passed for a "self" was coursing through the blender at high speed. When I did find my "voice" some years later, it turned out not to be so breezy and sure, so *Vogue* probably wouldn't have wanted it, anyway. Meanwhile, the basso profundo I had trumped up for the occasion seemed to be working. For the moment, anyway.

The elevator came, finally, and with no other passengers to stop for, dropped as if the cable were broken. Outside, the street was lit up and noisy and full of people—some dressed-up couples out for the evening; some out-of-town businessmen in twos and threes, laughing, looking for a bar or coming out of one; a woman in net stockings hailing a taxi. I looked up at the sky which was dark and clear, inhaled the air, felt it shoot up my nostrils, and, humming a little, began to walk home.

Had I had other jobs, I would have been acquainted with the following principle: in the workplace, the tasks one is given are not necessarily those which match one's inner gifts and personality structure, but, rather, the ones which need doing. Housewives also deal with this principle when they first experience the irrelevance of gourmet cooking skills, say, in the face of a toilet which needs cleaning.

The toilet which needed cleaning at *Vogue* was the society department. Nobody called it "society," by the way. "Society" was like "wealthy" or the unthinkably gross "swanky."

Nothing was wrong per se with the society department, only that it lacked a writer (enter yours truly) to cover and write up the social events—parties and charity hooplas, mostly—which blossomed forth in each issue of the magazine under the purposely dry title "Vogue's Notebook."

The precise social value of each event and person at each event was determined by a cranky octogenarian named Margaret Case, a thin, stylish woman, given to frequent and flowery snits, which caused her to growl and mumble to herself as she stalked the corridors each day. Handling frustration was not Margaret Case's forte. And when she became frustrated on the telephone, it could be dangerous for anyone else who happened to be in the room. If she was not hearing or getting what she wanted from the person on the other end, she'd occasionally express her irritation by hurling the telephone receiver, as if it were a softball, at the opposite wall. Miss Case had some difficulty keeping secretaries. But, while they were there, the smart ones paid attention while their boss was on the telephone.

Margaret Case never called anyone by name, not even Miss Talmey, and she had a way of looking at you as if she didn't know who you were. More specifically, she looked at you as if you had just come up to her in the street, dressed in rags, and asked for a quarter. Recognition hit, however, when she wanted something. At a party, for example, you'd know she meant you when you'd hear that voice from somewhere in the room: "HEY!" (Which meant she wanted your attention.) Usually, "HEY" meant, furthermore, that she wanted you to instruct the photographer to be sure to photograph this or that socially pivotal person. She almost never addressed the photographer herself. I think she felt it was beneath her, like placing your own telephone call, instead of having your secretary do it.

Once I was covering a big charity benefit at the Plaza Hotel and there were a lot of fast, fancy entrances in the midst of an unusually large crowd of both guests and press. The photographer and I were behind and slightly to the right of Miss Case, and I suppose she didn't realize how near to her we were. Suddenly, a striking woman, in a long black sequined dress lit up by a serious amount of serious jewelry, wafted into the room. Just as suddenly, I heard the rasp I had come to dread—louder than usual because we were nearer than usual. "GET THE PRINCESS! GET THE PRINCESS!" Then, *thwack!* she flung her right arm back, hitting me in the chest, at which point I lost my balance, fell on the photographer, who, in turn, lost his, and fell on someone with no sense of humor from *Town and Country*.

The truth was, Margaret Case was right not to trust me. I never did get the hang of who mattered and who didn't. The reason, at least in part, was that certain names automatically made certain people matter and, except for a few obvious ones like Rockefeller and Whitney, I didn't know what those names were. And when I guessed (on the basis of a Roman numeral III after a name, or because of an inordinately thin nose or a funny way of speaking), I usually guessed wrong. Nor did it help that in the sixties qualifications for social acceptability were changing. For example, the people on Long Island and in Lake Forest who had pedigrees but who didn't do much except clip coupons, play golf, and drink Chivas Regal were slipping somewhat. Whereas some accomplished people of questionable parentage—some Jews, for example, not necessarily Guggenheims or Lehmans either, and even an occasional black—were now let In, assuming *they had distinguished themselves at something suitable*, like running a country or conducting a symphony orchestra.

The relationship between Margaret Case and the features department, which is to say, between Margaret Case and Allene Talmey, was that of a lion and a Bengal tiger. There seemed to be a taut, careful, wordless agreement that each would live without bloodying the other. Strictly speaking, Talmey was boss; but she didn't mess with Margaret Case unless she had to. Talmey didn't give a damn what got covered or who got photographed—that she left entirely to Case—but she did care about the words. And, since all I wanted from life at this point was to please Allene Talmey, so, too, did I care about the words.

But there was a lot more to caring about the words than merely finding the most correct or even the most decorous ones. It meant writing surprises. Surprises, I had learned from Miss Talmey, were the opposite of clichés. It wasn't easy to surprise, and you had to be careful not to try too hard or the strain would show.

A surprise—an original thought or word or phrase—came most easily, I found, on the scene. That's because one's first (emotional) reaction to things is usually the truest, and the truest reaction is often the most original. Even at those silly parties, I found if I paid attention both to what I saw and to what I felt about what I saw, words would be there, the way steps to a dance are there when you're feeling the music. I'd scribble those words down—in the dark if I had to—and they were always better, fresher, more right, than anything I'd try to choreograph the next day at the typewriter.

I had worked up some faith in this method and some confidence in its results and that's probably what gave me courage for the big showdown with Margaret Case.

The source of the dispute was a scrawled notation I made at the opening of Shepheard's, a new discotheque in New York. The place had been jammed with celebrities, including, of all people, the Duke and Duchess of Windsor. It was dark and uncommonly noisy and one of my scribbles, which had to do primarily with the darkness, turned out to be just right. Or so

I thought when I looked at my notebook the next day in the office. It took no time to write the piece since I had already written most of it in my head, so after no more than an hour or so, I handed it over to Margaret Case. According to the routine, Case got first look, then it would go to Talmey for final approval.

The piece began:

> If you didn't know better (and everyone does), you'd think it was a teen-age hangout—without the teen-agers. Shepheard's is darker than the back seat of a car, more jammed than the senior prom, and when "Roll Over Beethoven" isn't on (the phonograph) "Hot Pastrami and Mashed Potatoes" is . . .

Not more than ten minutes after submission, Miss Talmey's secretary, who spoke only when it was absolutely necessary, ran into my office to warn me that Margaret Case was on her way to see me in what I gathered was a highly volatile state. I appreciated Fran's gesture and told her I did, but I knew from the look on her face that it was like alerting the defenses of Pearl Harbor on the morning of December 7, 1941. The bomb was already falling toward the ground.

I heard her voice before I saw her. "We can't have this! We can't have this!" Then, louder and nearer, "I won't have it! I won't have it!" By the time she got to my office, she was trembling. When I saw her, it occurred to me that she might fall over and die on my desk. "Darker than a back seat? Darker than a *back seat?*" she screamed, waving the paper in my face.

"Of a car," I added unwisely.

"Of a car! of a car! of a *car?*" she screamed louder, like a parrot gone berserk.

"Well, it was," I said evenly.

"NO PLACE," said Margaret Case, leaning on my desk now and glaring down at me, "ATTENDED BY THE

DUKE AND DUCHESS OF WINDSOR CAN BE—
DARKER THAN THE—THE BACK SEAT OF A CAR!
GET IT?" When she got to CAR, she began, inadvertently,
to spit. I stood up. At that point she slammed the paper on my
desk and stomped out.

I had to hand it to Margaret Case: she cared. I hated her and
her stinking values, but I had to respect the way she fought for
them. Which is not to say I didn't plan to fight back.

My two colleagues had come into my office now, followed
by Miss Talmey. "What was that about, dear?" said Miss
Talmey, standing in the doorway, wearing one of her ever-so-
slightly poisonous smiles.

"Miss Case says that any place that the Duke and Duchess
are in can't be darker than the back seat of a car," I said.

Miss Talmey frowned. "Why not?"

That was all I needed to hear. War was declared. It ended at
the end of the following day with a closed-door meeting
between Miss Talmey and Miss Case, which lasted about
seven minutes. Everyone in the outer office stopped typing
and speaking in order to eavesdrop. But we couldn't hear a
thing except the clock. At the end of the seven minutes when
Margaret Case clomped out, her mouth set, her eyes blazing
like headlights, we knew who had won. I almost felt sorry for
her. Almost.

Later that year, I was covering another party for *Vogue*
when, once again, there appeared the illustrious couple. Midway into the evening, I was introduced to the Duchess, who
was abundantly friendly and lively and, to my surprise,
seemed very curious about the nature of my work. (Had she
been anyone else, I would have thought she wanted the job.)
During our conversation, Margaret Case stood on the other
side of the room, eyeing me like Cinderella's stepmother. I did
not tell the Duchess about our little set-to. Winning, I
decided, was enough.

In September 1964 Miss Talmey fired me. "I'm letting you go, dear," she said one morning after one of my more witless caption errors. Exactly nine months had passed since she had hired me. I cried, of course, in the usual place—on the back of my door—but there was some relief in those tears. Lately, I had been writing more and more Notebooks and captions, and fewer and fewer articles, which, it turned out, the magazine could just as well buy from free-lancers.

The department's need, Miss Talmey explained, was not for long pieces, but for the Notebooks, captions, and miscellaneous paragraphs. For this, she explained further, she needed strong, sophisticated, knowing, speedy, and experienced writers. Not me, in other words.

"You're a good writer, dear," she said, her eyes pinned on me behind her round, red eyeglasses, as they were that first day. "In a way, I hate to let you go, but you don't know enough."

I looked right back into her eyes. "I understand," I said. And I did. I stood up, moved toward the door, then turned around. "I want to thank you, Miss Talmey, for teaching me how to write."

"Nonsense, dear. You have talent. Nobody can teach you how to write."

Then, for once, I contradicted her. "*You* did," I said.

And that was all there was to say.

CHAPTER
9

I must have had a date that year, but I don't remember having one. Of 1964 all I remember is: write, fret, eat, sleep, and shrink. And then it was over.

All the while, I did keep my promise to myself to "live somewhere"—my own place with my own family photographs, remember? Except, I happened to be going through a stage in my analysis of blaming everything on my parents, so I wasn't about to prop up their likenesses on bureaus and end tables. All the same, I no longer had to look at anyone *else's* parents . . . well, not strictly true. I had a roommate—an apartment-mate; we each had our own room—who put up *her* family's photographs. But they were in her room. Besides, I liked her family. I liked her. Molly Haskell was a girl from the South, as they used to say, with brains, looks, character, and a thorny sense of humor. We had met by accident, at a bridal shower of all things, just before I went to *Vogue*. As it happened, we were both looking for apartments, so we sized each other up and decided to face the perils of sharing. It worked. (Proof: we still speak.)

The place we found—how else? Through an ad in *The New York Times*—was a quirky walk-up, perched like a birdhouse, and not much bigger, atop a narrow, three-story building at the corner of Forty-ninth Street and Second Avenue. What must have been forty airline stewardesses and their trim legs, matching luggage, and assorted boyfriends lived in the apartment on the floor below; and underneath us all, on the ground floor, an Italian pastry shop, the smells from which floated up the stairs and continually lured us back down.

The apartment was considered four rooms because of the two bedrooms, but that was a laugh. The living room began at the entrance, like a foyer. In fact, it *was* a foyer, even smaller than the smallest bedroom, which was small. The "kitchen" turned out not to be a room at all, but a row of appliances on the farthest wall of the living-room-cum-foyer. Such was the noise from the traffic on Second Avenue that for five years we slept with earplugs, and kept spares for visitors. We were able to have intimate conversations with our guests, provided we sat in their laps. Otherwise, it was necessary to lip-read.

We were robbed twice—both times on Thanksgiving while we were having turkey up at my parents' house. (We wised up the third year, put the chain up on the door, and had turkey at home.) One year the bakery caught fire. No one got hurt and firemen put out the flames pretty quickly; but the smoke blackened our furniture, draperies, and most of our clothing.

Otherwise, it was a swell apartment and, now that I had graduated from Basic Training—i.e., *Vogue*—I could, at last, enjoy it. Ah, the pleasures of sleeping late, eating real breakfasts, and moving from one end of the day to the other without one moment of apoplectic terror. I even began going out with men again. No one elevated my pulse rate, but I liked knowing I'd be emotionally intact if it happened. Had Prince Charming surfaced and given me the magic kiss during the *Vogue* ordeal, I think I would have just opened one eye and rolled over.

I met some of my new dates through Molly, who had a

flotilla of gentlemen callers and didn't mind sharing them. Although, as I recall, she was less than amused at my calling them that. Molly loathed even the most oblique teasing about her Southern origins. I grew to understand why. In those days, if, in addition to being female, you were young and pretty and Southern, and on top of that, smart, the smart part, if anyone noticed it, was considered cute. But Molly had grit. The less that was expected of her, the more she delivered. In time, she became a film critic and lecturer, wrote a stunning book about women in film (*From Reverence to Rape*), and made an unconventional and rather late marriage to a brilliant film critic and scholar. She's still pretty, but no one mistakes her for Scarlett O'Hara anymore.

The women's movement had begun to roll in the middle sixties, but not so that anyone like Molly and me would notice. We read *The Feminine Mystique*, of course, but we couldn't see that suburban women's problems had anything to do with us. On top of which, I didn't get it. Here was I, steeped in fantasy about the joys of a normal life, i.e., husband, house, tree, child, car, and vacuum cleaner, only to find out that, according to this book, the women who had all of those things hated their lives and were having fantasies about mine!

If they only knew, I thought. Then I thought again. And read the book again. And I began to get it. Maybe I was lost and lonely, but I wasn't trapped. Maybe I was nowhere, but maybe nowhere was better than being somewhere you don't like. If nothing else, I thought, nowhere is easier to get out of. But the more I said that to myself and to Molly, and the more we talked about our wonderful freedom, the sour-grapesier it sounded. I pretended to think we were lucky. Meanwhile, I held onto my old fantasy.

Not that fantasies were uppermost in my mind then. Realities were. Like: now that I was unemployed again, where was the rent/food/shrink money going to come from? The booby prize for being canned turned out to be eligibility once again for unemployment insurance. That plus my savings plus my frugal ways would tide me over....But then what? I knew I should look for a job on another magazine. But I had lost my nerve.

Acting crossed my mind, but only for three seconds. Why return to an *old* punishment? During the *Vogue* year friends asked me sometimes if I ever missed acting, whether, when I went to the theater, I felt sad or nostalgic. "Sure," I'd say out of the side of my mouth, "just like an ex-hooker walking her dog gets nostalgic when she passes Eighth Avenue and Forty-third Street."

So: no magazines, no acting. That left one possibility: another book. Okay, on what? I thought and thought and snooped in bookstores and thought some more and, finally, in the middle of a warm tomato juice cocktail, on a boring date with a man who didn't drink (neither did I), it came to me: *The Non-Drinker's Drink Book*, starring, as the jacket eventually proclaimed, "Over 300 Non-Alcoholic Drink Recipes."

Another heist. Given the severe limitations of my culinary aptitude, that I convinced a publisher to give me real money to do anything that could be categorized as a cookbook, which this was, fractured my friends—not to mention my parents. "B-b-but," sputtered my father when we began speaking again, "what do you know about drinks?"

Poor father. I think with the signing of that book contract— Doubleday, again—his faith in America began to slide. Again, he was right. I knew nothing, as usual. But I had this other friend from Sarah Lawrence who had this mother who had this kitchen in Great Neck who had this time on her hands. We made a deal. For a credit, my friend's mother agreed to concoct (never has the word been more apt) non-alcoholic drink recipes, which I, in turn, would give names to and write up. Needless to say, the training I had received at *Vogue* in how to write about nothing came in handy.

I hung around the kitchen in Great Neck more than I had to. Funny that I did, because the place reminded me of that normal life I wanted and didn't have, and that got me down. I felt envious of my friend's mother. It was, I knew, ridiculous to feel envious of my friend's mother. But I did. For the usual reason. She had what I wanted. She had a place where she belonged, where other people expected her to be—a house, a very pretty house, a husband who did something serious (serious, meaning lucrative) and safe (safe, meaning lucrative)—and she did little projects such as this one, on the side, like (remember?) coleslaw.

I'd sit on a stool in her big, orderly, square, polished kitchen and feel, in contrast, like a bug—the sort of creature who flies in, flies out, lands here, lands there, and belongs nowhere, to no one. That, I also realized, was silly. I lived somewhere. My parents loved me, my friends....But the more I'd try to reason my way out of it, the downer in the dumps I'd get. Even so, as if my nose were glued to her window, I kept hanging around.

My reasons for hanging around were not purely masochistic. I was also curious to know what on earth my friend's mother was throwing into her blender. I wanted to know what the thing I wound up calling Phony Island Rum had *in* it. We had plenty of good times, too. Like the afternoon we tried to make gin without gin. We mashed no end of juniper berries, my friend's mother and I, threw in some other stuff, and, for a few enthralling hours, we thought we were on to something.

We weren't.

Books, like babies, always turn out to be a bigger deal than you expect. Even slapped-together books like this one. Recipes weren't enough for Doubleday. They wanted me to say cute things *between* recipes—a lot of cute things. And that is why and how I wound up for two months in the Frederick Lewis Allen Room of the New York Public Library, a fact which so shames me to this day that I recently made the library a beneficiary in my will.

My need for the room was reasonable enough. It's hard for a woman socialized in the fifties to write at home. The minute you stop typing, which you constantly do, and look up from the typewriter in order to ponder a word, your eyes inevitably fall on a torn slipcover, or a lampshade that seems suddenly too big or too small; not to mention all the plants that seem suddenly dry and spots on rugs that seem suddenly to have grown bigger, and on and on. Male writers don't have this problem. Men have not been socialized to see spots on rugs.

Neither sex, on the other hand, is impervious to the telephone. The problem with the telephone, I find, is not only the obvious one of receiving calls, but the ongoing temptation—in order to escape the tyranny of an unfinished sentence or paragraph—to make calls. To anyone. To friends to whom you have nothing to say, to gather information you don't need. Once I stooped so low as to telephone a movie theater for show times of a movie I didn't want to see.

It's also lonely to write at home. You know you're lonely when you find yourself in the basement shooting the breeze with the man who's come to read the gas meter. Also, working at home doesn't feel like work. That sounds nice, but it isn't. All it does is make you feel guilty at worst, peculiar at best. That's because work, as everyone knows, is what you "go to," not "stay to." So, on top of everything else, writing at home makes you feel like a parasite.

Enter Frederick Lewis Allen, a writer himself, who understood all of this, and as a result of his understanding and his money bequeathed to the library a room for writers, consisting of about ten cubicles, in which it is possible not only to type, but to leave your typewriter and other paraphernalia overnight for the duration of your book. The only requirement is that you have to have a book contract—a black and white confirmation that a publisher does, indeed, plan to print what you type. More than that, they don't ask. They didn't ask me, for example, to articulate the literary or historical merit of *The Non-Drinker's Drink Book.*

So I got in, not realizing how it would feel to have a poet and novelist in the next cubicle, writing about the firmament; James Thomas Flexner on my other side, laboring over his definitive biography of George Washington, which won both a National Book Award and a Pulitzer citation; while I sat in between, typing, "Ginger ale isn't all bad. It just needs help."

Whenever anyone in the room got up to go to the bathroom and passed behind my chair, I would smile inanely and, casually, throw my body over the manuscript. I tried not to make friends with anyone because I knew, sooner or later, they would ask about the subject of my book. But I made friends, anyway. It was impossible not to. I was the only female in the room under sixty. So when they did finally ask what my book was about, I said drinking and changed the subject. As a result, I think they assumed I was an alcoholic and that my book was a confessional, which was fine with me.

Summer '65: I finished the book and began to think about magazines again. I felt too nervous, still, to try for a staff job, but I needed money again, so I had to do something—a single piece, perhaps, on a safe subject—but for whom? Not *McCall's*, certainly. And because of my history at both *McCall's* and *Vogue*, I thought it wise to steer clear of the other ladies' magazines. There were the newsmagazines—*Time* and *Newsweek*. But I had heard they ran assembly lines at those places—that one person researched, another wrote, another rewrote, and nobody got a by-line. No, thank you. *Reader's Digest* struck me as too pure; *Esquire*, too male and too jaded; *The Atlantic* and *Harper's*, too intellectual (for me); *The New Yorker*, too exclusive. That left *Life* and *Look*. I liked *Life*, but its emphasis seemed to be on pictures more than words. Besides, *Life* was part of the *Time-Life* empire. Too big. That left *Look*.

I didn't want to lean on Henry Ehrlich again. But I knew from experience how much it helped to know someone on the inside. I asked around. A female photographer whom I knew because she had photographed me once for a magazine when *I Thee Wed* was published, told me about a woman *she* knew at *Look* who, according to the photographer, had both brains and power. In those days, the power was the unusual part. There were a lot of smart women around and some of them had top jobs on the women's magazines, but *very* few women had anything resembling power on any of the general-interest, mass magazines. Pat Carbine at *Look* (today she's the publisher of *Ms.*) was an exception. She got to be an exception, I suspect, because (1) she had brains and a good commonsensical way of using them; (2) the editor-in-chief liked her and made her his protegée; (3) nothing in her personality made him—or any of the other men in power at *Look*—feel that she wanted power; and (4) they were wrong; she wanted power.

My first visit to *Look*, then, engineered by my photographer friend, resulted from some early "networking," women-helping-women sort of thing. But there were a couple of outstanding differences from today's version. Today, first of all, networking is as common as the Heimlich maneuver. In the middle sixties, even if anyone had decided to push the notion, it wouldn't have amounted to much because there weren't enough women at the top—or even in the middle—to make it work. Nor can I say that Pat Carbine, one of the few women who was up there, gave me an assignment the first time I went to see her because of my sex. *However*, because of my sex she might have seen in me someone who wouldn't flinch at doing the kind of "light" pieces most *Look* men wouldn't do. And she must have known that, not only because of my girlish ways, but because of the article ideas I brought along when I went to see her.

I did not march into *Look* with ideas on the Soviet tank buildup or the fluctuating economy. Because of what had happened at *McCall's*, I didn't even march in with ideas about minority women or mental hospitals. Instead, I minced in with something sufficiently silly for me to feel capable of pulling it off. A fancy new reducing salon had recently opened in the East Fifties where, for a grand sum, women got wrapped like mummies in bandages soaked with a "secret solution" and sat around for hours, sweating like Japanese wrestlers and theoretically—and, it turned out, *only* theoretically—getting thin.

Unlike the *Vogue* militia, Pat Carbine wasn't a killer. She was a nun. I don't mean the perpetually self-blessing sort, but rather a kind of saloon nun, the kind that laughed loud and hugged hard and made you feel that you could tell her anything. She had a no-fooling-around round, full, firm body and a pretty, unmistakably Irish face and loved to tell about the Catholic school she went to in Philadelphia, where patent-leather shoes were forbidden because they reflected your underpants.

Carbine got from people what Talmey did, but rather than using terror she employed instead a potent lure of charm and morality. You obeyed her because you loved her, and also because you knew whatever she asked you to do had to be Right.

Unlike Talmey, Carbine was not a word person—maybe she knew an adjective from an adverb, but I don't think she knew a cliché from her elbow. Rather, her interest, and her skill, lay in thinking up ideas for stories and matching those ideas with writers. Pat Carbine had a way, too, of telling you about an idea—which is to say, of giving you an assignment as if it were a present, a wonderful present she found especially for you. "Close the door," she'd say, as if she didn't want the other children to hear. "Sit down." By now, she had your pulse going. Then she'd clap her hands together, and lean forward on her desk. "Tell me," she'd whisper, face flushed, as if she were about to burst from the excitement, "have you ever been to Mexico?"

One week later, you'd find yourself at the original homesite of Montezuma's Revenge, trying unsuccessfully for the third day to get the hotel to get the toilet fixed; but such was the job Pat Carbine would have done on you that not until the fourth day would it fully register that the assignment was not such a swell present, after all. You'd return home, then, weary and thin and pale and cranky, and she would kiss the top of your head and tell you (and tell everyone else, if she thought you'd like that) how great you were, how *courageous*, how *talented*, until she had you back in her lap, purring—and ready for the next assignment.

Thinking back now, I realize I never worked for companies or magazines. I worked for (not necessarily benevolent) bosses. I didn't work for *Vogue*, but for Allene Talmey. And from the end of 1965 through 1971, I didn't work for *Look*, but for Patricia Carbine. I have not the slightest doubt that my devotion to these women, given its slavish extent, had a neurotic component. I had an obvious need for authoritative, surrogate mothers and their approval. I know all about it. (With the time and money I spent on the couch, I *should* know all about it.) But my craziness was a useful craziness. And I had good taste in surrogate mothers. Needing to please Talmey and Carbine made me better at what I did.

Plighting my troth to female magazine editors, however,

was not bringing me any closer to plighting my troth to anyone else. Sometimes I felt as if, by mistake, I had gotten on the wrong train. I *knew* it was the wrong train—everything that flashed by outside the windows told me so—but, oddly, unexpectedly, I had begun to enjoy the trip anyway. I enjoyed finding the right words to say things and writing those words down. I enjoyed—especially after acting— aiming to tell the truth. What I told the truth about—trivia or non-trivia—didn't seem important. For now, it seemed important only to get better at the telling.

I didn't know where this train that I was on was headed. But I figured it would probably be better than where I'd been.

CHAPTER
10

L*ook* didn't propose right away. We had about three months of dates first, during which time I wrote pieces freelance—besides the one about the dummies in bandages, a profile of Barbara Harris, the actress, and one or two more. Then, one bright, cold afternoon in January, in lieu of an engagement ring, they gave me Johnny Carson.

To be given someone to write about for *Look* meant hanging around the person for days, sometimes weeks, watching him work, watching him play, watching him do anything he would let you watch—until you felt that you had absorbed enough to write the story. All the while, a *Look* photographer would circle the person like a hornet, shooting hundreds of pictures in order to wind up with the three or four which, eventually, accompanied the story.

Somewhere in the middle of the hanging around, there would be an interview, but by that time, you, the writer, would know, from all the watching, whom you were interviewing. It was a fine system and a fair system—assuming the writer was fair—because the writer would write mainly about what he or she saw of the person rather than what he or she was told by the person—or by anyone else. The most rudimentary exposure to public relations teaches a celebrity how to lie with words (which is why most television interviews are baloney). Lying with behavior is harder, especially a week's worth.

Once I did a story for *Look* about a woman in Washington, D.C., who, to listen to her words, was canonizable. On the third day of hanging around, however, I happened to notice the contemptuous and snooty way she treated her secretary. Then—as often happens—having seen one clue, I saw others like it. When the story finally appeared in the magazine, it was not a portrait of a Saint Theresa, but of the woman this woman really was. She didn't like it, and, in fact, tried hard to get me fired. An interview, alone, no doubt, would have resulted in a story which would have pleased her.

The Johnny Carson story was preceded by summit-length negotiations between *Look*'s managing editor and Carson's "people" (stars and politicians always have people around them who are called their "people"), after which the terms of coverage were agreed upon, as they would be for any business deal. The most basic part of a deal between a magazine and a star, however, is understood without being written or spoken. It goes something like this: in return for thousands, even millions, of dollars' worth of free publicity, all the more valuable because it's "journalism," not paid advertising, in a magazine deemed worthy by the star's "people"—publicity which they may want at this particular time in order to publicize the star's new movie or television special—the star agrees to make her or himself available to the reporter from the worthy magazine. Further, it is understood that the star will open him or herself up to the reporter to a reasonable extent, so that the reporter has access to the person behind the public image, and so that the journal gets a story which, while it satisfies the star's wish for publicity, doesn't reek of it. That's the basic deal.

In addition, depending on the star's importance, needs, or quirks, there may be a further agreement to keep off certain subjects—the fifth marriage, say, or the plastic surgery. Or there may be photographic restrictions—no shooting during the final rehearsal and the like. No unusual provisos were made in the Carson deal, only that the formal interview time had to be limited to an hour, or maybe two; and that we were to do our hanging around mainly in Las Vegas, where Carson would be performing for a couple of weeks during a break from *The Tonight Show*.

Also understood and also unspoken in a deal between magazine and star is the risk, on the star's side, that the story may not be flattering—a risk a star and his "people" are usually willing to take, particularly if the magazine is "respectable," which, mercy me, *Look* certainly was.

So, a *Look* profilee could count on the piece not being sleazy, and know that, at worst, it might be inane. And should it cut a bit, or belie the star's image—well, he and his people could always face the East, inhale, and focus on the proverbial solace: that we spelled his name right.

The first meeting: me, the photographer Stanley Tretick, Carson, and Carson's "person"—on that occasion, one lone public relations man—took place in Carson's hotel suite and had all the spontaneity, warmth, and ease of a first meeting with one's mother-in-law.

I was sure it was me. Not used to big stars and all that. The second meeting was worse. By the third (these were short, informal encounters, by the way, not interviews) I began to think it wasn't me. The problem with Carson was not that he wouldn't speak. He spoke. He even joked. He was polite. But it was all patter. And there didn't seem to be any way to get behind the patter. When we tried to get near him, he'd jump back, almost literally. I began to feel less like a person than a land mine. He needn't have loved us, or even liked us, in order for a story to happen. Nor did he have to give us any dirt. We didn't want him to strip. We only wanted him to take his tie off, to let go enough for us to get a small sense of who he was. Instead, every time he saw us coming, he put on an emotional tuxedo. The photographer wasn't getting anything, either. Every time Stanley raised his camera, the man in the tuxedo went one further: he turned to stone.

After three days of this, I started to worry. "Stanley," I said to my bronzed colleague one afternoon at the pool (our tans at this point were progressing far more rapidly than our story), "I'm worried."

"Don't worry," said Stanley, turning over on his stomach with a small grunt.

"Okay, but tell me *why* I shouldn't worry," I said, aware that Stanley Tretick had about fifteen years on me in this business and knew a lot.

"Because," he said, "life's too short."

I wasn't having a nice time. It wasn't only the story (or lack of one). It was the place. I hated Las Vegas. I hated it the moment I saw it. I hated everything about it. I hated, most of all, my room. It wasn't merely gross—I had expected that— but *grossly* gross. It wasn't a room merely to suit a gangster, but a giant gangster. The bed would have accommodated any seven people I knew, and the plastic-cum-crystal chandelier overhead would have, had it fallen, crushed all seven to death. The dimensions of the coffee table matched those of my bathroom at home and on the bed, windows, chairs, hung an ersatz gold brocade so dense that, had seven other friends been under *it* when it fell, they, too, would have been flattened.

The lobby was equally frightening. In the lobby— carpeted, of course, and gargantuan since it spilled into the gambling area—not only was the decor alarming, but so were the people. The people, that is, as they gambled. The way they looked when they did it, lunging over the roulette table, like horses at a trough; propped up on stools around the blackjack tables as if stuffed; or wandering between and among the tables as if the keys in their backs had jammed. There was on their faces a look of such cheesy vacuity I knew it had to be the place that did this to them—and that at home, celebrating Christmas, or in their backyards, raking leaves, they wouldn't look that way.

The Las Vegas air should be mentioned here. There wasn't any. I knew in my head that whatever was hanging out there had to be air, but whatever-it-was had no smell, no freshness, nothing about it that reminded you of the sensation of air as you had previously known it.

Nor was there time in Las Vegas. Outside, the sun went up and down, as in other places; but since there was no air outside—and, more to the point, no gambling—nobody went outside; and inside, day and night were the same. Had they tested Las Vegas on rats first, it probably would have been kept off the market.

"Maybe human contact isn't possible here," I said to Stanley over dinner that night. (I had just lost my way coming back from the salad bar; we were in one of the town's best-known "steak pits"—aptly named, I thought, given its enormity, darkness, and the fact that, once inside, you felt you had been lowered into a vermilion hole.)

Stanley laughed. "Somehow," he said, "I don't think our problem is geography."

"Hi, I'm your waitress. My name is Bunny," intoned a young girl with almost nothing on.

"Hi," I said. Then, turning back to Stanley—who, understandably, had moved his attention from journalism to Bunny—"Okay, I give up. What *is* our problem?"

"We'll be ready to order in a minute," said Stanley to

Bunny as she stood there, smiling with her mouth open as if she expected us to place a peanut on her tongue.

"I'm not sure what our problem is," he said, looking at me again. "I've seen guys like that before—skittish with the press—but I don't think that's it. I don't think it's us."

"You mean you think he's like that with everyone?" I said.

Stanley shrugged. "Could be."

Smart Stanley. Very smart. The next day I went to see Carson's (now ex-) wife, his (now ex-) producer, and his brother and (now ex-) director of *The Tonight Show*. I mentioned that we were having some trouble "getting through" to Johnny. His wife had a terse explanation. "He just doesn't go in for people," she said with a short (very short) laugh. I saw the producer next. "I'm Johnny's best friend because I'm not interested in his friendship. I don't try to make contact with him. Sometimes we go to dinner together. If he's altogether uncommunicative, I just leave ..." And Dick Carson, the star's brother: "We're not close. Nobody in our family ever says what they really think or feel to anyone else."

"You know what?" I said to Stanley later. "I think the thing that has been getting in the way of the story *is* the story. We've been in such a state about not getting near the guy, but what you said in the restaurant was right. He's not hiding anything. That's *him!*"

That evening Stanley and I decided to go backstage before the show. A half hour or so before curtain, we spotted Carson standing by himself at the end of a long hallway near an exit door, smoking a cigarette, staring at the painted bricks on the opposite wall. Stanley and I were at the other end of the corridor. He knew we were tailing him that evening, but at that moment he seemed not to see us. I looked at Stanley, Stanley looked at Carson, and slowly he lifted one of the cameras around his neck to his face. "Click." Then he raised the other camera. "Click . . . click . . . click." Then Carson's head snapped around. "Hi," he said, flashing his public smile. "How're ya doin'?" And the moment was over. But we had it.

The following morning I called the press agent and asked for an hour's interview time. At four o'clock that day, I went to his hotel suite, which was almost as large, and about as cozy, as an airport waiting room. Carson greeted me and asked me if I'd like a drink. "Ginger ale would be fine," I said, trying to decide when to say it. He went toward the bar. Now, I decided: "We've been having a hard time doing this story on you."

"Oh yeah?" he said, sounding interested. His back was to me as he poured the drinks. "How come?"

"Well, you're not easy to know . . . you're not very— open."

He slapped the bottle down on the bar and turned around. He looked sore. "What's the matter?" he snapped. "I'm friendly, aren't I? I'm polite, aren't I? I'm honest." He turned back to the bar, picked up the two drinks, walked over to where I was sitting, gave me my ginger ale, and sat down on the other end of the seven-foot sofa. He looked at me again. I said nothing. "All right, my bugging point is low. I'm not gregarious. I'm a loner. I've always been that way. Is that a crime?"

I laughed. "Of course not! But it's *interesting* that you're that way." Quietly then, I asked him how a loner wound up as an entertainer, and as such a gifted one.

"I don't mind a crowd of people in an audience," he said, as if it were the most obvious answer in the world. "I'm detached from them."

I couldn't wait to find Stanley. I called his room. Not there. I went down to the lobby, then the restaurant. I finally found him in the pool. He was easy to spot because he was the only one swimming. The others, mostly women, stood or strolled in the water in full makeup, not to mention hats, sunglasses, and earrings. "Stanley," I shouted, waving my notebook, "I got it!"

I realized later that everyone at the pool probably thought I had broken the bank. In a way, I had. Thanks to good old leave-me-alone Johnny Carson, I went home not only with a story, but after it was published (*Look*, January 1966), with a job on the magazine—and a title: Associate Editor, which was changed, about one year and twelve stories later, to another title: Senior Editor.

When something is good, you don't always know it. When it's over and life starts getting rotten again, *then* you know it. Happily, that was not the case with me and *Look*. I knew while it was happening that it was good. And when it was over and when, during the first few years in television, life got rotten again, I just knew it more.

Let me count the ways: First, *Look* was a family. That sounds corny, doesn't it? In fact, *Look was* kind of corny; I would even go so far as to say triumphantly corny. Notwithstanding the glut of uplifting stories about quadriplegic swimmers, the magazine managed to be wholesome without being sloshy. And at the office, such a palpable sweetness ran through the place as to make you wonder if they had put something in the water cooler. Maybe it was because the magazine had originated in Iowa and continued to be printed in Des Moines. Working there, one did get the feeling that a chunk of the heartland had split off from the rest and landed, intact, on Madison Avenue, between Fifty-first and Fifty-second streets.

Look seemed small-towny because of its size, too. At its peak, the writing population hit about twenty, plus not more than about a hundred others—hardly anyone at all compared with its rival, *Life*, which as a weekly and as a half-news-magazine, needed more people to get stories faster. *Look* covered no news as such, only features, and it published biweekly; so that, too, accounted for its exuding more of Des Moines's flavor than Manhattan's. People were not required to move as fast at *Look* as at the big-city news places. So they didn't. And as a result of moving slower, they paid more attention to one another.

Look had its bad apples—or should I say rotten ears of corn?—and not all of the good-hearted people were good at their work. There were also snits and jibes and rivalries and losses of temper and all of those normal ignobilities which rise to the surface whenever two or more people convene on a regular basis. But there was, at *Look*, less of all that than at other places—no scientific survey here, just observation and hearsay—and far more of the good stuff: civility, kindness, support, loyalty, and merriment.

I was struck by all of this right away—and moved by it. To me, *Look* felt like a good adoptive home after a lot of crummy foster care. All of this did *not* add up to being coddled, however. Pressure to perform ran alongside benevolence like piccolo and trombone in "The Stars and Stripes Forever." If one story worked, congratulations-and-on-to-the-next. So, feeling loved did not keep me from feeling anxious. Goodbye, General Talmey; hello, general fear. Fewer tears, more indigestion.

And what was the little girl afraid of? That's easy: being found out. In my mind, I was an imposter—not a real writer like the others, not smart enough, not this enough, not to mention that enough. Surely, therefore, sooner and probably not later, one of those grown-ups would get wise. You'd think that the rapid-fire production of thoroughly acceptable pieces might have altered this perception, but no. By this time, terror felt normal. It wouldn't have occurred to me to question it or its source.

It occurs to me now, however. I know, partly, it was my background—having been an actress, or, at least, how I felt about having been an actress. (Ashamed.) I think, too, it had a lot to do with being a woman. I say that because I've heard so many other career women—and not so many "career men"—whisper, to each other, usually, about feeling the same way. Before the women's movement took hold—and even today, to a lesser extent—women did not feel that they really belonged in the workplace the way men did and do; nor did they feel as capable. (Nor did they feel as bad about not feeling as capable as men do.) Cleaning women, nurses, receptionists, and secretaries were exceptions. The lower-level the job, in other words, the more "comfortable" it was.

Anyway, female shops like *Vogue* were, in those days, what Harlem used to be for Negroes. You may not have liked the place, but at least you were pretty sure you got off at the right stop. In going to *Look*, then, I left the ghetto and moved for the first time into the male work world. I liked it—and felt far more warmth from the men at *Look* than from the female collection at *Vogue*. Even so, it was their turf, not mine. They had invited me in; and they made me feel welcome, but I never forgot my place.

When ambitious blacks and women make it out of their respective ghettos, they usually arrive at the new place with an emotional knapsack packed with awe, gratitude, discomfort, fear, all of which add up to pay dirt for employers; because, chances are, an employee with that kind of baggage is going to knock him or herself out working. I did—although I probably gained as much as the company. I was still young, after all, and needed and wanted to learn, and I've always learned best when I've been scared or upset. Even during school days, all I needed was to have a fight with my parents or break up with a boy and my grades would jump.

Which, by the by, reminds me: it wasn't as if my labor at *Look* was keeping me from anything or anyone *else*. I had, remember, no husband waiting at home at the end of the day for his hug and his chicken surprise; no children who needed help with long division. Nobody wanted anything of me, except my mother, and all *she* wanted of me was that I get a husband and children who wanted something of me. I wanted that, too, as I guess I've mentioned a couple of dozen times before. I was lonely. But working hard kept me from noticing that I was lonely. I had a family at the office. They needed me, and that was good enough. Except for a moment at the end of each day when I'd realize, without especially wanting to, that my "family" was going home to their real family.

Like any other, the *Look* family had a structure. Pat Carbine, who was officially titled Managing Editor—which placed her among several number twos in the hierarchy— was, of course, Mother (sometimes called Mother Superior). Mother *pretended* to defer to Father—a succession of male editors—but we children knew who really was boss. Martin Goldman, senior copy editor at the time, reigned as the eldest sibling. (Guess who the youngest sibling was.) Martin was bony and professorial and had a big Adam's apple and wore bow ties, and made a wonderful older brother. He pretended to be gruff, but the louder he growled the more certain you could be that he was fooling.

Editing sessions with Martin Goldman were like playing word games. He'd read your piece alone, first; a telephone summons would follow. "Rollin!" he'd bark, causing damage to your inner ear, "Sharpen your little pencil and get over here." His stern tone of voice usually made me giggle— and run.

"Hmfff," he'd say through his nose when I got to his office three seconds later, "what took you so long? Siddown!" Then I'd pull a chair up next to his at his desk under a bulletin board on which was posted his most cherished nut note, which began, "Dear Nigger Jew," and with the manuscript spread on his desk like a chessboard, we'd start to play. There was Kill the Adjective, Goose the Verb, Find the Buried Meaning (his favorite), Pick-A-Title (my favorite), and Cutouts (my least favorite).

At the beginning, because Martin was not terrifying, I assumed he wasn't any good. This attitude, I learned on the couch, mirrored the one I hold in my private life. If a man was kind and liked me, I thought he was weak. Sad to say, the moronism of that view registered at the office years before it did at home. It didn't take me long at all to absorb the fact that Martin was far from being weak.

He was, however, crazy. Martin carried on about words as if they were children. Sometimes he behaved like an overconscientious headmaster of a school—the sort who, if confronted by a student with the sniffles, would track the parents down in the African bush to let them know. Once I was on location, covering a movie in a remote, hilly place in northern California. At the same time, a piece I had finished was about to be shipped to the printer in Des Moines. I had just begun on the movie story and was trying hard not to get in the way. The movie had a cast of, if not thousands, hundreds, not including the animals (the big kind: horses and cattle), and there was enough dust to choke the lot. They had only one portable telephone rigged up, clearly for emergency use, period. So, when the assistant director came up to me during the shooting and whispered that I had a long-distance phone call, I raced to the telephone, expecting to hear that one or both of my parents were dead.

But no, it was Martin, bellowing about an adverb. "NOW HEAR THIS, ROLLIN! I KNOW IT'S HARD TO CONCENTRATE OUT THERE UNDER THE PALM TREES, BUT IF YOU DON'T GIVE ME SOMETHING BETTER THAN 'SAUNTERED HAPPILY' BEFORE FIVE O'CLOCK TODAY, OUR TIME, THERE WON'T *BE* ANY MORE PALM TREES! NOW THINK!" Click.

Given the chance, one would try to counter Goldman's long-distance diatribe with hauteur. "Really, Martin," I'd intone with a Dietrich sigh, "go bother someone in another time zone, will you?"

But I knew perfectly well what a fine thing it was for a magazine—in the person of a mad copy editor—to be chasing its writers on the far side of continents over a small assemblage of letters. A much saner and cheaper way to operate would have been for Martin himself to change the word. But that was not done. The unwritten code said: the writing belongs to the writer. The editor may criticize, recommend, or even insist on any manner of alteration and/or destruction. But it is the writer who performs the alteration and/or carries out the destruction. An editor doesn't rewrite, any more than he or she would spank another person's child.

Most good magazines follow the same code. But you can't count on it. Many years later, after *Look*'s death, the magazine was revived—in name only, but I didn't know that—for about a year. The new editor asked me to write a piece and, in a wash of sentimentality, I said yes. One of the nastiest surprises of my small, sheltered journalistic life was to open the issue, read the piece, and discover words I had not written, conclusions I had not made, and entire sentences reassembled like sheets of scrap metal in a munitions plant.

On another occasion the *New York Post* shortened a piece I

wrote by lopping off the final paragraph, which was like helping a person lose weight by cutting his feet off.

I've never been a princess about making changes in a piece. On the contrary, I like editing—good editing. But an edit is not the same as an assault. Unless he's reporting from the front, the writer should always get a crack at making the changes the editor wants before the editor makes them—not only for reasons of politesse, but for the sake of consistency of tone and the rest. A person's writing is not so different from his handwriting. If someone else crosses out some of your letters and writes in some of his own, that sentence is going to look funny.

As injustices go in this world, the rape of a sentence shouldn't count for much. And I know it is wrong never to forgive a person merely for fiddling with a bunch of words. But it does, and I don't.

*L*ook, that is, the old *Look* showed respect for its writers in other ways than editing. For example, the kinds of surprises that *McCall's* had spurned were revered at *Look*. They actually liked it when you found something out there that hadn't occurred to them in the office. And because they were so corny, they liked it when you told the truth. They were also wise to the probability that the truth reads better. In short, they trusted the writer. They believed what you wrote. They believed *you*. They believed you, moreover, even when it was your word against someone else's. Even when the someone else was Cary Grant.

The Cary Grant set-to happened during my first year at *Look* when, as the opposition knew, I was still vulnerable. I had been sent to California on what a person who gushed would call a dream assignment—to do a quiet, at-home story on Cary Grant. I arrived on a Tuesday with a first meeting set up for the following day. Then I got suddenly sick—food poisoning or something—so the date was postponed until the following afternoon. Grant knew about the change, of course, as did his California "people" (when you're really hot stuff you have "people" on both coasts), but later it became clear that his people in New York hadn't known. Because when they called *Look* Wednesday morning to renege on the story—why, I never found out—their excuse was that I had, in some way, offended Mr. Grant (a small gaucherie, but you know how sensitive he is). Since I hadn't had the pleasure of meeting Mr. Grant, nor he me, my alibi was golden. But what I remember best about the incident was the telephone call from Pat, and the strong sense I had that, even if a meeting between Grant and me had taken place, she would not have believed that I had acted badly if I said I hadn't. That was important to me. Very. It matters, after all, that your family trusts you.

CHAPTER
11

My head was definitely shrinking. I wasn't a whole lot happier, but I was smarter. (I was also poorer. This was not turning out to be one of your overnight head jobs.) Unfortunately, my craziness was not the nice, focused kind—a fear of tinfoil or caterpillars or shrill noises—the sort of thing you can zero in on and expel like a cyst. What ailed me was both more diffuse and more ordinary: in the main, too much mother and not enough father. I never (consciously) blamed my father for his indifference. In those days fathers were not required to get involved with their children—especially daughters—unless they wanted to; and my father did not want to. It was nothing personal. My father simply never knew what to make of me.

Also ailing me was a touch—okay, more than a touch—of masochism, a vat of guilt, and the usual medium amount of repressed anger and sexuality—the same bunch of stuff everyone has, and nothing that the good German couldn't fix. But, clearly, I would not be ready, as they say, before Christmas.

Meanwhile, my external life had improved mightily. I had a terrific job, a cheery apartment—notwithstanding the din and the less-than-grand dimensions—a good-humored roommate in Molly, and in spite of psychoanalytic wallet depletion, I even had a little money. All that stuff about feeling like an interloper at *Look* didn't keep me from holding them up. It's amazing how far you can get with a toy gun. All you do is hold it steady and they think it's the real McCoy. I asked for money as if I expected and deserved it, and whap! they handed it over. Easy.

By now, I also had a fine collection of (mostly unmarried) friends. Besides Molly and Leo, the Sarah Lawrence pack reemerged: my old singing roommate from West End Avenue, Joanna Simon, who had moved into her exotic-romances-with-foreign-conductors phase; Erica Abeel, just divorced and shaky and a long way from writing her book about it (*Only When I Laugh*); and Pat-from-Cambridge, the only one of us who had gone the normal route—husband, babies, suburbs—but who stayed connected to us through two-way girlish letters in longhand and occasional visits to New York, after which we'd all be hoarse from "telling everything" in turn.

If you're not married—and, on top of that, are an only child—friends often become more than friends. They also turn into the husbands, brothers, sisters, and children you don't have. We trusted and loved and comforted each other, my friends and I—all the more for those other people we were replacing—and for the sense we had that the men in our lives might come and go, but that we would not.

Hallelujah, sound of trumpets, I also managed to find a beau in the late sixties. What helped that along, no doubt, was getting the word that Dan had married—someone in the Project who sounded far holier than me (and was, I hoped, uglier). What helped even more was the new intelligence I had been receiving on the couch that my attraction to Dan had a lot to do with his low-key but powerful contempt of me.

Psychology has often been said to kill romance. In this case, death was welcome.

I met the new man on a cross-country flight. Except for his state of origin—California—he was a different breed from Dan altogether. He had a mustache, a suave but not oily manner, and fell into the "older man" category, which is to say he raised me by eighteen years. However, since he was a Californian, he had a perfect body—and a sweet center, like a cream-filled chocolate. I wasn't gone on him, but he was funny and kind and I liked him a lot; and for a while I felt like a "two" instead of a "one," and that, in itself, made me feel refreshingly normal and whole. I still had not gotten the word that I could feel normal and whole without a man. (When I finally got it, I felt *sort* of normal and whole; but I didn't feel good.)

The romance ambled along agreeably for two years or so, until my battery gave out. Then I was a "one" again. But being a one didn't feel quite as bad as it had before. I still wanted to find someone to love, as the song says, but I no longer needed marriage to go with it, as the other song says— at least not the way I used to. Alone or not, I still had a life. I had an apartment, friends, a doctor, parents whom I was learning, at last, to love in an adult way, and a growing sense of what feminists call being "your own person." I hate the language, but the concept's on the money.

I also had, by almost anyone's standards—and certainly by my own—one lulu of a job.

Look had put me on the movie-star beat, an odd beat to be on in 1967–1970. America was having convulsions: we were at war—there was a fearsome rise in crime—revolution in the schools—drugs—assassinations—and where was I? Hanging out in Beverly Hills, trying to get a handle on the Smothers Brothers.

I would *like* to report that I felt shame and guilt about what I was doing. I felt no shame and no guilt. I felt happiness and gladness. I felt lucky. I felt whoopee, at last I've found the sort of work that suits me: i.e., dissecting people on paper....(And southern California in the winter ain't bad either.) Throughout that period there were two questions I did not ask myself. (1) Is this work serious? and (2) Where will this work get me?

The question of serious didn't come up because, although I had had it up to here with the *Vogue* parties, I still didn't think of myself as capable of serious work; and at that point the women's movement hadn't yet told me that I ought to be serious. Just as well, because this way I went about the Hollywood profiles as if they really mattered. I *slaved* over those Smothers Brothers.

Not until years later did I find out that "serious" is most often in the mind of the beholder. I also found out that sometimes the best way to be serious is not to be.

As far as where-it-would-get-me went: I didn't think about that because there was nowhere else inside or outside of *Look* I wanted to get. In psychoanalysis I had picked up the habit of looking "in" a lot more than looking "up." I wanted to find the *right* place, not a high place. I never wanted to write lead stories in the magazine, although some of my stories turned out to be lead stories. I never wanted to be in charge of anything, or anyone, or to rise, in the sense of becoming powerful, or to get to the top, wherever that was. My mother had pushed me, but she never said I had to be president.

Besides, for a woman, going for power in the middle 1960s would have been like trying to move up a ladder with someone standing on your fingers. In those years, the notion of a woman trying to be in charge of anything besides her shopping list was still considered slightly aberrational. And those who considered it so were men *and* women.

Like me. I was sure—at least, unconsciously—that if I got to the top, one of two things would happen: either I'd disintegrate from incompetence or, worse, I wouldn't disintegrate and, instead, simply turn into a man.

Notwithstanding the Glamour of it all, the routine on the Hollywood beat was the same as any other: hit the location with a photographer; hang around the subject, both at work and, when allowed, at play (or their idea of same); do the interview; fly back to New York. Then, with the ghost of Miss Talmey hanging over my typewriter like a spider, I'd write the story.

After a few months of this, having spent more than one less-than-fascinating day sitting next to Dean Martin in a golf cart, I began to think I would have preferred to dissect a few more civilians and a few fewer movie stars. But famous people— i.e., performers—are whom other people want to read about and, therefore, whom one gets assigned to write about. So be it. Performers, I soon found out, are no more interesting than anyone else; but they're no more boring, either. I take that back. They are more boring, but their situation is not. The situation of being a star is so peculiar and unnatural that it can make the person interesting even if the person is boring.

Every star, for example, is at least two people: the person he or she projects on the screen, or whatever, and the person(s) he or she is. It was always at least mildly interesting to discover who was behind the image. Sometimes nobody. As in the old Hollywood joke about what you see when you look behind all that phony tinsel: the real tinsel. Take Doris Day. Not that Doris Day was phony. That's the point. Doris Day—as far as I could see—was what she appeared to be. The person on the screen and the real person were, in her case, identical twins. That, in itself, was pretty interesting; I'd even call it a shock. I had never seen a middle-aged woman who, from a distance on her bicycle, looked as if she were in the fourth grade and, close up, looked as if she were in the eighth. "Wanna lick?" she said, offering me some of her Rocky Road ice-cream cone. She laughed, baring every tooth in her mouth; she wore funny hats; she slapped her knee when something tickled her, which it continually did; she hugged her dogs as if they were stuffed. I had never seen a grown-up person who was so authentically—cute. Except, of course, that lady she played in the movies.

Then, on the other hand, there was Bob (beloved-by-all) Hope. For three days in the state of Oregon, virtually every minute of which it rained, a *Look* photographer and I schlepped after Hope before, during, and after a set of performances he was giving at the university in Eugene. The shows were fine—I'll give him that—the usual incandescent one-liners, deftly timed. But during the day, what I remember best about the man was driving around the campus, with him leaning forward in the back seat making nasty remarks to the captive audience in the car (me, the photographer, and a university official) about every kid he saw with long hair, who, I think, in Hope's view looked like an antiwar pinko. The style was pure red-neck, slurs and smirks intact.

He wasn't even funny. I respect and accept a comedian's right not to tell jokes during daytime hours; in fact, I prefer it. But even my dry cleaner says something funny now and then. Not Bob Hope. Once or twice in the car I got the feeling that his cracks about the long-haired kids were supposed to be funny. They weren't.

This puzzled me, but not for long. A few days later, in California, the "explanation" revealed itself in a room in the star's house—a room so full of file cabinets it looked like the basement of the Pentagon. Instead of plans for weapons systems, however, these cabinets were packed with jokes—hundreds, maybe thousands, of jokes on paper, written by other people, indexed and arranged according to subject. (A: Airplanes, America, Animals, et cetera.) At that time, he also had as many writers on-staff pumping out more jokes as Snow White has dwarfs. Most comedians use writers, of course, but few can afford so many writing so much.

Since Bob Hope buys his humor, his gift, then, was/is clearly that of a performer. It's a fine gift, to be sure, and one he has given generously of—throughout his life and throughout the world. But that doesn't make him funny. And that doesn't make him nice.

One good thing about the famous-movie-star beat was that when you got tired of the movie star, you could always watch the fame.

Fame is fascinating. Fame is weird. It's not weird at a rock concert because fame is part of what that kind of situation is about. It's different in a supermarket at the produce scale. Raquel Welch once told me about a petrifying experience she had in her neighborhood market in California, when she wound up hiding—unsuccessfully—behind several cartons of toilet paper from some teenage goons who wanted to rip her clothes off. And once, sitting in an unpretentious little restaurant in Santa Monica which, among other things, made me think better of pretentious, big restaurants where stars can get protection, I watched Steve McQueen try—also unsuccessfully—to get a fork from his plate to his mouth, in spite of the pieces of paper that kept getting shoved between him and it for him to sign, along with commands like, "Write 'for Richie'!"

The experience of fame is not necessarily one of assault. But even when it's polite, it's peculiar.

Near the end of the story on Bob Hope, I accompanied him

on a late flight from Oregon back to California. We arrived in Los Angeles at about midnight. The airport was almost deserted; but as we walked down the long corridor from the gate in the harsh fluorescent light, we saw a soldier coming in the opposite direction. He was walking slowly, half-dragging a duffle bag. As he got nearer, he stopped, and dropped both his duffle and his jaw. "My God," he gasped. "It's Bob Hope!" Then, as we walked by, we heard him say again, to no one in particular, "That's *Bob Hope*," over and over, as if he'd seen Jesus. Hope said "Hi" and padded right on, barely taking notice. And why would he when, no doubt, someone drops dead at the sight of him every time he walks out of his front door?

How is it possible for a person not to be affected by that? It's not possible. For example, I don't think Bob Hope thinks he's Jesus, but I do think he thinks he's royalty. You can tell by the way he looks at you while you talk to him. He looks Out. You can tell by the way, when people ask questions of him, he doesn't ask any back. You can tell by his entourage—a band of people in the royal person's employ (Hope's masseur, among others, came along to Oregon) whose sole job it is to minister to the wants and needs of the royal employer. You can tell by the way that in any given room—except, perhaps, in the White House—he assumes he is the most important person in it; and he usually is. (Bob Hope may also assume that, in any given room *including* the White House, he is the richest person in it; and he'd be right about that, too.)

It should be said that there were—are—a lot of Hollywood stars who seem almost pretentiously *non*-royal. Paul Newman came by for me one day during a *Look* profile, not in a Mercedes, nor even a Chevrolet, but a Volkswagen. Some of my best friends have Volkswagens, but they don't make a million dollars or whatever a picture.

What is that? I wondered. Guilt? There is, in fact, probably as much guilt in Hollywood as there is royalty. It shows up in different ways. Some stars fervently attach themselves to causes. Others wear old clothes and act cranky. Some do both.

Some seem thoroughly thrown by all the attention and money. One difficulty has to do with the nature of public love. Public love, unlike the other kind, isn't for you, exactly, but for the public image of you. So, to interview a publicly loved person is to confront a person who is continually nervous that the person he or she is (who, he or she assumes, sometimes correctly, is less lovable than the image) will show.

If I were a bettor, I'd bet that one of the main reasons Elvis Presley was so revered is that during his life the public never got to *know* Elvis Presley—thanks to the intractable policy of his manager, that crusty old fox, Colonel Parker, who never allowed his boy to be interviewed. A risky ploy from a public relations point of view, but it worked.

Poor Steve McQueen. He would have done well to have Colonel Parker taping *his* mouth shut. One afternoon, a good ten years before his death, I found myself seated in the low leather passenger seat of his green Porsche. As my body lurched against the door with each left turn, he began his regular-guy routine. "I've always had itchy feet," he said, as southern California blurred by. "When I was fifteen all the room I needed for my freedom was the room for my hands on those little handlebars, and every once in a while a bug goes splat on yer forehead, know what I mean?" Then, the following day at a board meeting of his movie company, seated at the head of a conference table, sunglasses on, yellow pencil tapping on yellow legal pad, he launched into a different role: "Conception-wise," the star began in new, lower vocal register, "in my estimation, there is a necessitude for . . ."

The identity problem gets even more acute for actors with

running parts on television series, where the fusion between the actor and the character played is continual. It does not help, needless to say, if the character is (literally) masked. I remember being sent by *Look* to do a story on Adam West, a handsome, blond actor, better known at the time (and, it looks like forever more) as Batman. I watched him gnash his teeth as a bunch of kids crowded around with autograph books asking him to sign, not his name, Adam West, but Guess-Whose.

What of the stars who are neither royal nor guilty nor pretentious nor trapped in a character, nor, in fact, troubled in any way; who, on the contrary, are as blissful as pigs in mud? I saw a few of those, too, but none so blissful as Dino Crocetti from Steubenville, Ohio, alias Dean Martin, who greeted his success as if it were a feed. One afternoon, sitting on his Beverly Hills sofa, as wide as a beach—the wall-to-wall carpeting stretched before us like the sea—he told me what, next to golf, he liked to do best. "Sit aroun'," he said with a look of such cheerful stupidity I had to laugh. Then he thought a minute, which seemed to be a terrible strain, and came up with something else he said he liked—working in Las Vegas. "I do two hours a night," he said with his endearingly dopey smile. "Then I go to bed. I get up at ten and my buddies are waitin' for me to have breakfast. I'm on the tee at eleven, finished at three. I go to a health club, shower, shave, get a rub. Then I get dinner, put on my tuxedo, go out on the floor, go back for a rub, go back on the floor, then go to bed. Tha's what I like."

Being a reporter is a kind of enforced education. As you write about things, you *have* to learn about them. Admittedly, the view from the trenches of Beverly Hills was—special. But so is the view from a kitchen table in the house of a welfare mother. Thanks to this profession which legitimizes snooping, one gets to see both—and quite a bit in between.

You like what you're good at. And I was good at writing about movie stars. And the more movie stars I wrote about, the better, if I do say so, I got.

Among other things, I got wise to them.

Never, I soon learned on the star beat, trust a celebrity. Every celebrity, except Elvis, Jackie, and the Queen, has been interviewed to death. They've all been burned. As a result, they've all learned tricks. Like answering questions with non-answers (politicians excel at this) or like exuding pseudo-spontaneity. A media-wise celebrity, for example, is perfectly capable of looking deep into the eyes of a reporter from *Look*, say, and "spontaneously revealing" something thoroughly intimate which, it turns out later, he—or, more often, she— "spontaneously revealed" to *Life* a week earlier.

An interviewer has two choices when confronted with a star: you can take it as they give it, type it, punctuate it, and hand it in to your editor, who probably won't know that it's baloney; or you can learn a few tricks yourself. When I wrote for *Look*, I tried, as best I could, to report on what I saw, not what would have made a better story to see; I didn't bend the person to fit the profile; I didn't change quotes; I didn't exaggerate; and I didn't unveil surprises where there weren't any to unveil. But I was tricky.

My best trick—and one I doubt they teach in journalism school (what, by the way, *do* they teach in journalism school? and what, somebody please tell me, are Communications?)— was writing things down in the bathroom. Nobody lies all the time, and chances are if you hang around long enough, you'll not only see something real, you'll hear the person *say* something real, something worth noting verbatim. It doesn't have to be all that intrinsically fascinating; but sometimes you just suddenly hear the person's true lilt, tone, and vocabulary, as opposed to what the person uses for interviews and in public—and when a moment like that happens, you don't want to start flapping the pages of your little steno pad any more than you'd want to turn on a fluorescent light in the middle of a steamy embrace. On the other hand, you want to get the thing down right. So what do you do? What you do is go to the bathroom, where you can close the door, write down exactly what the person said before you forget, flush the toilet, and reemerge with your notebook and pencil back in your purse. Until the next authentic moment.

This trick has one catch: having done time in their bathrooms, I'm sure that Goldie Hawn, Barbara Harris, John Lennon, Tom Smothers, Sally Field, Bill Cosby, Jackie Gleason, Dean Martin, Mike Nichols, Paul Simon, and Steve McQueen all thought I had a kidney disease. But what if they did? I never planned to see any of those people ever again. They weren't my friends. And as long as the subject of friendship has come up, I should add that I was never (well, maybe once, early on) so foolish as to mistake the rush of warmth and intimacy that can happen during a story for friendship. It's the *business* of a star to be warm during an interview. It's the *business* of the writer to respond to the warmth. The purpose of all the shmoozing is clear: business. Most profile writers, unless they are star-struck hacks, understand that.

Good old psychoanalysis provided me with a couple of interview tricks, too. Since an interview is something that happens *between* two people, not *from* one to another, it matters what the questioner is like. It helps if the questioner is not, him or herself, defensive and hidden, if, instead, he seems pretty willing to show *his* cards. I don't mean that you sit there and yammer about the details of your own less-than-fascinating personal life—even if you did, most stars are so self-centered that the mere mention of a subject or person other than themselves causes an immediate glazing-over of both eyes—but the *spirit* of openness often encourages the person answering the questions to respond in kind.

Also, knowing something about your own defenses and denials makes you smarter about other people's. Smarter about seeing them and dealing with them. You know, for example, how to ask a question so that you'll get an answer, rather than a defensive sidestep. Let's say you want to get someone to level with you about his or her drinking problem. If you ask about it flat out, they'll usually deny it. But if you say, "A lot of people think it's easy to stop drinking, that all you need is a little willpower—what do you think?" then you'll hear how it's not easy. And that's probably not all you'll hear.

One reason such trickery works, by the way, is that, at bottom, most people, even stars, seem to *want* to tell you about their true selves—if they have one and if they think you'll still love them anyway. The pleasure in spilling is great—like throwing up without any of the mess.

When you're trying to get someone to talk, location can count, too. People are most likely to let go, I used to find in *Look* days, when they were moving—that is, when they were *being* moved, in planes, trains, back seats of cars, whatever. There's something about being *between* here and there, as opposed to *being* here or there, which lowers one's guard—and opens one's mouth. I got far more out of Bob Hope on that plane ride from Oregon to California than I did during the official interview. I still remember him leaning back in his first-class seat with the words—apropos of what, I did not know—"Sometimes, my stomach don't move so good." The information was not startling, but after the royal routine the syntax was, and therefore worth noting. (In that instance, I used Air West's bathroom.) I also got far more out of Paul Newman in his Volkswagen than in the living-room interview with him. So I guess the point is that anyplace is better than the official interview place.

Of course, the interview, at least for *Look*, was not all. What you saw and heard when you hung around, as I've said before, mattered as much—more—than what you saw and heard in the question and answer period. I remember watching Judy Garland on what turned out to be her last day on a Hollywood movie set. She had been cast in *Valley of the Dolls*, but was so wrecked from pills and alcohol that, ultimately, she had to be let go. On this day she appeared four hours late, propped up by two young, effete-looking men who resembled an attractive pair of bookends. Another hour later, she emerged from her dressing-room trailer, and the shooting finally began— only to be interrupted continually because Garland kept blanking out when it was her turn to speak. Each time it happened she'd get fluttery and giggly and apologetic and ask for another take, and the camera would roll again, and again she'd go glassy-eyed.

The other actress in the scene, a young, particularly vapid starlet who, like everyone else, was losing patience, came up with what she thought was a swell solution: "Miss Garland," she said in her sugary, breathy, oh-wow starlet voice, "our feet are off-camera, so when we get to your line, I could remind you by giving you a little kick!"

"Ooooooo, no," said Judy Garland, her small, thin, trembling fingers shooting up to her face. "Don't kick me! I'm just a little girl!"

Probably any reporter would have picked up on that one, but, again to give psychoanalysis its due, any reporter who has been on a couch for a couple of years would *have* to have picked up on it.

Most of that stuff about tricks sounds pretty shady, doesn't it? It sounds that way because it is. Is it necessary for journalists to be so sneaky? I think so. Is it moral? I'm not sure. For myself, I've always justified it this way: to trick someone in order to get something out of them that isn't true is bad. But if the point of the trickery is to get what's really there, it's okay. I know, I know, that smells of bad means justifying questionable ends. I admit it. I can't defend it in any grand way. And sometimes trickery makes me feel low. But most of the time, especially when it works, it makes me feel terrific.

CHAPTER
12

I developed an addiction on the star beat. I got hooked on a hotel, although I knew if I were deep I wouldn't have felt the way I felt about the Beverly Hills Hotel.

It happened the first time I saw the place, in 1966: The taxi swung up the grand, curvy driveway and stopped before a pink edifice, which had the powerful allure of the sort of country club that won't have you. The air was filled with ancient, undulating palms, and the ground with new, parked Mercedeses. As I reached for the door handle on the inside of the taxi, Robert Redford reached for it on the outside. It wasn't really Robert Redford. The doorman at the Beverly Hills Hotel was handsomer than Robert Redford (and from what I remember about the tipping, he was probably richer). Once I was out of the car, the thick, rich, leather smell of someone else's luggage hit me like Oberon's love potion. Whose luggage is that? I thought. A maharaja's? As a matter of fact, yes. One time, the hotel had three maharajas at once.

A sight more common than maharajas, of course, was stars. Elizabeth Taylor, Ringo Starr, Ingrid Bergman; not to mention Kennedys, Rockefellers, etc. People didn't do much staring at anyone, since if they did, they would have been staring at each other. In fact, the only time I ever remember seeing heads really turn was when the late Colonel Sanders of fried chicken fame marched by in an ice-cream suit.

There were also TV and film executives, company presidents, real estate tycoons, and dogs. Dogs register; in those days they paid five dollars a night. A typical customer, then, was anyone for whom excess was not exactly boring but was no great thrill either. I was an exception. For me, excess was a great big thrill.

On your way up the rose-red carpet to the main door— only in Beverly Hills do they have wall-to-wall carpets *outside*—you usually got to see a costume parade. Some of the paraders were locals en route to a catered affair. (That reminds me of a joke, but never mind.) Now, the people who were in costume didn't *think* they were in costume. *They* thought they were wearing regular clothes. But would you call a pink-fleece jump suit, like Dr. Denton's without the flap, "regular"? Or a black riding habit? When there isn't a horse in sight? And in Beverly Hills the men play dress-up with the same enthusiasm as the women. In the Polo Lounge I saw moguls making deals in blues brighter than the sun, in sherbet-colored shoes softer than the dew, with complexions to match—men who had clearly spent all of May and half of June at Elizabeth Arden.

Having ogled the natives, I would then turn to the registration desk, where the blend of efficiency and affection would envelop you like a down quilt. Then, ah then, to your room. "We try to be perfect," the vice-president, Burton Slatkin, said to me once. "We try to have a hotel that is as little like a hotel as possible. There is no printed matter in the rooms—no folders telling you about the wonderful shops—*no maroon-flowered carpets.*"

There is a gray area of love that the hotel provided, especially for special guests. For example, if someone got a fix on a certain waiter—Orson Welles did— the hotel tried to arrange for that waiter alone to serve him. To help everyone's love memory, there was an elaborate file system of guests' likes and dislikes. "When we see Mr. Kahn, we come running with the hot milk," said the breakfast-room hostess. It was carefully noted in the room-service file that Mrs. Ziv did *not* wish to have the customary rose on her tray because she got depressed when the rose died. And after the president of Prudential mentioned his liking for oranges, the good fairy would leave him bowls of oranges. Speaking of fruit, most guests received a basket upon arrival. Or flowers. Or both. Who got flowers and who got fruit was a matter of vast speculation. All I know is, it was a sorry day when one was scratched from the Fruit or Flower list. When it did happen— like most misfortunes, unexpectedly—most people just sulked for a day, or maybe they'd have lunch at the Beverly Wilshire. But there were some who lost control and went running to Public Relations. Those people got their fruit and flowers. But it wasn't the same. Needless to say, royalty never asked, it just got. The day Queen Juliana of the Netherlands arrived, tulips bloomed on cue around her bungalow. When it was learned that Lord Snowdon fancied filter-tip Gauloises, they were flown over from Paris.

Once in your room, you were ready for a cardinal event: your first phone call. Whether you chose the custard-colored phone in your bedroom or the one in your bathroom, the voice you heard belonged to your grandmother. "May I help you please, Miss Rollin," she'd ask in a tone as soothing as a hot lunch. (I've heard the hotel now has direct dialing, but I refuse to believe it.) It is important here to explain the whole telephone hang-up in the Beverly Hills community. This, I know, has not changed. The most dangerous thing that can happen to a person in Beverly Hills is to lose contact with unreality. So in case one feels oneself slipping, there's always a telephone nearby. In the BHH, there were phones every-where, and everywhere everyone was being paged. To spend time, at the pool or bar, say, and *not* get paged was to have social dropsy. Even if you *didn't* want to be paged, they found you. Once I snuck out of my room to go to the drugstore downstairs. As I waited for change, the phone rang. It was for me. Once, in the Polo Lounge, I saw a man with two phones. One at each ear. He was placing a call *and* receiving one at the same time.

The pool area, a big, azure play-pit, collected bodies after ten A.M. On weekdays, wives of the moguls, their rippling thighs gleaming with sun oil, shot the breeze in their dressmaker bathing suits that never got wet. Some ladies lying in the sun had black telephone receivers lying down next to them like Teddy bears. The moguls themselves, who looked less than alluring in their swimwear, showed up on weekends, as did the starlet brigade.

The funny thing about the pool was that nobody went swimming. It was like the scene at Las Vegas. You'd see heads with hats, dark glasses, eyelashes, and red mouths, gliding on top of the water. That meant someone was taking a walk in the water.

After two or three years of sopping all of this up—during that 1967–1970 period, I was in residence at the hotel about two months a year—I did what lovestruck writers have always done: drooled on paper. "I don't drink. I don't smoke," I wrote. "I go to the Beverly Hills Hotel ..."

The piece ran as a full page of text with a small, extremely silly photograph of me lying on the diving board, talking on the telephone; and it turned out to be the beginning of something I neither expected, dreamed about, nor pursued, nor was sure I even wanted (I got sure in about five minutes): a column. My own column.

It was like a present. And when the ribbon was untied, they told me to write about the nicest thing anyone can be told to write about: Write about anything, they said, anything at all.

So I did. I wrote about the women's army of Israel—and, of course, got to go there. I wrote about Brigitte Bardot and Coco Chanel in Paris—and got to go there. I wrote about the Los Angeles Rams, the revival of comic-book superheroes, the wives of presidential candidates (in '68 they were the Mmes. Reagan, Kennedy, McCarthy, Nixon, and Humphrey); and, occasionally, when I ran out of ideas, I'd write about myself. About some experience I had had, that is, like getting hit— well, grazed—by a speeding taxi on Fifth Avenue.

"Rollin, I can tell by your voice that you're not dead," barked Martin Goldman into the telephone the day after the accident, "so I hope you took notes while you were unconscious because we're expecting a column out of this, and it's due YESTERDAY!"

My, it was fun. Then, suddenly one day, the fun stopped. What killed it was that I got a serious idea. I didn't want to get a serious idea. I knew I wasn't capable of writing anything serious. True, the women's army story wasn't fluff, but I wrote it fairly fluffily and, besides, it was reportage, rather than an essay; I wrote about what I saw, rather than what I thought. Whereas this new idea smelled dangerously like an essay. But once it arrived in my head, it wouldn't leave.

By now, 1970, the women's movement had registered, even on me, and I began to do what a lot of women began to do: think about certain things that we had always thought about one way, another way. Things like motherhood. In 1970 I was thirty-four years old. I had a boyfriend (silly word, but "lover" is too randy and implies that all you do together is go to bed). I liked this man. Cautiously, I thought I might even love him. He was a writer. I felt a certain kind of comfortable with him I hadn't felt before. We understood each other, liked the same people, got each other's jokes. What does that have to do with writing an essay on motherhood? Officially, nothing. Except that writing a column had brought me around to the view that "professional" and "private" are not church and state; that sometimes—maybe even all the time—it's a good idea to write about what stirs you personally; and at the moment what stirred me personally—outside of the possibility of marrying this man—was the fact that —for a bunch of reasons—marrying him probably would mean not having children. And what bothered me about this news as much as anything was that, somehow, this news did not bother me. And that got me thinking. As much as I had always liked children (who, in the abstract, doesn't like children?) and assumed that I would have them (what woman before the seventies *didn't* assume that?), the thought of not having them did not make me feel awful, as I thought it should.

When you've been analyzed you tend to blame odd, that is, unconventional, thoughts or feelings on your own neurosis. Although my time on the couch was drawing to a close, I didn't—and don't, by the way—doubt that a lingering neurosis played a role in my lack of maternal longing. But I suspected that my own craziness wasn't the only craziness involved here. Because what else besides crazy would you call compulsory motherhood? Which, for most women, pill or no pill, motherhood was. Like it or not, any good at it or not, motherhood was something women were simply expected to do. As I thought about this, I realized what anyone would realize who thought about it: that there were plenty of mothers whose maternal competency and pleasure were strikingly low—mothers who would survive motherhood, and who might even like it now and then, but who, on balance, might have been better off doing something else. If— big if—they *had* something else to do.

Were there no women's movement, I probably would have dismissed the whole issue and gone back to movie stars in golf carts. Instead, I thought about it more and more and finally, slowly and informally, began talking to other women about it. Of those I talked to, I took particular notice of two groups: childless women who didn't seem miserable, and women with children who did. "No one told me what motherhood would be like," said one Long Island housewife in such a low, even, dark tone of voice that I knew she was having more than a bad day.

Then I hit the literature, keeping an eye out for anything that questioned the premise of motherhood as a must. Since the issue was academic before birth control, I didn't expect to find anything old; but outside of a couple of diatribes against *mothers*, as opposed to motherhood, and Simone de Beauvoir's less-than-sentimental view of maternity in *The Second Sex*, there wasn't much of anything new, either. . . . That left the academics. So, early one April morning, I opened my office door, sat down at my desk, put my finger in the phone, and called everyone I could think of—sociologists, psychologists, plus a psychoanalyst or two—people who I knew knew the field, had proved reliable in the past, and had no ax to grind.

By the time I made those calls, I already had a good stack of anecdotal information—nothing scientific, but enough testimony from enough women to convince *me*, anyhow, that maternal dissatisfaction existed, ran deep, and was underreported. However, I didn't know—and what I hoped the social scientists did—was whether, in spite of the negative testimony, the wish to reproduce was instinctual. If it were, the case against motherhood would be weakened, and might not even be worth pursuing.

The experts gave me an answer, all right, accompanied, in most cases, by a contemptuous snort: it was a unanimous "no." "Motherhood instinctive?" said Jessie Bernard, a distinguished sociologist—and mother—as if I had asked her if elephants could fly. "Biological destiny? If it were biology, people would die from not doing it!"

"There is no innate drive for children," said Dr. William Goode, past president of the American Sociological Association, pronouncing each word slowly, as if he were addressing a class of third-graders. "Otherwise, the enormous cultural pressures that there are to reproduce wouldn't exist. There are no cultural pressures to sell you on getting your hand out of the fire!"

"You know," I said to Goode, "when I listen to your answer, I realize it's a dumb question. But if it's all so obvious, why, then, are most people in the United States of America under the impression that motherhood is instinctive? I mean, how come you people haven't let us in on the news?"

"Because," said Goode brightly, "that's not our job."

Oh yeah? Whose job was it?

Don't tell me, I know.

Time, I decided, to have a little chat with Carbine....I found her seated straight up, as usual, behind her desk, the top of which was loaded, also as usual, with what looked like the contents of two attics. She smiled at me merrily above the debris. "What's up?"

"Pat," I began, then stopped, remembering suddenly that the woman sitting across from me looking so agreeable in her Peter Pan collar was Catholic and might have some personal difficulty with what I was about to say. Then I had a second thought; I'm not giving her enough credit.

"Pat," I started again, "how would you feel about my doing a piece that suggested—uh—that maybe motherhood isn't so—uh—hot?"

She laughed. "Oh, great. Last month we took on Bob Hope. Now you want to dump on motherhood. What's next, Santa's reindeer?"

"Wait a minute," I said, somehow not amused, "I don't mean a—cantankerous sort of piece, about how motherhood is awful and kids are rotten."

"Well, *that's* a relief," said Pat, trying not to smile—and not succeeding.

"It would just say," I went on, "that motherhood is awful *sometimes*" (groan from the other side of the desk) "and that there's no reason every woman should feel she has to do it!" She gave me a look. "I'm serious about this," I said.

"I can see that," she said, and nodded the way a mother nods after her daughter has told her that she plans to marry a convicted felon.

"Look," I said, lowering my voice, "most women don't choose to be mothers; they become mothers *automatically* because it's what everybody does. Well, it's time to *question* this because some of these women muck *up*—I mean, they muck themselves up *and* their children—and—and it's crazy!"

"But—" said Pat.

"—*and* guess what?" I went on. "It turns out the *premise* of motherhood—that it's an instinctive wish—isn't even true!"

"How do you know?" she asked, looking very sober now.

I sat back and pushed my hair away from my face. "I talked to six heavies, and they made me feel stupid for asking the question."

Pat leaned back in her chair and, for a few seconds, said nothing. I had never seen her look so unsure.

"I take it you've done some—uh—research," she said.

"A little," I said, and told her what I had found out.

"Hmmm," she said. "Interesting."

"How interesting?" I asked.

"Very," she said, giving me a hard look.

"Interesting enough for me to go ahead and do it?" I asked with my best nine-year-old-can-I-go-out-and-play voice.

Silence. She leaned back in her chair, looked at the ceiling, and sighed.

"Why don't you put everything you just told me in a memo, and I'll—circulate it around?"

I stood up. "I'll do that right away," I said—and did. And got it to her in triplicate that afternoon.

A few days passed. Not a word. Meanwhile, I had been wading through a piece about the author of *Everything You've Always Wanted to Know about Sex But Were Afraid to Ask*, trying not to overreact to a piece of intelligence I had just gained in an interview with the author and his wife. During their stay at the Plaza Hotel, it seemed, Mrs. David Reuben washed and ironed her husband's shirts herself, because the Plaza "didn't do them right."

I was on my way back to the office, thinking about ironing, when I half-collided with Pat on the corner of Fifty-second Street. "Hi!" I said in a way that must have sounded like a question.

"Soon," she said, and smiled her most reassuring smile, which, somehow, did not reassure me.

I found out later that the idea was met with something less than enthusiasm on the executive floor. Not a big surprise. *Look* had a reputation as a family magazine, after all, and, as one three-piece-suited executive reportedly said: "There are *limits*." Someone else was surprised that such a radical proposal came from cute little me. I was and am not either cute or little, but I knew some of the gentlemen in charge liked to think of me that way.

I finished the Reuben piece, and still not a word about Motherhood. I decided to keep on with the research anyway. The more people I talked to, the more certain I felt that I was on to something. Which, on the one hand, pleased me, and on the other, got me down because I knew all the corroboration would make me feel even worse if the story were turned down. I had another worry, too, a recurrent question that went: isn't this whole idea awfully obvious? Answer: yes, it *was* obvious. I hadn't yet learned that good ideas *always* seem obvious—after you have them. And I still hadn't found anything or anyone who had put this particular obvious idea on paper. So I kept going. In fact, I couldn't stop.

"Can't you think or talk about *anything* else?" my writer-sort-of-fiancé—Arthur, by name—barked at me one night.

"No!" I barked back. But I knew he had a point. "If they let me write it, I promise not to be so boring about it."

"Hmfff," he said, sounding not at all sure that he wanted to stick around that long.

A week passed and still no word. Then, finally, late one afternoon, I pulled my coat on to go home and the phone rang. It was Pat asking me to come by. I decided not to run. Instead, I sat back down at my desk, opened my compact, and smoothed the lipstick on my lower lip with my finger. Then, slowly, I combed my hair and told myself to prepare for a letdown, the way I used to do when I was an actress.

Pat liked drama, so I couldn't tell right away how the verdict had gone. "What do you have lined up next?" she asked. I looked for the beginning of a smile, which would have been a clue, but it wasn't there. She closed the door. ... That's a good sign, I thought; or maybe she just doesn't want anyone to see me cry. Or maybe I'm about to get some kind of a swell booby prize: the Beverly Hills Hotel Revisited....

"Nothing," I answered, my feet still locked in a standing position near the door.

"Sit down," she said. I sat down. "How would you like to take a couple of months," she said slowly, still no smile (definitely the booby prize) "and do a major piece questioning the premise of motherhood? You know"—considerable twitching around the corners of her mouth now as she swung into her imitation of me—"*not* to say that motherhood is *awful*, but just that it's awful *most of the time!!*" Full regalia of teeth now on display. Pat, you old fox. That *is* why you closed the door. You *knew* I'd cry, didn't you?

CHAPTER
13

God, what a sweat. Literally. One entire, steamy summer. *Three months* it took me to write that thing. With marriage plans on hold—a mild case of cold feet on everyone's part—Arthur and I had taken a summer house in East Hampton, Long Island, with another writer friend of his, Betty Friedan of Betty Friedan fame, along with a (male) sociologist friend of hers.

A restful summer it was not. A culinary summer it was not. True, Betty Friedan spent most of her time in the kitchen, and Betty Rollin spent most of hers in the dining room. But Betty F. chose to hole up in the kitchen because that's where the telephone happened to be, and the telephone was the baton with which she happened to be conducting the women's revolution. And Betty R. spent her days in the dining room only because in its center lived the biggest table in the house, which she needed for her voluminous and rather untidy notes, otherwise known by her housemates as her "crap," as in the sentence, "Get your crap off the dining-room table." The two men, meanwhile, had two books going—on killer bees and Prestige, respectively—in each of the bedrooms upstairs.

The house was yards from the beach, but as I recall, the

only one of us who went there with any kind of regularity was the dog. My mother, who has always had an irritating habit of looking on the bright side (unintentional pun coming up), reminded me cheerily on the telephone that the sun ruined one's skin, anyway, and that it was "just as well that I had something interesting to do indoors." (After the piece came out, she didn't think it was quite so interesting.)

There were a few problems in our little house, which Betty F. insisted on calling our "commune." Although no one in the group had the slightest enthusiasm about preparing food or cleaning up after its preparation, everyone had a lot of enthusiasm about eating it. This led to (1) many repulsive meals, (2) many complaints, (3) many ants. Toward the middle of the summer, we devised a camplike work-assignment schedule, which I Scotch-taped to the refrigerator door. That improved matters somewhat, although there were still occasional disputes ("I was on cleanup *last* night!" "You were *not!*"). At one point in August, when everyone's books, articles, and revolutions heated up, and domestic sabotage seemed near, I assigned titles to the chores. Overnight on the refrigerator door "Cleanup" became "Queen (or King) of Cleanup"; I scratched out "Salad" and wrote in its place, "Sultan of the Salad"; "Main Course" became "Master of the Main Course," et cetera ad nauseam.

Given the personalities of the group, the royal flourish made a difference. Everyone's mood improved. Unfortunately, nothing else did. That was because the problem was not only one of attitude, but one of skills. Which is to say, no one had any. The lack of skills, however—at least on the part of the two Bettys—resulted in the kind of equality Betty F. was fighting for. The men cooked because, they soon learned, when they did they ate better. At cleanup, everyone stank equally. Not that we didn't give it our all. As Queen of Cleanup, no one threw herself into the role more fervently than Betty F. It was touching how hard she'd try. I'll never forget the sight of her bent over the kitchen table, attempting to clean it, her finger—that's right, one finger—inside a cloth, pushing it around and around, leaving it, when she had finished, looking as if a first-grade finger-painting class had just been held on its top.

Also, although the house afforded each of us adequate working space, it did not afford us adequate working *silence*. I know one cannot run a revolution by whispering—and it wasn't Betty's fault that my dining-room office lay adjacent to her kitchen office—but Betty F. did respond vocally to each phone call as if it were coming from Moravia. Given that I was writing the most difficult piece of my life, I realized—too late—that I probably could have chosen a better place to do it than one in which fifty percent of the population was being mobilized for action.

As the revolution peaked, along with the decibel level, I decided to purchase earplugs. They worked fine and I thought the problem was solved until, one day, I lost one of the little buggers inside my ear and had to be rushed to the East Hampton Clinic to have it removed. After that, I wore earmuffs, but they weren't as good. They also gave me hot ears.

Of course, the biggest drag of all was the piece itself. I was right about its not being my sort of thing, at least as far as the writing was concerned. No story to tell, nothing to describe, nothing that moved or breathed—except those sociologists, and they didn't move or breathe much. The more I typed— and retyped and retyped—the better I got at typing and the more my head hurt. Never again. The next time I get a big idea about how society should be different, I thought, I'll give it to Margaret Mead.

And then, thank God, it was finished. And then it was published.

And then it hit the fan.

With one exception, the piece got more mail, I was told, than any other piece in *Look*'s history. To say the mail was vicious would accurately describe some of it, but would be far too mild for the rest. It seemed the entire Bible Belt wished me dead. And worse. All in God's name, of course. They called me a lesbian, a Communist, and a kike. "That's odd," said Arthur, trying to be funny, "you don't *write* Jewish." They told me my soul would rot in hell and that my mother must have "had the spirit of Satan in her belly" when she had me. Meanwhile, my mother received so many condolence calls from friends and relatives she unplugged her telephone.

I hate to admit that some of the letters made me cry. I told one of the other writers, but instead of commiserating, he congratulated me. "Mean mail means you've hit a nerve, kiddo," he said, putting his arm around my shoulder. "Enjoy it!"

Of course, not all of the letters were scathing. Some were just sad and, in a different way, equally affecting. "I love my children, but . . ." they began, and one went on (in wobbly handwriting) to say, "I wish someone told me I din't haf to have them becaus then I think maybe I wuddent have. Do you now wut I mean?"

I knew what she meant. I also knew what the woman meant who wrote, ". . . I used to think I was some kind of a monster because I didn't want children."

A couple of publishers called and asked me to do a book. I thought hard about what it would be like to quadruple the summer I just had and said no. The piece was reprinted in some college textbooks, though, and it ran in several other magazines in foreign countries, including New Zealand, which tickled me because I didn't know where New Zealand was.

When I reread the piece now, I do what writers do: I wish I

had written it better. I wish I hadn't felt obliged to be quite so Clever, and I hate the title: "The Motherhood Myth," they called it. Then, in huge print, a subtitle: "Motherhood: Who Needs It?" Gross. I also wish I hadn't been quite so tough about the whole thing, especially now that the pendulum has swung the other way. Ah well.

Soon after the motherhood piece was published—in September 1970—Pat Carbine left the magazine. She went to *McCall's* and became the editor, a job she never would have been offered at *Look* because of her sex.

As it turned out, her sex wasn't the only reason she wouldn't have had that job. One year later, the job didn't exist.

CHAPTER
14

I can't call September 3, 1971, the worst day of my life, only the most rattling. To begin, at ten A.M., nine-fifty, to be exact, I rose—two stages, as always: sit up, feet on floor, then stand—for the last time from the analytic couch. Socially, it was awkward. I didn't know how to say goodbye. Goodbye and thanks for decreasing the size of my head? Goodbye, it's been nice to know me? Goodbye, and I hope you get rid of that cough? Goodbye and thank you for making me a healthy, independent person and, by the way, how do I get from here to the door? Goodbye and—look, now you can tell me—weren't my dreams terrific?—especially the one about me and the—? Goodbye, and is this as weird for you as it is for me? Say yes.

We shook hands. I don't remember what I said.

When I got to the street, I felt light. I remembered when I was twelve and the braces on my teeth were taken off. I don't know what made me think of that. That was so much nicer. I remembered running my tongue across the top row of teeth, then, very slowly, across the bottom. Smooth! Slippery! Like glass! Like ice! Like teeth! It took awhile, though, before I began to smile again. I had lost the habit.

I couldn't figure out how I felt now. Not marvelous. I knew that much. I stopped at the curb and waited for the light to change. It was a clear, beautiful day. I wished it weren't. . . . Maybe I quit too soon. Eight years *sounds* like a long time, but . . . stop it.

I ran down the subway steps. A low rumble sounded through the tunnel; then it became a roar; then a train clanged into place. I got on. There were seats, but I stood. "I'D RATHER FIGHT THAN SWITCH" read the advertisement overhead. *I'd*, contraction; *rather*, adverb; *fight*, verb; *than*, particle. Or was it a preposition? *Switch*, verb . . . or object verb? Was there such a thing? I couldn't remember. Fiftieth Street. My stop. What if I stayed on the train? No one would know the difference. No one on the train knows me or knows where I'm supposed to get off or knows what my life is supposed to be. I could stay on and no one would notice. It wouldn't matter.

I got off. . . . I felt as if something other than me was making my legs move: one at a time, knee bends, toe, lift off, step. Look at her go! Walking! All by herself!

When I got to the office, I knew right away that something besides me was peculiar. As soon as I got off the elevator, the sounds were different. Not the usual low editorial hum, but something louder, more urgent. I pushed the double glass doors open and followed the sounds inside. People were milling around the way they did at the Christmas party. But this was September and nobody looked drunk. There must have been a fire drill. But it didn't look like that, either. Suddenly, I noticed some people I had never seen before. One of them, a large man in shirt-sleeves, held a camera—a big camera, like a movie camera, or a television—what was a television camera doing—?

And then I knew. "What's going on?" said my voice when, finally, I found it.

"You didn't hear?" said a man from the photo lab, who was standing nearby.

"No, what—"

"Miss Rollin!" I turned around. It was one of the strangers, a vaguely pretty young man. Of course; he was on one of the news programs—Channel 2, or was it 4? "Could we talk to you for a few minutes?" he said, almost too politely.

"Okay," I said, "but I'm not sure if I know what's happening."

"You haven't heard?" said the young man, his eyebrows moving slightly. I shook my head. "The magazine has folded," said the young man pleasantly.

"Folded," I repeated. My God, I was right.

I turned to find the lab assistant—someone in the family—but he had gone. I turned the other way and saw one of the secretaries. "Folded," I said to her. Slowly, she nodded. "What happened?"

"There's a meeting at noon," she said and pulled a Kleenex out of her purse and blew her nose. I turned back around and walked into the television reporter. "I'm sorry," I said.

"That's all right," he said with the same pleasant expression on his face. Which I now realized wasn't an expression, but an engraving.

"Is this a good time?" he said.

"Is it *what?*"

"Is this a good time for the interview?"

"Oh," I laughed. "Sorry. It's thirty seconds since you asked. I have a lousy memory." I was babbling now, and he, engraved smile intact, was politely waiting for me to stop. "Sure, sure," I said. "Now is fine. My office is this way."

"We'll follow you," he said and turned and signaled two men behind him, one small and dark, the other tall and big-bellied, like a wrestler. On cue, the two of them bent down; slung over, around, and across their bodies a formidable load of equipment—camera, lights, cables, and a big box that looked sort of like a portable radio; and, with surprising speed and agility, they began to move.

"Oh," I said half to myself, half to the reporter, "you guys take pictures while you interview, don't you? I guess I should—uh—comb my hair."

When we got to my office, I surveyed the face in my compact. Decidedly unalluring. Bags under the eyes, smudged mascara, lipstick eaten off . . . "Do I have time to fix myself up a little?"

"Oh, yes," said the reporter. "It'll take us a few minutes to set up." Then he turned to the two other men and began to speak in another language: "First, let's go for a two-shot, then a zoom . . ." Then to me: "Ready?"

"I guess so," I said, trying to pull a knot out of my hair.

Suddenly, the wrestler reached for my neck. I jumped. "It's a microphone," he said in a flat tone of voice that reminded me of the attendants at Bellevue.

"Oh!" I said with a laugh, hoping I hadn't hurt his feelings.

"Okay, Jim, roll it," said the reporter over his shoulder to the cameraman. Then a bright light clicked on and I heard a hum that sounded like the noise my electric typewriter made when it wanted me to write.

"I—I don't know where to look!" I whispered.

"Look right at me, Miss Rollin," said the reporter in the voice of my dentist. "How long have you been working here at *Look* magazine?"

"Um—six years," I said.

"Would you speak up just a little, Miss Rollin?"

"Oh, of course! EXCUSE ME!" I shouted.

"Perhaps just a *tad* lower," the reporter said. "Now—how did you feel when you first found out about the demise of the magazine?"

184

"How did I feel?" I repeated stupidly. The young man nodded; the camera hummed. "Well, I haven't had a chance to feel anything yet. . . . I mean, I just found out—a minute ago—in fact, you told me, didn't you?" I laughed a little. He didn't. "I guess it hasn't hit me yet." I trailed off, sensing failure. I know, I thought. He wants me to cry. Like one of those women on the news whose house has just burned down. The camera hum sounded louder than before. I *can't* cry, I thought, in a sudden panic. I locked eyes with the reporter. "I—I guess this is what it's like when somebody dies," I said, hoping that would do.

"Cut," he said. And with that, the camera dropped and the light popped off, and he said goodbye and thank you and I said goodbye and thank *you* and they cleared out and I was alone in my office, standing next to my desk as if I had an appointment with myself.

I sat down. I got up. I sat down again. I called Arthur, who had just replaced Molly as my roommate.

"Guess what just died," I said.

"Your cactus, I hope."

"Very funny."

"Okay," he said, "I give up."

"*Look. Look* just died."

He sighed. I could hear him light a cigarette. "Well, you were expecting it, weren't you?"

"Sort of, but not this quick. Not *today*. I had my last analytic appointment an hour ago."

"Oh." He whistled. "You okay?"

"I guess so. If I weren't, wouldn't I know it?"

He laughed. "Not necessarily."

"Well," I said, taking a breath, "I'll see you later."

"What's the big rush?" Arthur hated long phone conversations but he liked to be the one to end them.

"I think I better find myself another job."

I put down the receiver and picked it up again and dialed NBC. I had called them two weeks earlier when the rumors about *Look* began to sound less and less like rumors. For that reason, I can't explain why I felt so stunned by what had just happened. It was the difference, I suppose, between hearing a person is dying and finding out, as I had tried to explain to the television interviewer, the person is dead. I truly hadn't thought it would happen so soon, but I had called NBC, anyway, probably because of an old reflex—a maxim, really—from acting days: look for work when you're working because if you wait until you're not, you'll look too hungry.

I had decided to try television because I couldn't think of another magazine, except maybe *Life*, and I reasoned— correctly, it turned out—that if *Look* was dying, could *Life* be far behind? I picked NBC rather than one of the other networks (1) because I liked David Brinkley's snarl, and (2) because NBC was in Rockefeller Center, a direct ride on the crosstown bus from where I lived, not necessarily in that order.

When I called NBC the first time, I asked to speak to the president of NBC News, whose name, the operator had told me, was Reuven Frank. When (to my surprise) he got on the phone, I decided not to beat around the bush: "There's a rumor going around that *Look* might croak," I said, "and I have a feeling it's not a rumor and if it's not I'm going to need a job; and since I've also heard it's television that's killing us [only partly true] I figured I better join the enemy. So, would you like to see me, and if so, when?" You're a nervy broad, I said to myself, waiting to hear if I played it right or wrong. "Sure," he said with a laugh.

Right.

"How about late this afternoon?"

The difference between Reuven Frank's office and the executive offices at *Look* was three television sets, all of which, to my astonishment, were on and remained on—the picture, that is, not the sound—during the length of my visit. Frank, who was older and also scruffier—less buttoned-up—than I expected, ignored the simultaneous triple feature, which I found difficult to do, especially when a woman on the middle set began jumping up and down and turning pink. I think she had just won something. I wondered if everyone working in television had a television set in the office and, if they did, how did they get any work done? Or was it like working in a chocolate factory?

I did not voice these concerns to Mr. Frank. Anyway, after three and a half minutes of unfocused conversation about *Look* magazine, the interview, such as it was, seemed to be over. He had risen from behind his desk and was leading me out of his office into a smaller one next door. There, he introduced me to a thin man, whose name was Wald, a vice-president of news, whom I liked right away because he snarled almost as endearingly as David Brinkley.

"You don't expect to get anywhere in this business, do you?" he said, grinning with one side of his mouth.

"No," I half-grinned back, suddenly wanting to get somewhere. "I just thought it would be more fun than going to *Field and Stream.*"

"Don't count on it!" Wald said cheerily and sprang up and led me into yet another (still smaller) office to meet another (still thinner) man called Margolis. At this rate, I mused, the reporters would turn out to be eighty-five pounds and work in supply closets.

Margolis talked faster than the other two, so I didn't catch every word, but there was one word that I did catch: the word audition. . . . Audition? Oh God, I thought, am I back to that again? I'm a journalist, for Christ's sake. I won't audition!

"What kind of an audition?" I asked Margolis sweetly.

"We'll send you out with a producer and a camera crew. You'll do a spot for us and we'll have a look at it and—we'll see."

"What's a spot?" I asked.

"A piece," he said, "a story on film." Why didn't you say so, I thought. He smiled—not a real smile, but a facial tic he was using in place of a period. That was my cue, I knew, to spring up and get to it. But I couldn't get to it because I didn't get it. "I don't get it," I said.

The funny thing was, when I finally did it—a day or so after getting the word about *Look*—I still didn't get it. Oh, I understood what the piece *meant*—it was my idea, after all—I just didn't understand how we did it. It was like surgery. In surgery, they knock you out and do things to you and you wake up and it's over and you sort of know what happened, but mostly you don't, and all you do know is that you don't feel wonderful.

At least this operation seemed to be a success. First, the idea itself had juice. Margolis had told me to think up a local story that would be visual. Visual. I knew what the word meant from working with still photographers, but this visual meant good *moving* pictures and, moreover, good moving pictures with sound. Not so easy. But I got lucky.

The day after I spoke to Margolis, an invitation arrived in the mail from Saks Fifth Avenue's beauty shop to participate in their "Miracle Makeover." For $100, the card said, you could get yourself redone from head (literally) to toe, including all ten of the latter. Nothing that would have fired up Woodward and Bernstein, nor, in itself, would it have fired me up; except that, of all splendid coincidences, "the kick-off," as they called it, for the first Miracle was set for August

28, which happened to coincide with the date set for a big march down Fifth Avenue of the women's liberation movement. That meant, while one portion of the female population would have taken their bodies to the streets in pursuit of equality, another portion, at the same moment, would have hauled theirs up to the fifth floor of Saks Fifth Avenue in pursuit of blonder hair, smaller pores, and prettier cuticles.

As soon as I got the go-ahead, I did what I would normally do on a story, and had done for all of my seven years as a reporter. I went over to Saks and hung around and took notes and wrote a piece—a short one, about five hundred words.

"Uh-huh," said the producer as he read it, nodding the way people nod when they're looking, not reading. "Uh-huh," he said again. He hates it, I thought miserably. When he got to the funny parts, he didn't even laugh. He didn't even *smile*. "Well, maybe we can use some of this," he said.

Yeah. Like about twelve words. It wasn't, he explained later when we got to be friends, that he didn't like what I had written. It was simply that what I had written was for a page, not a screen. "In television," he said, "the camera does most of the writing. The writing you do has to follow the picture. See what I mean?"

"Yes," I said and nodded because he was being kind and not because I understood, which I didn't. I knew only that my final draft consisted of one page of typing, which read like *Dick and Jane*. Never mind, I did it. They loved it. They bought it. And before September was out, they bought me—initially for about $18,000 a year, a few thousand more than I had made at *Look*. Ironically, since I wasn't paying an analyst anymore, I didn't much care.

So that was how, two weeks after the death announcement on Madison Avenue, and one weekend after the death, my cactus and I, having cut the mourning short in the interest of pragmatism, found ourselves one block down and two across on Rockefeller Plaza, blotter in place, calendar tacked on wall, ready, willing—and not remotely able—to meet the needs of our new employer, NBC News.

Precisely *how* not remotely able, I didn't realize until I got to Haiti. Haiti? Yes, Haiti. I'll back up: Upon arrival in my new professional home, I knew only that I would be working on a "magazine" show, *Chronolog*, previously called *First Tuesday*. If nothing else, my audition piece taught me that doing a piece for something you hold, and doing a piece for something you watch, are alike the way an airplane and a sailboat are alike. Both move. Period. Since it was plain—to me, if not to NBC—that I didn't know how to do the job I had been hired to do (I didn't actually know what I had been hired to do, but I knew I didn't know how to do it), I figured at least I'd come in the first day with a story idea.

The trouble was, I didn't have a story idea. Something did kind of catch my eye in the *Times*, which I read on the crosstown bus on the way to work the first day—a piece about "quickie divorces" in Haiti. But that didn't count, because surely NBC News didn't need me to bring in story ideas from page three of *The New York Times*....Why, then, when I mentioned the idea did everyone react as if it were the hottest notion since the musical transformation of Eliza Doolittle? I didn't know the answer to that question then, and I don't know it now; all I do know is that the following Monday, accompanied by a producer, an assistant producer, a cameraman, an assistant cameraman, a sound man, and a light man, I landed in Port au Prince, Haiti, where, for six days in the steaming (and I mean steaming) heat, we interviewed everyone in Haiti getting a divorce, everyone in Haiti who had just gotten a divorce, every lawyer, judge, or official person who had anything to do with Haitian divorces; we filmed Haitian scenery, Haitian markets, Haitian buildings. If it moved and it wasn't a cockroach, we shot it. And then we shot it again from another angle.

Everyone in our little (not so little) group treated me sweetly—and carefully—as if I were both royal and retarded. It occurred to me that they probably thought I was having an affair with Reuven Frank, or with one of the thinner executives below him, or one of the (presumably) fatter executives above. Why else would the network have hired someone who thought that covering shots came from snipers and that a zoom described a hasty departure by Captain Marvel?

Certain aspects of the work seemed familiar. Operative word: *seemed*. When it came to an interview, for example, I knew what questions to ask. But soon I realized that in this ball game it wasn't enough to throw the ball; you had to throw it smoothly. Unlike a magazine interview, an interview for television included the questions as well as the answers. The questions might get cut out later in the editing, but you couldn't count on it. That meant the questions were part of the show, and, therefore, had to be mellifluous, smooth, and, most important, short. No more cozying up to someone and breathing vague queries into his or her ear; no more hanging around for the inevitable Revealing Moment; no more sitting back to receive droplets of truth in moving vehicles. No more going to the bathroom. With a television camera, intimation and nuance were worthless. A television interview was all sit up straight and fire.

Since this particular story had nothing to do with per-sonalities or human beings per se, but rather with the mechanics of Haitian divorces, the destruction of intimacy through rapid-fire questions didn't really hurt. Still, I didn't like it. And having to doll up the questions because they "showed" was only part of what I didn't like. Having to doll *me* up because I showed was the other part.

Don't get me wrong. I have always liked looking nice. I like making the effort and—when it works—I like the result. What I didn't like was having to look nice and think at the same time. Especially in 100 degrees Fahrenheit (my hair died on the first day) plus 80 percent humidity. The more days that passed (my journalism died on the second day), the less I worried about investigating the two American lawyers who seemed to have cornered the Haitian divorce market, and the more I worried about whether I should wear my sleeveless red dress, which I thought made my arms look fat.

Once we were back in New York, it took a full day just to screen the film (thanks to a long shot, my arms looked like linguine), then ten more days to edit it. The cost, I was told, approximated $40,000, the equivalent today of about $100,000. Running time on the air: three minutes and forty-five seconds.

Above all, the Haitian experience had given me a much better grasp of my ignorance. Now, at least, I *understood* what I didn't understand. The job, I now knew, was film producing, and I didn't know how to do that. The kind of work I did know how to do, writing, was only a small part of this job. Words—narration—mattered only in relation to picture. You used words, moreover, only when you had to. Words were like galoshes. If you didn't need them, you didn't use them. And when you used them, you used plain ones.

A few days after I got back, Leo came to dinner and over dessert I tried—unsuccessfully—to explain to him and Arthur the workings of my new career.

"So it's like a whole new—uh—beginning!" said Leo, trying to sound jolly.

"Yeah," I said sourly, pouring the coffee.

"What's wrong with that?" he said.

I put the pot down and looked at him. "I'm too old to be a beginner."

"What crap," said Arthur sweetly.

I looked at *him*. "It's not crap. Being a beginner means feeling like a fool half the time and being scared *all* the time. Who needs that?"

"Wellll," said Arthur, lighting a cigarette, "it looks like *you* do."

CHAPTER
15

Now what did he mean by that? Just because I had a high tolerance for terror didn't mean I *liked* it. Anyway, I was scared only for the first three—well, maybe five—years. After that, I got the hang of it. I didn't get the hang of it sooner because the "it"—the job—kept changing. The first year, for example, I did a profile of Bella Abzug which included a singular, if I do say so, interview with her mother (her mother made my mother seem like a Lutheran). That piece was followed by a couple of others which also worked out pretty well, and I was just beginning to feel vaguely competent, when the local station popped up suddenly and pronounced me their new theater critic.

Okay, I won't pretend that I stood by helplessly, little wrists up, while a masked gang of executives dragged me to the theater and tortured me into revealing what I thought of the play. I could have said no. Except that because of an odd memory lapse, I had forgotten the word for no.

Besides, I thought it would be fun to be a theater critic. For the first time in my professional life, I even felt sort of qualified. I knew a thing or two about the theater, after all, and I knew how to write consecutive sentences. Best of all, here was one job in television that didn't require messing around with film. As I understood it, being a critic meant simply going to plays, writing reviews, and reciting them to the camera on the eleven o'clock news. Easy! Fun!

Wrong! Every job has its trying side, of course, but some jobs sound so monumentally swell that the job's penalties come as a shock. One big penalty of reviewing plays, for example, is that you must watch them. That may not sound like punishment, but when you have to see a play almost every night of the week and 90 percent of what you see is drek, that which would seem like perquisite is indeed punishment.

It's not that 90 percent of the plays running in New York are drek. I'm not talking about plays that *run*. I'm talking about plays that *open*. That includes all the plays that run *plus* all the plays that are so execrable that they open and close before anyone, except the critics, gets a chance to see them. Remember *Heathen*—a rock musical about Hawaiian missionaries? Or *All the Girls Came Out to Play*, a spoof about frustrated housewives and a homosexual who turns out to be straight? Of course not. No one remembers those plays, with the possible exception of the saps who invested money in them, because they closed almost as soon as they opened. Nobody remembers those plays because nobody saw them. The critics don't remember them, either. But the difference is, the critics saw them, every one.

And here's the really sad part: it's not much fun to be a critic, even when the play is okay. There's a gulf the size of Mexico between watching a good play when all you have to do is sit there and enjoy it, and watching a good play knowing that in less than two hours you'll have to regurgitate a cogent, pithy assessment of it. It's the difference between doing anything pleasant for its own sake or for a result—not unlike the difference, from what I've heard, between having sexual intercourse when you feel like it or having prescribed sexual intercourse during ovulation because you're trying to get pregnant.

During the opening night of *Grease*—probably the best musical that season—a girl with a bow in her hair moved center stage and sang, "Look at me, I'm Sandra Dee / Lousy with virginity." It was a very funny moment and most people in the audience laughed. Normally, I would have laughed, too. But you can't laugh at something when you're worried sick about how to describe it.

After my tenth or twelfth play, I eased up and finally reached a point where I actually *could* laugh at what I saw—or be moved by it—without instantly trying to seize upon the world's snappiest word or phrase for it. But that's still a long way from having fun.

Of course, plays like *Grease* and, in the same way, *Heathen*, were the easiest kind to review. When a play is clearly terrific or clearly bilious, all you have to do is figure out how to say so. It's the ones in the middle—the so-so plays—which lead to gastrointestinal spasms.

Will I, can I, ever forget the abundantly costumed *Vivat! Vivat Regina!* about Elizabeth I? Sure I can, and did the instant I left the theater. That was the problem. Watching that play was like watching a no-stick snowfall. Now you see it, now you don't get it. "What was that?" I thought to myself as I bolted up the aisle after the curtain came down. "What was that?" I thought as I sat straight up in the back seat of a taxi, the palms of my hands growing colder and wetter as the taxi moved nearer and nearer to Rockefeller Center: I don't know what that was and I don't know what I think and please God let this taxi have an accident so that I will have to go to the hospital and not have to review this play (and please God don't let the driver get hurt, just me, okay?).

I paid the fare and got out of the taxi and walked into the

building and stopped. I could say I got sick. I could go home and say I developed pleurisy (too exotic); a heart murmur (not believable); menstrual cramps (not serious enough); an attack of food poisoning (perfect!).

I couldn't do it. I don't know why. Maybe because in the back of my mind I knew what would happen once I got to the newsroom. What happened was I sat down at a typewriter, looked at a clock—which said 10:10, which meant that I had fifty minutes to type—so I typed. And when I read what I typed I knew what the play was about and what I thought of it. And the funny thing was, the next day, when I read the other critics, they thought the same thing.

Theater criticism was my first introduction to the "magic" (i.e., horror) of live television. To a person watching, live television means immediacy. To the person on-camera, live television means if you screw up, you can't fix it. Reading one's own fifty-second theater review from a TelePrompTer does not sound like something fraught with potential mishap. It isn't. Everyone, from friends like Leo to the director, told me so. But it was like telling someone who is afraid of flying how much safer, statistically, a plane is than a car. That is also true. But a person who has white knuckles in the air receives little comfort from hearing about traffic fatalities on the ground below.

My biggest fear, for some odd reason—even though I had no allergies and possessed nasal passages clearer than the Vermont air—was that, as I began to speak, I would contract a fierce respiratory ailment which would make me cough, sneeze, choke, and possibly die. Or, worse, that I would get the hiccups. In order to be safe, I walked into studio 3A each night armed with Kleenex, water, and two kinds of cough drops. The desk behind which I sat to give my review looked like a first-aid station.

"Look, it doesn't *matter* if you make a mistake," said my colleague, the friendly sportscaster. "If something goes wrong, make a joke of it and go on."

"I could never do that," I replied glumly.

"Sure you can!" he said.

But I was right and he was wrong. Because when it finally happened, I couldn't think of a joke. Not that what happened was the sort of thing I had been worried about. It hadn't occurred to me, for example, that the screw-up might originate in a place other than my own throat. For that reason I never thought to check on what was going on around me because, to the same extent that I distrusted myself, I trusted everyone else. The old the-grown-ups-know-what-they're-doing fallacy.

Therefore, not until the director cued me and the camera light went on and I began to speak did I notice that the camera, instead of being in its usual place a few feet from where I sat, was clear across the room, about fifteen feet away. The distance of the camera would, I knew, in no way affect its view of *me*. But it seriously affected my view of it—or, more to the point, my view of the TelePrompTer in it. I began to read, assuming, I suppose, that the camera would realize it was being bad and move closer. But it didn't, and the type began to look like a line below the bottom line of an eye chart. I squinted, I faltered. Still the camera didn't move. I leaned forward over the first-aid station; I stood up; and then I did the unthinkable: I looked into the camera and wailed, "I can't see!"

I forget exactly what happened next. I think someone handed me a copy of the review, which I read.

When it was all over, I noticed something: although I didn't make a joke, I also didn't die. In fact, no one died. In fact, no one even mentioned it—except the news director, who, when I came in the next day, made a crack about getting me a Seeing Eye dog.

It was then I learned three important lessons: (1) that which feels like a catastrophe usually isn't; (2) trust others at least as little as you trust yourself; and (3) only an imbecile goes on camera without a copy of the script in hand.

Through some union weirdness, the wage for reviewing plays on television in 1972 was fifty dollars per play. As far as the union was concerned, a critic, like a weatherperson, was a species of performer. Fees were based on the amount of time spent on the air, and the "performance" of a review took less than a minute.

Both in terms of prestige and money, the job of television theater critic, not unlike the job of state senator, guaranteed you two things: a proud mother and the need for an additional job. Luckily for me, I already had another job on *Chronolog*. Although lucky was not what I began to feel when, each day, I punched in at 9:30 A.M. and punched out at 11:30 P.M. What I began to feel after a few weeks of *that* was punchy.

I also began to feel like Clark Kent and You-know-who. I'd go off to work in the morning dressed in my office skivvies, my theater critic costume packed discreetly in a dress bag— nothing flashy, but a conservative little frock, which I thought would make me look unsexy (in other words, intelligent).

Each day, then, at six o'clock, when the *Chronolog* people put on their coats and headed home, I'd close my office door, lower the blinds (in case the dentist across the way was working late), pull one dress up over my head, another one down, and tear off to the makeup room where a small Latin man slapped an abundant amount of pancake on my face.

The usual order of things would have been to get made up just before going on the air. Doing it this early meant that by the time 11:15 rolled around, my powder caked and turned into an unlovely shade of orange, especially around the eyes and crevices near the mouth, euphemistically called laugh lines. But getting made up before the theater rather than after gave me twenty extra minutes to write a review—worth the orange laugh lines. Such are the compromises of television journalism.

The people at the station, meanwhile, voiced no opinion on how I looked, what I wrote, or how I said what I wrote. I was told by an old-timer that this was normal. When I asked him why the people in charge never say what they think of you, he said, "Because most of the time they don't know. But count your blessings. When they think they *do* know, somebody usually gets fired."

I didn't so much long to hear about my laugh lines as my spoken ones. What I missed was a clone of Martin Goldman to bark at me once in a while about an adjective. But I kept forgetting: surely one reason no one criticized my adjectives was that adjectives didn't matter the way they used to.

Early on at *Chronolog*, I had seen words accompanying film get short shrift. Now I saw the same thing happening to words on their own. Words were treated as if they were terminally ill, and not worth the trouble. I could see why. In television, as soon as a word leaves your mouth, it's gone. A word said is a word dead. Sooner or later, I guess somebody would have noticed if every sentence I uttered was ungrammatical, or if every opinion off the wall. But the only criticism or guidance I ever got from a person in charge during my term as a theater critic—and this only after I asked for it—was from the same news director who had suggested the Seeing Eye dog. This time he said, "Don't use big words."

I decided not to ask what big meant.

By the time the theater season ended, NBC News had a new president: Richard C. Wald, the first of the thin men I had seen that first day. He summoned me one June morning to his new office.

"How would you like to be a network correspondent?" he said as soon as my bottom hit the chair on the other side of his desk.

"A what?" I said.

"You cover news for the network," he said. I looked at him. He wasn't kidding.

"How do you—do that?" I said, trying not to let my voice lose volume.

"You'll learn," he said brightly.

"Who—who's gonna teach me?"

"The kind people who bring us our local news," he said.

"Local? I thought you said network!"

"I did. You'll learn at local and then you'll *do* what you learned on the network."

"I see," I said, not seeing. "Uh—when do I start?" He shrugged. "If there's no rush," I said, "how about next September?"

He looked surprised. "Why September?"

"Because that'll give me time to get married and go on a honeymoon."

Now he looked really surprised. "Mazel tov," he said, sitting straight up in his chair. "I didn't know you were getting married!"

I smiled. "I'm not sure if the groom knows, either."

CHAPTER
16

In 1972, for the first time in my adult life, I no longer felt like a freak because I was single. On the contrary, by 1972, the single career woman had, at last, come into her own. Housewives envied us, younger women respected and admired us. The term "old maid" was dead and displaced by a heady new term: "liberated woman."

From a card-carrying feminist's point of view, if, in 1972, you had married long ago when, presumably, you didn't know any better, that was one thing. But, in 1972, to *get* married, especially if you didn't plan on having children, was considered, at best, quaint. And among the people I knew, quaint had all the cachet of cute.

I was not impervious to this view of marriage. Intellectually, I respected it. And it amused me to find my failure to get a husband suddenly considered a sort of triumph, a show of independence on my part. (Ha!) When feminists gathered— and I considered myself one of them—and compared marriage to slavery, I offered no opposing view. I didn't really have an opposing view. I had an opposing feeling. I didn't care what the hell marriage was. I wanted it before there was a movement, and I wanted it now. I didn't even know why, anymore. I just knew that I was sick and tired of being a solo act. I wanted a partner. Children or no children, I wanted to be a member of a family; and I wanted the family to be the person at home, not the people at work. Anyway, with all the job changes I had at NBC, the people at work kept changing and did not, therefore, constitute a proper family as I had known it at *Look*.

The marriage idea thrilled Arthur not at all. But when I put it to him as either/or—either marriage or so long—he (sulkily) changed his mind. His terms were a little strange, but I went along. We had already planned a trip to Europe during my summer break. I had thought it would be nice to get married before the trip. "Then," I ventured cheerfully, "we can have a sort of—honeymoon!" The suggestion was not a hit. "No no no no no, absolutely not!" he said, shaking his head fiercely. If we *had* to do this thing, we could do it *on* the trip, not before. Where? Somewhere. Promise? Yes. . . .

I settled, attributing all of his static to premarital jitters, and off we went.

First to Greece, but we couldn't get married there because they had just had a revolution. Then to Hungary, but we couldn't get married there because Hungary had a Communist government. Then to Czechoslovakia, but ditto. Then we went to Denmark, where, we both knew, it was here and now or never, at which point Arthur got *lungebetaendelse*, which is Danish pneumonia. When he rallied, we went to buy a ring. I liked the ring—a thin, gold, sort-of wire—but I left the ring store in a snit because he flirted with the salesgirl ("I did not!" "You did so!"), who was blond, of course, and ravishing. Then we stopped speaking. Then, that afternoon, we marched—not quite as if to our execution, but something like it—to the town hall in Copenhagen, a pretty building that looked as if it were made of candy. And then pale (him) and trembling (me) we stood in a grand and beautiful marble room before a woman judge who, in English, pronounced us man and wife. Which made us feel somewhat friendlier toward each other. We even stood on the steps of the hall and asked a passerby to take our photograph. I remember thinking I should smile, so I did. (Later, by accident, the film was exposed to the sunlight and ruined.) Then we walked back to the hotel—a sweet place called the Hasnia, which, by an eerie coincidence, burned to the ground five years later to the day (by which time we were divorced)—and called my mother and father.

I returned to work in September and reported to local news for basic training, where I felt about as welcome as an illegal alien with a prison record. I couldn't really blame my hosts. The local news department was understaffed and overpressured. They could hardly be expected to cheer the arrival of an incompetent trainee who, as soon as she got competent, would be shipped off to the network. The chill came mostly from the higher-ups, however. The reporters, exhausted and bedraggled, were as friendly as children in a sandbox. Not until much later, and then only from one or two, did I sense a speck of resentment about my guaranteed job on the network. . . . Which brings up the question of why some reporters stay on local and why some go to the network and why. And the answer is, I don't know why. I know only that no science and, often, very little sense, governs these decisions. I've heard people in the carpeted offices talk about "network material"; and sometimes, when you know whom they're talking about, you know what they mean. And sometimes, when you know whom they're talking about, you can't imagine what they mean. Most often, it's a matter of a person in charge getting a fix on someone on-camera. If the fix is positive, the someone-on-camera has it made—at least until the next person in charge comes along, who may or may not have the same fix.

Whatever judgment is made about a television news reporter, however, two separate areas are always under consideration: the area of one's journalism and the area of one's kisser. In the journalism area what counts is how intelligent—and fast—you are at news gathering, at covering a story; and how cogent—and fast—you are at writing it. What counts as far as your kisser is concerned is more complicated. It's all right not to be gorgeous; it's not all right to be hideous, messy, or strange—unless, with regard to the latter, you've been around for a long time and have managed to make a shtick out of looking strange.

They also like you to look "natural"; but, there again, one news executive's "natural" is another's French marionette. Generally, I got the impression that good looks—preferably blond—and an appealing personality—whatever whoever-is-in-charge happens to think that is—were more important on the local station (for anchor people, *all*-important), and that good writing mattered more on the network.

I didn't know what they saw in me and I wasn't about to ask. That I could write probably didn't hurt, but that I was a female who could write probably didn't hurt even more. In 1972, out of about fifty-five correspondents at NBC News, roughly five were women. In their collective heart of hearts, I don't think the big (male) guns wanted more women; but, given the political climate in those days—affirmative action, threatened lawsuits (one turned into an actual lawsuit)—they were beginning to think that they had better get some more. Audition tapes from twenty-two-year-olds on local stations in

The Heartland, hopeful of being whisked from Fort Wayne to the White House, rolled in with every mail delivery. Some of the blonds with hard *r*'s were smarter than they looked; but the good old boys seemed to have a hard time telling which cupcakes had brains in their centers and which had marshmallows.

Anyway, I think the gentlemen in New York felt safer with someone brunette and slightly aged like me, who had a background—like most of theirs—in writing, rather than speaking. Of course, there were scads of other brown-haired, slightly aged women writers around New York whom they might have hired instead of, or even in addition to, me. But those women hadn't come calling—yet. Few of the good women writers and editors I knew wanted to get into television then. If *Look* hadn't died, I wouldn't have wanted to, either. Print people were awfully snooty about the "boob tube" in those days. (Many still are, but more often now, when you scratch a writer who turns his or her nose up at television, you find a writer who was turned down after his or her audition.) You would think the network would have done more to try to lure good female, or male, writers. But for some reason—or more likely, none—recruiting efforts seemed to be minimal. And I don't think that's changed.

What all of that adds up to is that one big reason I think I got somewhere in television when I did was that in 1972 not too many female writers were pushing down doors to get in; nor were many doors being held open for them to enter.

I felt surprisingly excited and uncharacteristically un-terrified about this new adventure that loomed on my small horizon. I guess I figured that if I failed I could always be a writer again. And, besides, I was somebody's wife now, which meant that, whatever else happened, I had a life—a home to which I belonged, rather than a collection of walls within which I parked.

Little did I know, when I arrived for work the first day at the local station, brimming with gladness, that I had just walked into the aftermath of a revolution, and that the bodies had only just been removed from the main square. No signs had been posted to inform me that the old order had gone under the previous week and that the junta was just beginning to set itself up at police headquarters. Meanwhile, the lower-echelon militia crouched and quivered, waiting to hear who would be executed and who would be allowed to survive under the new order.

Nor did I have any way of knowing, once I found out what was going on, that in (particularly local) television, as in Latin America, revolutions come along as frequently as holidays. Had I known this, I might have been wise to the fact that the new rulers, having just gotten in, were by definition in danger of being summarily thrown out and thereby were far shakier than winners normally are. And knowing that, in turn, might, just might have prevented me from sticking my entire foot, ankle included, in my mouth during my first meeting with the generalissimo. "Hi! I hear it's your first day, too!" I chirped, as if we were both having a fun bounce on the camp trampoline, all the while noticing but not absorbing the fact that his features were beginning to tighten and grow smaller, as if they would soon gather in the middle of his face in a sharp point.

Nor, until it was much, much too late, did I notice the other signs: he was (1) *very* short, and had the aura of a man who would have preferred to have been *very* tall; (2) given to strutting; (3) fond of wearing three-piece English tailored suits in a profession with a dress code far from that of Wall Street's; (4) apt to keep his chin down at all times, the way bulls do when they're about to charge—not, in any case, a posture that connoted warmth or whimsy.

"Did you have as much trouble deciding what to wear on your first day as I did?" I cooed adorably, then waited for a charmed response.

Funny, there wasn't one. Not a laugh, nor smile, nor snicker; nor, in fact, a sound of any kind. He simply looked at me as if I were one of the condemned and moved on. I thanked God—or whomever I was thanking in those days—that since I was network property and had diplomatic immunity, he could not have me beheaded.

The old boy did manage an insult or two before I moved on ("I don't think women belong in the studio," he said to me once about my theater reviewing, "unless," pause, "they're beautiful"). But by then only sticks and stones hurt my bones.

Moments after that first encounter with Mussolini, a harassed underling in shirt-sleeves came by to show me to my desk. I looked at it, dumbfounded. There was nothing wrong with the desk itself. It was as unremarkable a desk as a desk should be. But something of importance which I had always thought surrounded a desk was missing: walls. I swallowed, remembering my vast corner emporium at *Look*. No office? I put the question to the harassed underling, who looked at me as if, having just been locked in a prison cell, I had said to the guard, "What! No down comforter?"

Since I had no choice, I decided to be a good sport about it. Until the second day when, judging from the number of messengers who relieved themselves on my desk of packages addressed to other people, I woefully absorbed the following equation: in the eyes of all beholders, a female behind a desk with no office around it = secretary. Click! The Working Girl's Moment of Truth. It was also the *New* Working Girl's (we-couldn't-care-less-that-you-were-hot-stuff-where-you-came-from) Moment of Truth—a moment familiar, no doubt, to many who have changed careers, male *or* female.

For me, that moment had been delayed for a year, and that

gave its slap all the more force. Big deal, I said to myself. What had happened, after all? A loss of status? Well, so what. Well, so plenty. I hadn't thought much about status before (when I had it). I hadn't thought of it as something I cared about. But now I felt its loss like a sting. And, having assumed I was above such feelings, I didn't like finding out that I wasn't.

As it turned out, I didn't need an office, or a desk, or even a chair, because, within a couple of days, my orders had come through. I was to trail one of the big kids for a couple of weeks—follow a reporter around town as he covered the news. At the end of the two weeks, the plan was, I'd have a go at a story myself.

The reporter who played Batman to my Robin was Bob Teague, a tall, swift, quirky black ex-athlete and sports writer, who called me "princess" (affectionately, I *think*). In any case, he seemed not to mind my tagging along, and went out of his way to show me the ropes, even though the rigors of his job would have prevented anyone of normal energy from doing anything of the kind.

The rigors were, in a word, frightening.

First the hours: to me, the hour of eight A.M. has always been a time by which with difficulty I have often been forced, during an otherwise agreeable professional life, to rise. In the local news business, the hour of eight—sometimes seven!— meant, instead, the time a reporter was expected to arrive. Arrive. *Get* there. Contacts in. Pantyhose pulled up.

Worse, when reporters showed up at that hour, they were not permitted to do anything reasonable, like drink a quart of coffee, decide which pencils need sharpening (leaving the more arduous task of sharpening them until later), or study the *Times* movie page. Instead, they had to—get this—go to work! No sooner would Teague arrive than the sadist on the assignment desk would dispatch him to a location. And with instructions which seemed to me appallingly cursory: "Some old lady got mugged, third time this week. Saint Clare's Hospital. Room Three Fifteen. Says she'll talk." Teague would be in motion at the sound of the room number. Seconds later he'd hit the street, with me panting behind, where a crew would be waiting in a parked car on Forty-ninth Street, and we'd take off like bandits (vroom, vroom, vroom!), Teague in the front seat next to the cameraman, who usually drove, me in the back, squeezed (happily, since at that hour it was always freezing) between the electrician and the sound man.

Besides warm bodies, the car held other compensations. My favorite—a splendid adult toy by anyone's standards—was a two-way radio which had a way of transforming the car from the ratty Chevrolet it usually was into a Batmobile.

Officially, the radio made it possible for the reporter to communicate with the assignment desk and vice versa—usually vice versa. Calls from the desk had a range of purposes—from the correction of errors ("Sorry, guys, wrong saint. The old lady's at Saint *Luke's*. Repeat: Saint Luke's Hospital. Oh, and guys? It's an old man, not lady. Repeat: muggee is man") to the transmission of late-breaking story information ("Hey, the fire is out. But you're in luck. There's another one in the South Bronx . . .").

What I liked most about the radio was that you got to say things like "over" and "out" and "that's a Roger" and my favorite, "that's an affirmative." There were also certain things you were not supposed to say—four-letter words, for example (including "help!"). In addition, you'd try not to say anything which would give the story away, because other crew cars from other stations were plugged into the same frequency.

I never understood why everything was such a big secret

because everybody was out covering the same stories, but the secrecy did enhance the theatrics of it all, to say nothing of the language. Say you had to talk to the desk about one of these (ostensibly) veiled missions. You wouldn't use the car radio; you'd pull over and use a telephone. But nobody called it a telephone. In local newspeak a telephone is a "landline."

I seemed to have a real aptitude for the part of the job that took place in the car. I learned, for example, how to drink my morning coffee in the back seat: by leaving the top of the Styrofoam cup on, in case anyone's interested, and cutting a small hole out of its edge. In later years, I also mastered—if I do say so—the far more difficult task of in-transit false-eyelash installation. The trick there was to apply the glue as the car started up, then to slap the lashes on fast during a red light.

But eventually, sad to say, one had to get out of the car and cover the story; and the more I watched Teague—both what he did, and the speed with which he did it—the more that part of the job began to worry me.

Teague sometimes did two, maybe even three, stories each day, and they all had to be edited and written for the show that night. That's what it meant, I learned, to cover local news. News meant killing yourself. News meant interviewing people with whom you had no appointment, but rather catching them on the run—occasionally as they fled a burning building. News meant emergencies, and in emergencies you don't think; you do. And you do fast. Slapping a news story together, getting it edited, written, and ready for air was in itself an emergency. When you did that you had to skip a lot of things: things like digesting the material; mulling it over; rethinking a point; rewriting; expanding; pondering. News meant, "Do it"—as the assignment desk used to say when time was particularly short—"quick and dirty."

News: I didn't like it.

I didn't like quick and I didn't like dirty because, like everyone else, I knew perfectly well what that meant: slop. It meant "Get a little actuality" (e.g., the fire in progress); "get a talking head" (e.g., a person, preferably a victim, to say something emotional—but *short*); "lay down a track" (i.e., a recording of your voice, telling the story); and "Cut" (edit, and fast).

News made everyone run. Even the newspaper reporters with spiral notebooks had to hustle to and from the scene of a story. But when they got there, all *they* had to do was write down what was going on, not produce a short motion picture about it.

However ratty the results, however choppy and superficial that two-and-a-half-minute movie turned out to be, make no mistake: it took consummate skill to make it. And once a story was in the can, I could tell that the reporter lying in a heap on the floor of the editing room (assuming his vital signs were still in evidence) experienced a certain pride of completion. But as I looked at him, I remember feeling like a dog eyeing a fish. I knew—aside from the less-than-inspiring product—that my own metabolism was all wrong for this kind of racing, nor did I thrill to its high. Nor, in spite of what Arthur said, its particular brand of terror. I liked to be frightened into *thinking*, not running.

One part of the job involved standing still, but that turned out to be the most nerve-racking part of all. As far as I could tell, the function of a "stand-upper," as it was called—the short, on-camera recitation delivered by the reporter, usually at the story's end—was to show (prove) that the reporter was at the scene and not back at the office eating bonbons or smoking grass. So, naturally, the stand-upper had to be filmed on the spot. And, therefore, written on the spot. The spot, more often than not, turned out to be a fire hydrant or car fender, where one had not only to compose grammatical English sentences—and fast, before the fire went out—but, since these were *concluding* sentences, one had to compose them while trying to imagine what one might wish to say in the narration *before* the conclusion, which one would write later, sometimes in the car on the way back from the filming, and record, still later, in a recording booth.

If one were writing the piece for a magazine, it would be like trying to work out the last paragraph of the story without having written, or even thought about, the beginning or the middle. In addition, one had to *memorize* what one wrote on the fire hydrant in order to say it into the camera, as if it were talking, not writing. Teague's technique, I noticed, was to compose on the hydrant and memorize while pacing up and down the block, talking to himself like the neighborhood loony. Meanwhile, at the sight of the television camera, the children of the neighborhood would have shot out of every apartment house, street corner, and schoolyard within a two-mile radius, and by now would be screaming, "Take my pitcher! Take my pitcher! I wanna be on TV!"

When the filming was done, it was rush, rush back to the building to get the film in the soup—nowadays, they use tape, which can be viewed right away, but the tempo is the same—pop a Bufferin, grab a sandwich, write the rest of the narration (while eating), and edit.

Editing happened in a small, dark, airless, icy room with an editor, Italian, usually, built like a boxer, and impervious to cold, who would sit bent over the machine and, magically, transform the scraps from Queens into a cut story with a beginning, middle, and end; while, behind him, the reporter would call out instructions and pace like an expectant father (or aunt). Meanwhile the producer upstairs would be calling up at ten-minute intervals with "How're ya doin'?" and

"Howzit goin'?"—euphemistic, as everyone knew, for "if you don't step on it, it's not gonna make the show," which, somehow, it usually did.

Teague covered a lot of crime. If it was big-deal crime—a major drug bust, say—the first stop was usually the D.A.'s office for a press conference, which gave the cops a chance to describe their cleverness at foiling the criminals—or the "alleged poipetrators," as they were called in Brooklyn.

I remember liking Brooklyn drug busts better than those in other boroughs because the Brooklyn D.A. in those days, Eugene Gold, had a plump, motherly secretary who always laid out a table that looked like a wedding brunch: coffee, Danish, rolls, jelly, and indecently sticky sticky buns. After the press conference, everyone would belch (except, as I recall, *The New York Times*), pack up the gear and head on over to the slammer—or wherever the poipetrators were being held. Then, when everybody was good and ready: cameras on sticks, lights on, sound plugged in ("Testing, one, two, three . . . Geddowda my light, Irving!"), the press honcho from the D.A.'s office would give the cue and, cotillion-style, they'd appear, two by two, criminal and cop, the cops beefy and expressionless, and the criminals—well, you couldn't tell what the criminals looked like because most of the time they'd use the hands that weren't handcuffed to pull their coats or shirts over their heads. And the cameras would roll and the flash cameras pop and, still in twos, like God's creatures boarding the ark, into the police van they'd go, and the first door would slam, then the second door, then the obligatory shot of the van moving away and that's it, boys, everybody can go to lunch.

Which usually produced more controversy than the story. "I don' wan' Italian," from the electrician. "We had Italian yesterday." Cameraman: "Yer crazy. We had Chinese yesterday. All day I had heartburn from that monosodium whaddyacallit—gluckamate." Soundman: "That was Toosday. Whaddabout the deli over on Canal Street?" I loved Jerry Gold (no relation to Eugene), but if he didn't get his pickle at lunch, he'd be cranky the rest of the week.

For the crew, who, by the way, may have sounded like palookas, but who were often smarter, sweeter, and almost always saner than the guys in suits back at the office, the story was over the instant the camera clicked off. For the reporter, who usually got an earful of the lunch fight without getting the lunch, the end of the shooting merely ended the first phase. The second phase—writing, editing, and narrating— began back at the office. So, usually, I'd follow Teague uptown, unless Italian won, in which case I'd stay downtown and have lunch with the crew, and in either place I'd find myself thinking still about the procession we'd just seen. One thing that always stuck in my mind were the sneakers which so often showed at the bottom of the pants legs, which meant that the person with the shirt over his head was a kid. Of course, that was before I learned about the kind of kid most of these kids were. . . . That was before I learned a lot of things.

So we'd finish our ravioli and order zabaglione and everything tasted terrific and there were a lot of laughs, especially if an electrician called Jimmy Gleason was on the job—Jimmy Gleason was a real cutup, especially when his pal on sound, Jim Garrity, was along—but in between the laughter and the mouthfuls, I'd keep having flashes about those people under the shirts and coats and why they did it and how long they'd been doing it and where it all began and how they felt just now being paraded in front of us for a shot, and whether they had any children, and again, about the ones who *were* children themselves, and about whether they felt guilty and on and on. . . . All of which, as far as my new chosen profession was concerned, was thunderingly irrelevant.

Because news, television news, most often meant a minute-thirty of who did what to whom, when, and where, and what he or she would get for it, period. Maybe a little bit more if one of them was a Mob star, or if the crime were particularly flashy or vile.

So why did I stick with it? Partly, I suppose, for the same reason I didn't say no to a recent trip to the Soviet Union. Because sometimes you do a thing, not because you think you'll like it or because it suits you, but because it's a new ride—from which you can always get off and walk.

I also knew that the people who ran the place could, at any moment, realize their mistake in hiring me and tell *me* to get off and walk.

Meanwhile, I guess I wanted to see if I could do it. And as it turned out, with the greatest difficulty (I was right about stand-uppers. They were murder) I could.

CHAPTER
17

$\mathbf{A}$nyway, most of my worries were academic because when I moved to the network, which I finally did in
January 1973, having done a couple of local pieces on my own
and lived, everything was different. Different floor, different
furniture, different grown-ups in charge. Different, meaning
better. Also easier. Also nicer. Like having an office at last.
And eventually, I even got to do the kind of non-news news
stories—features—which I could do "slow and clean."

As a correspondent for NBC News, I now worked chiefly
for the *Nightly News* program, anchored in those days by John
Chancellor. What made life at the network better and easier
had to do with the length and breadth of that show. Instead of
an hour, the network news was only a half hour—twenty-two
minutes after commercials—and in those twenty-two minutes
they covered, as they were fond of saying, the world. Which
considerably diminished the chances of Eugene Gold's wedding brunches getting on the air, as it did the chances of
practically everything else going on in New York.

On the local show, if it moved, they shot it; if they shot it,
they cut it; if they cut it, it made, as the vernacular goes, air.
On the network, for a story to make air it had to be—as they

were even fonder of saying—Big. Unless it was a "closer" (pronounced like "bulldozer"), a piece which ends the show, in which case it could be Cute.

Fewer stories that were acceptable meant fewer stories to cover meant less work meant better work. When you showed up in the morning—far closer to ten than nine—you were not immediately thrust out into the cold. But if you were, there were a couple of crucial differences. For example, instead of being sent to Canarsie with three men, two hundred pounds of equipment, and a beat-up Chevrolet, you were sent to Canarsie with three men, two hundred pounds of equipment, a beat-up Chevrolet, and a producer. A producer who would direct the cameraman—especially if the cameraman was cranky and didn't like taking orders from girls (*sic*). A producer who knew what the story was about even if you didn't. A producer who would sit down with you on the curb next to the fire hydrant and edit your stand-upper—or, if you were too stupid, write it. A producer who would graciously assume the role of idiot-card holder for your stand-upper; so that, instead of having to swallow it whole in your head, you could write it down on a card. Then, as the camera rolled, the producer would hold the card up for you to read. The producer would make sure everyone got fed when their union and their stomachs (not necessarily in that order) said they should. The producer saw to it that everyone had a room at night with Kleenex coming out of the wall, if, in order to shoot a second day, we were farther away than Canarsie and had to stay overnight, which—another change from local— we frequently did.

Producers were daytime husbands. They were loyal, comforting, intelligent, funny, and, sometimes, if the occasion warranted it, chivalrous. (In 1973 at *Nightly News* they were also all males.) Once in Newport, Rhode Island, after a long, wet day covering the America's Cup races, the producer and I stopped at a bar. When a friendly drunk nearby got *too* friendly and put his hand on my arm, the producer, who happened to be only slightly smaller than a large bear, took the man's upper arm in his hand, raised the forefinger of his other hand in front of the man's face, smiled with the sweet assurance of the one who knows he's bigger, and said in a voice so intense it sounded louder than it was: "We may talk to the correspondent, but we never *touch* the correspondent." Then he paused, tightening his grip ever so slightly on the man's arm, and added, "*Do* we?"

That same producer, Michael Silver by name, repeatedly saved my little neck, not to mention my not-so-little seat, in the early days by, among other things, preventing me from saying something dumb in a stand-upper. (I could always turn a good phrase, but it was not always the *right* phrase.)

It's really not fair. Field producers, which is what news producers are called, generally do most of the work on a story, while correspondents get all of the credit and, usually, a lot more of the money. Which is how the system rewards journalists who don't show. On top of that, producers are frequently saddled with correspondents who are not only fairly incompetent (like me) but ungrateful for their help besides (not like me).

In the early seventies, if you were in a field underpopulated by women, you always got asked about the "special problems" you had as a woman. I had trouble with those questions because I knew I was supposed to tick off abuses, but I didn't, myself, feel any. I knew women had a tough time getting good jobs in television. Even today, when they *do* get good jobs, they are rarely on the off-camera managerial level, and if they're on-camera, the contour of their noses and the color of their hair play a far greater role in their selection than such things do for men. I knew, too, that once hired, women did and do have "special problems" with rank, attitude, and salary. I felt as angry as anyone on behalf of those women. But I couldn't feel anything like anger about myself or my own experience.

In fact, I might have been benefiting from reverse discrimination. I knew that if I weren't a woman I might not have the job. If I weren't a woman I also probably wouldn't be getting the kind of help I kept getting from men *on* the job. When my feminist friends queried me about the nature of that help, I had to admit that, sure, sometimes the help had chauvinistic overtones—big-guy-comes-to-rescue-of-helpless-female sort of thing. And as a female, raised in the forties and fifties, I knew I might have been more willing to be—and act— helpless than I should have been.

However, the other way of looking at it is: because I was female, maybe I was more willing to admit what I didn't know, and to ask for help when I needed it and maybe that helped me to learn. A producer told me once that both male and young female correspondents had a noticeably harder time doing both of those things than I did.

But, if my memory is accurate, the man who said that was kind of bossy. So who knows? I only know that when women producers came along, I found that I respected them, too, and got as much help from them as men. I also knew that during those early days in the trenches, I was much more interested in getting help than in trying to figure out why or from whom I was getting it.

All the more because, incredibly, the first year I was at it, I also *was* it—NBC News's only network correspondent covering New York and, can you believe it, the entire Northeast. (CBS had twelve people in New York alone.) So, if something Big—or Cute—happened in New York, Connecticut, Rhode Island, Maine, New Hampshire, Vermont, Massachusetts, New Jersey, and it happened on NBC News in 1973, it happened with me in the foreground. And once, because the flight from Kennedy Airport in New York would get me to Bermuda before a flight from anywhere else would get anyone else there, it was I they sent when the governor of Bermuda went for a stroll with his dog in his garden one evening, and got shot and killed by an unseen sniper in the bushes.

Murders, like most other unsavory news events, rarely occur at convenient hours. One of my most vivid memories of the Bermuda murder story is being summoned to do it at four o'clock in the morning. Not surprisingly, the people stationed at the news desk who do the summoning have developed certain techniques of getting the attention of people who are likely to be unconscious at the moment the summons occurs. Their fear is that even though the summoned person's voice may agree to go to work, once the phone is back on its cradle, the summoned person's body may go back to its bed. When my call to go to Bermuda came at four A.M., I knew right away by the tone of voice on the other end that I didn't have a chance. "Are your feet on the floor?" it wanted to know.

"Are my what?" I said foggily.

He repeated the question, louder and slower: "*Are your feet on the floor?*"

Now I got it. "Just a minute," I said. ". . . no. I just looked and they aren't there."

"Well, keep looking," said the voice, even as a metronome, "until you see them. . . . Okay, *now* do you see them?" A certain steadfastness in his approach caused my bedcovers to move. I put one foot on the floor, then the other. My husband, Arthur, meanwhile, was hanging over the other side of the bed, mumbling to himself and groping for his glasses, which had fallen to the floor.

"Yeah, I see them now," I said to the phone in the dull voice of the vanquished.

"*Good*, Betty, very good. Now I want you to stand on those feet. That's right. Stand right up on those same feet you're looking at." He had me now. I knew it and he knew I knew it.

"I'm standing on those feet," I reported.

"Good! Now get your ass to Kennedy because you're booked on a five-twenty flight to Bermuda."

"B-b-ber ..."

"The governor was assassinated a few hours ago. I'm sending Sandy Goodman with you. He'll meet you at the airport and fill you in....What are you going to do with those feet now?"

"I'm going to move them," I said in an extremely small voice.

"Good girl!" Click.

I tore into the bathroom, peed, and while on the toilet tried to think what one wears to a murder in Bermuda.

"What the hell is going on?" said the voice of my husband from the bedroom.

"I don't know what to wear!" I yelled over the sound of the flushometer. I opened the bathroom door.

"There's something you're leaving out," he growled. "Wear to *where?*"

"Bermuda, Bermuda. Somebody's been shot—the governor—they're sending me—Jesus, is it summer there or what? What do you think about my pink jumper? No, too cute. *Where's* my hairdryer?"

"How do I know where your goddam hairdryer is," said the husband, his head under the pillow.

"Well, try to think! *Please*, Arthur, this is serious. I can't go to a frizzy climate without my hairdryer." By now I had pulled out half the contents of two going on three drawers. "Oh no!" I screamed.

"What, what?" said the husband, lifting the pillow straight up off his head.

"I just remembered. I lent it to my mother!"

Never mind. No time to fret. I got down on all fours on the floor and pulled a suitcase out from under my side of the bed.

"Can't you pack with the light off?" said the muffled voice, back under the pillow on the other side.

"Let's see, stockings, bras, shoes—my God, I almost forgot shoes!"

"Are you leaving soon?"

"Bathing suit? Should I take a bathing suit? No. I don't know where it is, anyway. . . . Sunglasses. I'll need sun-glasses—"

In ten minutes, I was sitting on my suitcase, bolting it shut. I picked up the pillow and kissed my husband on his ear. "What do I tell your mother?" he rasped as I went for the door.

"Tell her—tell her I've gone to a murder in Bermuda—and—and not to worry—and not to feel bad about the hairdryer. I'll stick my head in an oven or something."

I've never minded working hard, but I don't like not sleeping. In Bermuda I learned another new television equation: the bigger the story—requiring, therefore, continuous coverage—and the more remote its location—resulting, often, in limited manpower, that is, one crew, one producer, one correspondent—the slimmer the chances of getting anything like the minimum hours of sleep deemed necessary for the sound functioning of mind and body. It wouldn't have been so bad were we just doing stories for *Nightly News*, but since we were the only people there from NBC, in the late afternoon when we finished feeding *Nightly News*, we immediately had to fill the next open mouth—the *Today* show's. Then, by around eight or nine in the evening, with the *Today* spot finished, we'd start hearing from radio. Radio—no pictures, at least—wanted not one spot, but one spot phoned in (they told me how to unscrew the mouthpiece in order to get better sound) every bloody hour throughout the night. (They finally settled for every other bloody hour.) "But nothing is *new!*" I'd whine into the telephone at the radio chief in New York. "It's *night*. People here go to *sleep* at night. The *cops* go to sleep. The *murderers* go to sleep ..."

"Then make the next one short," he'd say without any noticeable warmth.

Short Shmort. You still had to be awake. And for what? A three-sentence story that went on for three days with no new developments. The governor went out to the garden to walk the dog. He was shot. The dog was shot. They both died. Nobody knew who did it. The police suspected a radical group of blacks—no individual suspects, however, and no arrests. That was the story on Monday. That was the story on Tuesday. That was the story on Wednesday, and I reported it over and over and over, twice a day for television, and more times than I could keep track of for radio—each time adding a desperate embellishment, e.g., interviews with people on the street and on the beaches (me with makeup on, shoes off) virtually all of whom said the same predictable, trite things about how awful it was.

The governor's widow, a pretty woman with a fine, thin nose, held a press conference in a lovely, airy room with French doors on the ground floor of the mansion. Because of the extreme stiffness of her upper lip, Lady Sharples fascinated me and set me off on my usual private trail of useless, self-addressed queries: Was she brave, numb, or acting? What sort of a marriage had it been? How did she feel about having to perform on the subject of her husband's death, so soon, and in front of a pack of strangers—the international press, that is—whose job it was to get "something good" and run.

Meanwhile, the cameras—ours and the others—rolled on the rote Q's and A's: "What are your plans, Lady Sharples?"

"Well, to tidy up here, then to return home to England," she said with consummate poise, making hometoEngland sound like one word.

Who, I also wondered, were the radical group of blacks in this pretty, unperturbable-looking place which once I had heard described as WASP heaven? What, exactly, did the blacks want? Why would they have it in for the governor, who seemed to have been only a figurehead, and a benevolent one? But as long as there were no official suspects, that was not for us to wonder about, either. Instead, each day, the producer, Sandy Goodman (dear, good-humored Sandy Goodman, who, if you owned a department store, would be your first choice when December came for the person you'd dress up in a red suit and park in the toy department), would prop me up in front of a palm tree outside the governor's residence, make sure the camera was positioned so that coconuts would not appear to be growing out of my head, and hold up the idiot card on which we had composed an appropriately factual, relevant, to-the-point, which is to say boring, stand-upper, which I would then recite: "Three days after the killings here at Government House,* the hunt for the killer went on with as many hunters as this island has ever seen. They include eight men from Scotland Yard, the entire three-hundred-and-twenty-man Bermuda police force, and one hundred and twenty members of the local militia. . . . " Then I'd wipe the makeup off my face and we'd go to lunch, and maybe after

---

*It is customary in stand-uppers to say, "here at such-and-such-a-place" to underline the fact that you have actually dragged your little self to the actual scene of the whatever—although it is possible that's all you've done. Many a correspondent, especially on those show-bizzy magazine programs, has been airlifted to the story's location, dropped like a weighted leaflet, and retrieved immediately after reciting his or her words—often written by the producer—into the camera.

lunch, mosey over to the police station, which looked like the gingerbread residence of Hansel and Gretel. Here we'd have a nice chittychat with the chief detective on the case, who looked like Errol Flynn and spoke, not of poipetrators, but pehrpahtratahs, informing us, at the same time rather apologetically, that none had been found. Then off we'd go to find another palm tree, in front of which I'd recite another version of the world's most boring stand-upper for the *Today* show. Then we'd go back to the hotel and I'd start worrying about the bloody radio spots and Sandy would worry about his wife in Larchmont, who, at any moment, was about to have their first baby.

It was not the sort of life that helped perpetuate marital harmony. Not, by the way, because of on-the-road hanky-panky—there's very little of that, actually—but for a far more central reason: because of a rule which both the rulers and the ruled accepted with equal equanimity—that the body of a reporter belongs first to the network and second to his or her mate (and a very distant third, maybe, to those hanky-panked). For me, the problem got to be chiefly one of physical energy—not having enough for both Job and Life. It shot my wad to get up in the middle of the night to take a plane somewhere, then never quite to catch up with lost sleep when I got there. When I came home from Bermuda, it took days before I was good for anything; and when I was, they sent me back to Bermuda to cover the funeral.

It wasn't necessarily travel that sapped one of marital energy, either. I've never been more sapped than I was one January, right across the George Washington Bridge in Newark, New Jersey, after a succession of early mornings spent waiting outside in 4 degrees Fahrenheit for an eruption in a community war between blacks and Italians.

I have two sharp memories of that occasion: one is not being able to get beyond the first couple of words of the stand-upper because my face was so numb that, although I could make sounds, I couldn't make my mouth form words. I also remember the mercy some of the Italians showed the reporters by inviting us into their houses so that we could thaw out and use their bathrooms, and how some of the women even brewed big, fine-smelling pots of coffee. We held those coffee cups in both hands and let the steam hit our faces, and I remember feeling a rush of love for those women, even though—because of what was going on on their street—I felt pretty sure I didn't like them.

One particularly dark, cold morning we had just taken our places on the street when we got the word that the women in the houses were angry—not at everybody, it turned out, but at everybody from CBS. A report had aired on CBS's local station the night before which the block's residents felt was sympathetic to the blacks. So, that morning all houses on the block were closed to CBS; and, as far as I could tell, on January 14, 1974, no one working for CBS in Newark, New Jersey, went to the bathroom.

One does get crafty about at least *trying* to avoid physical discomfort. The same year my mouth wouldn't move in Newark I had been sent to Pittsburgh to cover a union leader's murder trial when, in the middle of the night (when else?) a prison riot broke out in Moundsville, West Virginia. Since the trial was winding down, and since mine was the nearest body to West Virginia, I got picked to cover the riot.

This time it was fall, not winter; but middles of nights are cold in most places in most seasons; and I had packed clothing in which to sit in a stuffy courtroom—nothing thermally suitable for the new assignment. But necessity breeds nerve. I simply pulled the blanket off the bed in my hotel room—a large yellow thing with an "H" on it—and dragged it, Linusstyle, through the lobby of the Pittsburgh Hilton. "I'm going to a prison riot," I explained to a stunned night clerk, and kept moving right out the door, "and I need your blanket to keep warm."

And, oh boy, did I. Prisoners had taken guards hostage inside, negotiations were going on, and all we could do was (what else is new) Wait.

The longer you wait for something to happen, the more you want something to happen and the less you care what does. Reporters are not genetically monstrous, but they get that way. One death, two, none, three hostages injured, four, none—after a while you become too emotionally dislodged really to care. You stand there and you wait and you shiver and you just want something—*anything*—to break, so that you can slap your eyelashes on, do your number, and get the hell out of there and go where it's warm and where you can get some food and go to sleep.

You don't even feel guilty for not feeling anything. I didn't. Guilt comes hard, it seems, when the body isn't getting what it wants. . . . And, to return to the original point, when a day like that is done, you do not come home to your sweetie full of get-up-and-go. You do not wish to frolic. You wish to flop. Which may not suit your mate. It did not suit mine, who stayed home writing all day and who, at night, wanted to burst forth on the scene. Or at least dine with someone who stayed awake through dessert. That's not what ended my marriage, but it didn't add to its longevity, either: me always pooped; he always irritated that I was always pooped. What if, I thought sometimes, then quickly put it out of my mind, we had children? Some correspondents did, I knew, have children. How did they do it? I didn't really want to know. I felt inadequate enough as a wife.

Nor does it help a marriage—it didn't help mine—if you

start to love the work that saps you. (Remember when this only happened to men?) In spite of my kvetching, I was developing a real fondness for my loony job. It did nothing for my writing, but I hadn't expected it would. I had gone into it for adventure and to try out new muscles, and that's what I was getting and what I was doing. And I liked it. I liked lunch with the boys. I liked hotels and airplanes. I liked tearing around and then telling what I saw. Once in a while I even ran across something that seemed important to tell. So I liked the job. Sometimes I even loved it.

I never did figure out which cart came before which horse. Did the job dent the marriage? If the marriage had been better, would I have focused less on the job? If the marriage had been better, would I have been able to love my job without its being a problem? Probably the winning answer is a combination of numbers two and three. Meanwhile, it should be said that Arthur focused plenty on *his* "job"; but writing books at home required about half as much physical energy as continually shuffling off to the latest disaster in Buffalo. On top of which, Arthur seemed to have twice the energy I had, anyway, and he didn't seem to need to sleep more than occasionally.

A lot of times my work got between more than me and Arthur. Like the time some American who had been living in China for thirty-five years chose to come home to Connecticut the same evening we were having a sit-down dinner for twelve. My bureau chief (more about him later) assured me that the helicopter would get me back in *plenty* of time to put in the roast. Well, (1) it didn't and (2) when we finally did whir and putter to the ground on the small landing pad next to the Hudson River, the pilot let us off and lifted off again, unaware—as we were, too, for about a minute and a half— that the heliport had closed for the night and that the eight-foot-high gate leading to the street was locked, leaving us, a three-man camera crew, a producer, and me, no way out unless we wanted to about-face and swim to New Jersey.

There are few strollers, once the sun has set, along Twelfth Avenue, and even fewer cars going under sixty. It took two hours before the driver of an ambulance, of all things, heard us yell, and swung around, drove up to the gate, and informed us, in fairy-godmother fashion, that he "just happened" to have an eight-foot ladder. (I didn't understand it then and I don't now.) He then got the ladder out, managed to get both himself and it onto the roof of the ambulance, and lowered the ladder down on our side of the fence. Now all we had to do was climb the ladder, jump onto the top of the ambulance, and jump down to the ground. Wonderful! we all thought and I, too, until I saw the eight-foot ladder in place on the (slightly swaying) eight-foot gate and decided I'd miss my dinner party and sleep on the pier.

"Aw, come on, Betts," said the electrician, Bill Ryan, a kind, bespectacled man who, until that moment, I had thought was my friend. "If you fall, we'll catch you!"

"Thanks, old buddy," I said, "but I'm not going." But eventually, of course, I did, with Bill Ryan and the sound man holding the ladder and cheering as if I were a sports event.

"C'mon, Betts! Atta girl! Don't look down now, don't look down! Almost there now, Betts!"

When I opened the door of my apartment at 11 P.M. I saw pillows which were normally on the furniture on the floor, with both the guests and the husband sprawled all over them, making the best, you might say, of the extended cocktail hour. Of the twelve, only two women seemed remotely sober. I found them wandering about in the kitchen, scouting for the dinner.

It was then I knew that with difficulty I could swing Brenda Starr and Wife, or I could swing Perle Mesta and Wife; but I couldn't swing Wife, Brenda Starr, and Perle Mesta. Perle Mesta had to go. And somehow, I thought, I will manage the remaining two.

CHAPTER
18

Nineteen seventy-three found me on my knees, praying each day for the continued good health of Bob Hager. Hager, a bright-eyed, ambitious young correspondent with a vigorous pulse rate, had just returned from Germany to become the newest member of the Northeast Bureau. And guess what. He liked hard news. He liked breaking stories. Exhaustion turned him on. Physical discomfort made him fight even more fiercely. His motor was perpetually on. When they didn't send him running, he ran in place. They called him Rabbit, and I loved him because the more he ran, the more I could walk. The more, that is, I could escape from hard news and work instead on the kind of feature pieces that allowed me to get answers to the kind of questions I always wanted to ask when the news part of the story was over.

But even with the new recruit, I still had to contend with the tastes and disposition of our boss, the bureau chief, whom I'll call O'Brien. O'Brien was a stolid, regular-featured (even handsome in a marine-captain sort of way), crusty man of the hard-news-is-all,-the-rest-is-fluff school of thinking, and he greeted my interest in feature stories as joyously as the coach of the Pittsburgh Steelers might greet his prize quarterback's interest in marijuana.

At the beginning we used to argue about features versus hard news. O'Brien would say features were junk and I'd say they were junk if they were done junkily. He'd say a network news program was no place for stories about basket-weaving. I'd say I agree, and that stories about how people lived their lives and how some of those ways were changing were not stories about basket-weaving. He'd humph and say, no matter, stories like that are soft. I'd say "soft" is a condition in the head of some reporters and that good features could be as "hard" and were easily as important as most of that political blather from the White House lawn. But after a while—a short while—we both gave up. As long as he got his hard news covered, O'Brien didn't really care what I did—or thought. And as long as I could do features, I didn't care what he thought of them. We also both got wise to the fact that what he thought didn't matter a whole lot.

The show producers—of *Nightly* and *Today*—decided what went on the air, not the bureau chiefs. If the producers of those shows wanted features, and wanted them from me, which they seemed to, that meant I did them. Which did not keep O'Brien from grousing behind my back. Nor did it keep him from taking me off a feature and throwing me on a news assignment whenever he could. No matter who was in charge of our finished pieces, O'Brien, as O'Brien continually reminded us, was in charge of us. When the News fairy on his shoulder whispered in his ear that a story should be covered, O'Brien, alone, decided whether to pay attention and whom to send. If the News fairy whispered loud enough and if, at the same time, Hager was busy on another story, I would almost surely get nabbed. "Rollin!" he'd yell—which I always heard as "Cinderella!"—and I'd scurry into his office. When I got there he'd squint and say, "What're you doing?" as if it mattered because whatever I would answer, he'd say, "Well, drop it! You're meeting a crew in ten minutes on Forty-ninth Street. There's been a bomb threat in the llama cage at the Central Park Zoo . . ."

I admit that sometimes O'Brien's decisions to send me running were reasonable. And I even got to understand why he sent me—or any of us—when it seemed less than reasonable. "Look," Mike Silver said once after we'd both been snatched off a feature, just as it began to percolate, to shoot Spiro Agnew mouthing off from the dais in the Hilton ballroom, "O'Brien's got to cover his ass. Suppose Agnew flipped out and took all his clothes off and suppose ABC and CBS were there and we weren't? They'd take *O'Brien's* clothes off and flip *him*."

Even so, O'Brien's News fairy cried wolf a lot, and when that happened, you'd find yourself on a thankless run of what we used to call WGCs: Wild Goose Chases. Nor, once he decided to send you somewhere, could you ever talk O'Brien out of it. And if you were smart, you wouldn't try. Never, the rule went, question O'Brien's News fairy. If you did, he'd *really* keep you running. I learned that lesson the hard way once in the middle of a stakeout, the most thankless of all WGCs.

In the news business, a stakeout usually means hanging around on the street in front of someone's house or office, waiting for a person who doesn't want to see or talk to you, in order to ask him or her a question he or she wouldn't dream of answering. If, by chance, you get lucky and the person emerges before you've died of exposure, and does, actually, open his or her mouth before the cameraman has also not died of exposure, you usually get something like, "I have no comment on that right now"; or "You'll have to ask *him* about that"; or "Would you excuse me, please" (as they swat you with the opened car door); or, as L. Patrick Gray said to me oh-so-crisply one sunny afternoon in Connecticut when he arrived home and found me and the crew waiting in the driveway: "You're trespassing." My reaction was prompt. I turned as red as the geraniums on his front lawn, stammered an apology, tumbled into the crew car, and fled. Not the instincts, O'Brien later remarked, of a person destined for news-gathering greatness.

But I can't blame everything on bad instincts. I also had a terrible attitude. On the William Rogers stakeout, for example, I could easily and justifiably have been charged with sabotage. The assignment to stake out Rogers came after Spiro Agnew's resignation. Everyone was playing guess-who's-going-to-be-Vice-President. Reporters were hounding anyone who had been so much as mentioned as a possibility, hoping for—what? I used to wonder. No one expected any of these people to admit anything resembling either fact or feeling. The likelihood of a potential appointee for such an office emerging from his house in Chevy Chase, looking into a network camera lens, and saying, "Yop, it's me" was not large. The chances were small even for getting an "I sure hope it's me," not to mention a "My wife keeps telling me if I get this one, I really *will* have to go on the wagon."

When, tell me when, in the history of television news, has a reporter, having staked out a politician or a defendant or a hotshot who doesn't want to talk, retrieved from such a person anything truthful, informative, or even faintly interesting as he moved at a clip from his doorstep to his car? I know stakeouts exist for a reason (I forget what it is) and I know it's wildly important to get whomever or whatever you're supposed to get first, and beat out the other networks (I forget why; after all, no one knows or cares who got there first, *except* the other networks), but time and time again, on each and every stakeout, even when I tried, the necessary surge of adrenaline never came.

Partly, I guess, it was the same old problem I had about racing. I've never liked moving fast for *any* reason, even in a sport; and beating someone out in a gang-bang, which is what a convergence of press is called and which describes, accurately, its charm and delicatesse, did not entice me. I don't know why. I used to think it was because I was female. In fact, I used to think one of the good things about being female was that you didn't have to get caught up in that huff-puff-I-won stuff. Of course, nowadays females race too, against men and against each other. I don't mean to sound less competitive than thou—I'm certainly ambitious, I definitely like *getting*—but I don't seem to need to get by *winning*. I suppose you could argue that all getting is winning. But, somehow, I don't think it is.

Anyway, if I had to run, I'd run. If I had to do stakeouts, I'd do stakeouts; but I wasn't going to stick one elbow in ABC's ribs and the other in CBS's to get to the front row.

Back at the bureau, meanwhile, word had come down that William Rogers, among many others, had been named as a possible candidate for the vice-presidency. That's all O'Brien had to hear on a slow news day. Next thing I knew, I was being ordered over to the Pan American Building, where Rogers had an office, in order to get him to talk about the nomination. Fat chance, I thought to myself, as I pulled on my coat and took a last swallow of coffee standing up. Fat bloody chance.

"The Pan Am Building," I announced, getting into the crew car and slamming the door. "And don't hurry." When we arrived we looked around in the lobby and neither ABC nor CBS (surprise, surprise) was there. Nor was the Twinkletown *Gazette*. I looked at the cameraman and he looked at me. "WGC!" we said in unison, and looked for a comfy place on the wall to lean.

Then I made a bold decision. Instead of lingering in the hallways like vendors of pornography—after all, no other press is here—why not be civilized for once, go up to Rogers's office, and ask straight out to see him? Which I did. And which, to my astonishment, worked. Sort of. Rogers would see me, said the receptionist, but alone, without the crew. Okay, fine, I said, and went in.

Rogers, handsome, tall, and dripping with dignity, greeted me, not only courteously but warmly. I was enchanted. Immediately, I explained the purpose of my visit. He told me he suspected as much but that, of course, he couldn't say anything about the vice-presidency: that first of all, he didn't know anything and, "even if I did," he said with a quick smile, "I probably wouldn't say so!" He asked me if I could understand that and I said of *course* and how gracious of you to see me, sir, and I'll explain what you said to my boss and I'm sure he'll understand, too!

"We're off the hook, boys!" I whispered to the crew, who were still parked in the reception area. They hoisted up their gear and we piled into an elevator and immediately began hearings on our next destination. "How about that Mexican place over on First Avenue?" "Mexican? Whaddayou, crazy? They got flies in the soup! Whaddabout the deli over on Lexington?" . . .

As soon as we reached the lobby I got on the telephone to O'Brien: ". . . so he said that he didn't know anything and will absolutely not utter one word about it and that we might as well go, so I guess that's what we'll do, huh?"

"The fuck you will," replied our leader. "You'll stay right there and nab him when he leaves the building."

"But I *know* he won't say anything," I wailed.

"Listen, Rollin, it's not your job to know! *I* know! You *do!* Now quit wasting time on the telephone. Get out there!"

Oh God, I thought, and leaned my head against my hand, which was still holding the telephone receiver. I cannot pounce on that kind, elegant man after we agreed there was no point. I looked at the crew, who were collectively propped up against a huge marble pillar. "We gotta stay," I said grimly, and I could tell by their reaction (none) that they were not surprised. "Of course," I said slowly, "just because we're here, doesn't mean we can catch him. . . . We could watch *this* elevator and he could come out of *that* one." Wink.

But Rogers did one better. Having gotten word, no doubt, that we were still hanging around, he left through the basement.

But what if, I asked myself later, he hadn't sneaked out? What if he had stepped out of the elevator we were watching? I couldn't pull the bladder trick again. I had already done that the week before on the Martha Mitchell stakeout. . . . The bladder trick (no relation to the bathroom trick from *Look* days) is when you wait for the moment just before you think the person will emerge, and then develop a sudden need to go to the bathroom. Then, if you've guessed right, when the person shows up, you're safe in a toilet across the street.

One virtue of covering hard news is that you never get stuck for ideas. That's because hard news doesn't come from ideas. It just comes. A hard news story is like a bomb. It goes off. You run. Toward it. (Along with everyone else. And chances are, when you all get there, you'll all wind up saying pretty much the same thing.) A feature, on the other hand, doesn't go off anywhere but in your head. It's got to be about something real, of course, but sometimes it's in pieces and sometimes the pieces are hidden and it's for you to find them and put them together. Then—maybe—you have a story.

It takes time to do that; it takes work; it takes thinking about what a thing *means* as well as what it is; it takes willingness to change the concept if, once you've examined it, the story looks different than it did when it was inside your head. And occasionally, it takes willingness, if the story turns out to be a lemon, to drop it.

Fine. Great. I had no problem with any of that. I had another problem. Every time I got an idea for a feature story and began to try to develop it, O'Brien made me feel as if I were having an affair. And it was all the dicier because, according to the system, I needed his permission each time to have it. Not only did assignments *from Nightly News* have to go through O'Brien to me, but *my* ideas for features also had to pass through him to *Nightly*. And, according to my spies at *Nightly*, O'Brien did not exactly pitch my ideas with verve.

So I began doing end runs. I'd dart over to *Nightly*, pitch my own idea, and, if they liked it, they would call O'Brien and ask for the story—and me—as if it was *their* idea. After that, O'Brien would be obliged to give me the assignment. Then, calling upon my old acting skills, I would feign surprise. Not delight, however. It upset O'Brien's sense of military decorum, I knew, if anyone reacted to an assignment with emotion, pleasure *or* pain. Anyway, he fell for it every time, and not since the third grade, when I told my mother we were playing word games at my birthday party when we were really playing Spin the Bottle, have I so enjoyed the fruits of devious behavior. In 1974 I went on a veritable binge of feature assignments, which went on, more or less, until my day of departure in 1980.

Like everything else on television, each piece died as it was born. But I keep them still in my desk like pressed flowers—filed on cards, alphabetically according to subject matter.

Thumbing through them, I can still spot my favorites:

Adoption, hard-to-place children
Ali-Frazier heavyweight championship fight
Army Lesbians
Ballroom dancing, return to, in college
Child suicide
Comden-Green, Betty and Adolph, a double profile
Drugs in the record business
Dying, better ways of
ERA
Graffiti, group trying to get kids to do them on walls
Homosexuals
Miss America (how come they all want to be lawyers, all
   of a sudden?)
Nursing homes, scandal
Pain
Pay-toilets, a movement to end*
Pedro, portrait of a kid in crime family, destined for
   same. (Nine years old and had just been arrested for
   stealing an ironing board. On a hunch I asked him if he
   knew his birthday. He didn't.)
Policewomen
Rape
Read, kids who can't
Sesame Street, tenth anniversary of
Single mothers, sharing homes instead of going it alone
Stepchildren

---

*Story never ran. Wald found footage offensive. What the hell did he expect us to shoot on a toilet story? Nasturtiums? Of course, we never should have flushed the toilet at the end of the stand-upper.

Surrogate wife, woman who rents herself out, days only,
no windows (joke)

Teenage pregnancy. (Fat, black, baby-faced fifteen-year-
old story subject had had intercourse once with a boy
she hadn't seen since. "It hurted," she told me.)

Vietnam veterans on drugs

I liked everything about features: the subjects; the time
allowed to do them—weeks sometimes, as opposed to hours;
the time allotted to them on the air—three or four minutes,
compared to one; I liked how hard they were to edit. And I
liked that most features were about ordinary people, whose
lives were about their lives, not about their images, and who,
therefore, seemed to have an easier time telling the truth than
famous or powerful people, whose expertise at the interview
game made every utterance a ploy.

Ordinary people, because of their innocence of interviews
and cameras—and because their livelihood most often does
not depend on public approbation—have an astonishing way
of looking at you and saying exactly what is on their minds.
Which usually turns out to be far more interesting and original
than anything a celebrity can make up. Ordinary people often
surprise you by what they say. A celebrity rarely does that;
politicians, most rarely of all.

Even when ordinary people try to hide or lie on-camera,
they fail because they haven't had enough practice to do it
right. But most ordinary people *want* to give you a straight
answer. They are flattered by your interest, thrilled to be "on
TV"; and they couldn't be more delighted to tell you
everything you want to know about anything, even when they
have nothing to gain and, sometimes, something to lose.
Ordinary people are *obliging*. Occasionally, I'd underestimate
how obliging:

Mike Silver and I once went to Florida to do a story—before it had been done to death—on sex and romance vis-à-vis the elderly. Our main interviewees were an enchanting pair of seventy-three-old newlyweds, who sat on their flowered print living-room sofa holding hands, and reacted to each question from me as if it were a little present. The crew, who had just come off a race riot, was happily overdosing on honey cakes the bride had prepared for us; even Mike looked cheery, and in the midst of a story he was never cheery. The only sober face in the crowd was mine. That was because I knew, once the little cakes were gone and once the little get-acquainted part of the interview was over, I would have to ask the big smarmy question, the one that would go (in not so many words, but the meaning would be clear): Are you still Doing It?

During a break I pulled Mike into the kitchen. "Listen," I whispered, "I can*not* look those sweet old people in the eye and ask them if they're screwing! I can't do it! They look like my grandparents!"

Mike stepped back, frowned, and said what I thought he'd say: "They're not your grandparents and you gotta do it."

"What if they walk out?" I said. "What happens to the story then?"

"Sh!" he said. "You *gotta* do it! That's all there is to it. We *gotta* establish that they're having sex—it's the crux of the goddam story—and the only way we do that is if they *say* so, and you *know* that as well as I do!"

Of course I knew it. I didn't want to know it, but I knew it. I inhaled, smoothed my hair back, and the two of us went back into the living room. I sat in my place, the electrician clicked the lights on, and the cameraman said, "Rolling" and the camera began to hum. I hemmed. I hawed. I stammered. "Th-there's something that I have to ask you that's awfully p-p-personal," I said, dying a little, "but if you don't want to answer you don't have to . . ." Oops, I hadn't meant to go that far. I looked over at Mike, but he was bent over, holding his head in his hands, probably wishing I were Barbara Walters. The camera, meanwhile, was still humming in my ear. I turned back to the couple. "Do you . . . I mean, do you still . . . are you . . ." And then, like a vision it came to me. I sat up straight and looked right at them: "Some people think that older people like you aren't interested in sex anymore. Is that true?"

"Oh, no!" said the pair in unison, shaking their little white heads and clucking adorably. Then they went on to say how very silly that notion was, with not the slightest discomfort. It was as if I had asked for directions to the freeway: "Would you mind telling me the best way to . . ." "Not at all. You turn right at the corner, then make a left, then . . ."

I still can't say I understand it. I've spent a large portion of my years as a journalist trying to get people to talk, and they keep talking, and I keep being amazed when they do. I think part of the reason is, simply, that most people like to talk about themselves and a reporter is one of the few people they're likely to run across who seems to want to listen.

On another occasion, if that's the word, *Nightly News* gave me an assignment to do an abortion story. It was the first anniversary of the Supreme Court's decision to legalize abortion and, in addition to covering demonstrations or whatever happened on the day itself, they wanted a feature story from me, to be prepared in advance, about the kinds of women who were getting abortions and why.

After a lot of telephoning, I began to get the picture, and it wasn't the picture I expected. Many, if not most, of the women getting abortions were white, middle-class, middle-American, church-going, God-fearing, conventional, and married.

Pretty interesting, I thought, not to mention underreported. But how to do a story? In television, I knew perfectly well by this time, you don't *tell* a story. You show it. And in order to show it, you have to find it and shoot it. And where the hell was I going to find a white, middle-class, middle-American, church-going, God-fearing, conventional, married woman who would talk about her abortion on national television?

I was sitting, I knew, in the middle of the classic feature-story sand trap, the sort that (almost) makes you long for a stakeout. You get an idea, you love it, they love it, then you remember that without a star, the play doesn't even open in Philadelphia. And the hitch is, the kind of star you need who, of course, will work for no money (even if we wanted to, paying interviewees on news shows is illegal) has neither an agent nor an eight-by-ten glossy. Nor, except for the phone book, is she on a list. She is, in short, invisible and possibly un-findable. But you know she's there. So you start looking.

Which means you start calling. If it's an abortion patient you're looking for, and you want her to represent Middle America, you start calling Middle America. That is, you call the national office of an abortion organization, get some telephone numbers of clinics in the Midwest and begin by dialing, say, Illinois. When someone answers, you ask to speak to the director and, slowly and carefully, you try to explain the kind of story you're trying to do and you ask for his or her help in finding a woman.

You can usually tell right away whether the person on the other end (1) gets it, and/or (2) wants to help. (Usually they want to help more than they get it, which you find out later when you start getting call-backs from unmarried teenagers.) When you've called all of Illinois, you move on to Minnesota, and when you've called all of Minnesota, you do the same in Ohio, then Iowa. Then you look at a map and see what else is out there in the middle. And you call *it*. And you keep calling until your right ear has turned bright pink and you feel that you cannot do the spiel one more time. Then you do it five more times. Then you hang it up for a day and wait. And when nothing happens, you start again.

By this time you *may* actually have some secretarial or research help. But probably not. Most news organizations don't consider research help sporting. According to tradition, the reporter—male or female—must stick his or her own finger in his or her own phone and track down every last piece of information by him or herself. The system is definitely unpretentious. It's also stupid, inefficient, and knee-jerk democratic. Once, I got so mad about the lack of help that I went marching in to see one of those people who have offices with sofas and trees.

"You're overpaying me," I said, guessing rightly that that might get his attention. "I spend half my days sharpening pencils and dialing numbers of people who aren't home. If I'm going to work as a secretary/researcher, you shouldn't be paying me as a correspondent!"

It sort of worked. I got some secretarial help after that. Too bad it lasted only about five minutes. What happened was O'Brien made his entrance that month as bureau chief, and predictably, O'Brien was against the concept of help for underlings—for correspondents and field producers, that is. The bureau had a secretary, but shortly after she arrived, O'Brien sent around one of his defense department memos saying that she belonged to him and that if we wanted her to do something for (the likes of) us, we had to ask him first. So after that, as far as we were concerned, she was as good as dead.

Meanwhile, I began feeling so desperate about the abortion story I started calling New Jersey. No soap. Pennsylvania. Nothing. Then Minnesota called back—as I accepted the charges I got so excited, I could hear my heart pumping—but the clinic director was one of those who had somehow missed the thrust: she had a woman lined up who was unmarried, "but she can *say* she's married!" I tried not to sound lofty while explaining that news was nonfiction television.

Ohio checked in with someone married, who, they said, would "*love* to be interviewed—as long as she doesn't have to say anything about the abortion because she doesn't want her mother-in-law to know."

Weeks of this.

Then, when we were about to throw in the towel (that's, at least, what you *say* you're about to do; in truth, once you've gone this far, you throw in nothing), Iowa calls: Someone is due in for an abortion next week who is married, has three children, goes to a Presbyterian church (by now I am listening so hard I have stopped breathing), is "definitely middle-class—not rich or poor—and the girl who sits at the desk here says she didn't look weird or anything—just normal. The only thing is . . ." (I feel my face turning blue from a lack of oxygen) "she's not really *sure* she wants to do it. She says she wants to talk to you first."

"OF COURSE!" I say, not meaning to yell. "Ask her to call me collect."

Then you stare at the phone the way you did when you were seventeen and waited for a boy to call. And when the phone rings, you pick it up before the first ring is over and it's who you want it to be and her voice is whispery and nervous, and your voice is whispery and nervous, too. Very gently, then, you explain the story you're trying to do—how the law is affecting women like her, and how important it is to tell that story, and that she will make it possible for you to be able to tell it.

You also remind her—trying, all the while, not to push too much—that it's NBC News after all, and that the story will be tasteful and discreet. Then you spell out exactly what you will need from her: film of her going to church, film of her walking into the abortion clinic, some covering shots of the actual abortion—nothing close up, only enough to suggest that the procedure is happening—and a short interview. Pause . . . Then you tell her you understand how this must be a trying time for her, even without the television coverage—she whispers, yes, it is—and that you and the crew will try to make it as easy for her as you possibly can

And even though everything you've said is true, you feel like a con artist. But you pay no attention to that feeling, because you have a job to do. And when you're through, when you can't think of one more thing to say, you ask her—carefully, quietly—if she understands what you have said and if she is willing to do it. And, incredibly, she says yes. And you hang up the phone and let your head fall on your forearm. Then you race over to *Nightly* and scream, I found her! to no one in particular. And then you race back to your office and get yourself on a flight, that is, several connecting flights, to Clinton, Iowa.

I arrive at twilight during a light snowfall. It has taken longer to get here than it would have taken to fly to Mexico. The producer and crew, all from Chicago, have come to the airport, bless their hearts, to meet me. We drive to the hotel or motel or whatever it is, where they have already checked in, and I check in and go to my room. I hoist my suitcase up on the bed and unsnap the lock, and the phone rings. That, I said to myself as I reach for it, will be the cameraman, with a report on the restaurant situation.

It is not the cameraman. It is the head of the abortion clinic, who tells me that the woman has changed her mind and doesn't want to do it and could we possibly find someone else; and, trying hard not to let my voice get shrill—and not altogether succeeding—I ask the clinic director to tell the woman that no, we cannot possibly find someone else and that we have come all the way from New York (partial white lie) and that it is very late for her to change her mind, that we are counting on her and why doesn't she call me directly so that I can find out what is troubling her.

Now I am feeling oddly calm. She calls. "It's not me so much," says the woman in her whispery voice, but ... her husband doesn't like the idea. She had talked him into it, sort of, but he still doesn't like it. "He's kinda worried about the men at work, y'know," she says. I refrain from asking her why she/he didn't think about that before, but I don't, because I am the wooer and she is the wooee and although I thought the wooing was over, clearly it's not. I am thinking on my feet now—literally; I am standing next to the bed, my eyes fixed for no reason on the night table on which there is a multiple-choice quiz about the motel services: Maid Service, (1) Excellent, (2) Good, (3) Fair, (4) Poor—and I'm thinking she will do it, she must do it, she just needs soothing.

So I soothe. I tell her it's natural to feel jumpy, but that once we begin, she will be *fine*. I try not to beg. I beg. I cajole. I babble. I tell her she is doing a service. I tell her that being interviewed on television is interesting—yes!—and that her husband will find it interesting—fascinating!—you should *see* the wires and cables and the camera, oh, the camera! Okay, she says, okay, with an enormous sigh, sounding more worn out than convinced. And I am more worn out than convinced she will do it.

I hang up the receiver and I lie down on the bed and read the rest of the questionnaire. Room Service, (1) Excellent, (2) Good, (3) Fair, (4) Poor. Then I call the producer and report the recent event and tell him I'm too tired to eat. He asks me whether she will be going to church the next morning, I tell him I forgot to ask and that I don't want to call her back because I'm afraid she'll change her mind again, and he asks if I mind if *he* calls, and I say of course not. He calls back later to say he called her and she is, indeed, going to church, and the next day he shoots it. I stay away and have room service, which is (3) Fair, and take a walk and watch politicians yammer on a Sunday afternoon panel TV show and read the local paper and wait for it to be bedtime and finally it is.

The original plan was that she would meet us at nine the next morning at the abortion clinic. The abortion itself had been scheduled for ten, but she was coming an hour early so that we could do the interview first. We were there at eight. At 9:05, I began getting nervous. By 9:15, everyone was nervous. The producer said he felt pretty sure she'd show up, eventually, for the abortion. He did not go on to say what we all knew—that if a lot more time passed, the abortion would be *all* she'd show up for.

She didn't arrive until 9:35, but as soon as she walked in, I knew, by looking at her head, that she was going to do it. I nudged the producer. "Relax," I whispered in his ear. "She had her hair done." Her husband, who looked faint, was also, in his way, gussied up. He had on a dark three-piece suit with striped necktie and from the way he held his body (as if it didn't bend) it was obvious that these were not his every-Monday clothes.

I decided not to say much. One funny move, I kept thinking, one wrong word, and we'll blow it. Everyone else— the clinic director, the doctor, the nurse, the crew, and the producer—seemed to have gotten the same message, and for the next few minutes we worked with the quiet, tense efficiency of a SWAT team. Gently, we eased the subject and her husband into the interview chairs and we began.

She was wonderful. He was wonderful. They were wonderful. And I was so relieved and grateful that even I was wonderful (which is to say I asked the right questions and knew when to keep my mouth shut). She talked about her decision movingly and with dignity. She said—in the same small, whispery voice she had used on the telephone—that she already had three children, that neither she nor her husband wanted another child, that her doctor had told her it would be dangerous for her to give birth again because of some condition in her uterus. But—and here her voice got *very* low—she said that if abortion weren't legal, she would have the baby. Because, she said, she would be too frightened to go to "a back-alley person" and they didn't have the money for her to go to another country where abortion was legal, and besides, she added, she would have been too frightened to do that. (I didn't entirely understand the last part, until she went on to say that she had never been out of the state of Iowa.) Then I asked her if she felt guilty. She looked at me for a moment before she answered. "This is hard on me," she said, "but the other way it would be hard on me *and* my husband *and* my children. So I had to pick. Didn't I?"

Cut.

CHAPTER
19

By 1975, O'Brien and I both had what we wanted. O'Brien had a flotilla of new recruits in the bureau, each one a loyal soldier of hard news. And, because of them, I had all the time I wanted to do my features, without being yanked off whenever a news bell went off in his wire-serviced head. Which, I noticed, didn't happen nearly as often as it used to. O'Brien's News fairy seemed to have mellowed. So, at last, we had a kind of truce. Hallelujah. Except something fairly unpleasant came along as a result of the truce, for which I was not at all prepared: O'Brien got friendly all of a sudden. Friendly, can you beat that? Smiles, jokes, the works. I couldn't stand it. The fact was, I couldn't stand O'Brien, whether he was bugging me or not. I *liked* having him as an enemy. This way, when he acted nice to me, I had to act nice back.

By 1975, there had been a few other changes at NBC News, as well—a switch from film to tape, for example. With tape, you could both look at what you shot and edit it right away, without having to wait for film to develop. Great for Quick and Dirties. But tape, at the beginning, anyway, seemed less suitable for editing features, because you couldn't cut and splice and change your mind and cut and splice again, and fool around with the order of things the way you could with film. In addition, the giant tape-editing machines (television's answer to microwave ovens), plus all kinds of rococo new union restrictions on the editors, made the process of editing seem far more mechanical than artistic, and a lot less cozy—although I did understand that coziness was not a priority goal of the news department.

In 1975 tape-editing machines were not the only new presence at NBC News; there was also a batch of new women. Almost none of them had been invited to occupy those offices with sofas and trees; but more and more women were showing up on the air—particularly on local news stations, first as reporters, then later as anchors, too. Women on the network were far fewer—there were only about eight or nine out of sixty or so men—but eight or nine was still twice the four or five who were there in '73, when I first started doing duets on the street with Mike Silver.

Unfortunately, I didn't get to know most of the new women on the network, because none was in New York. But I watched them on the air, of course, often on the big Sony in the newsroom, where comments ran in tone from admiring to scurrilous. The prettier the correspondent, it seemed, the more scathing the remarks—not all of which, by the way, came from men. "Willya look at those black roots?" is one I remember, referring not to heritage but to hair.

Occasionally, I'd rise to the defense of my fellow females, which told me that I must have felt some kind of kinship. Yet, I had a much stronger sense of distance—other than geographic—between me and them. They were true newswomen, this new crop, and some of them were good and some of them weren't so good. But they all meant business. That is, they were headed in one direction: Up. They wanted to be where the men (only) had been; they wanted to do what the men (only) had done; they wanted to succeed as (only) men had succeeded in this field before; and, naturally, they were hard news all the way.

I admired the new crop of women. I even felt proud of them. But I felt no more *like* them than I felt like most of the men. And later, when I did get to know some of them, and some female correspondents from the other networks as well, I occasionally sensed a kind of O'Brien-like contempt—too strong a word, perhaps, but not by much—for anything or anyone who covered anything less (*sic*) than hard news. Sometimes they'd compliment me on a feature story, but often in the spirit, I felt, of someone complimenting a child on a nice drawing of a flower.

It seemed to me most of these women had simply bought the—I can't even say male definition, because so many men were beginning to "soften" on this issue—the conventional definition, then, of what kind of news mattered and what kind didn't. Rare, in other words, if she existed at all, was the female correspondent who would be caught dead doing a story upon which someone else could conceivably affix the label "soft."

No question about it, many of the new women were sincerely and ardently interested in politics, and liked to run—and *could* run—just as fast as Bob Hager; and each had at least one funny and not-so-funny story about being diverted, in a previous job, to covering the wife of the candidate instead of the candidate, or getting assigned to the fashion show instead of the hijacking. Partially as a result of that, I think, stories about foster care or stories about fudge were, to them, in the same hated category. It was all sissy stuff, and better steer clear of it, or else you might lose your footing and slip back into the muck of "soft" reporting. To them, features, not unlike the nursing and teaching professions, represented where women had been, not where they were (all now supposed to be) going.

This is still going on today, and the effect it has on me is to make me feel closer to all of those housewives who feel put down by the women's movement. Sometimes I feel like a sort of housewife of journalism. I like what I do, I think the subjects I cover are as important as most others—hell, who really knows what's important, anyway?—and I feel insulted when my beat is lumped together with fudge. (Nor do I mean to sound snooty about the latter. The fact is, given a choice between hearing a great fudge recipe and hearing most speeches from the chambers of the United States Congress, I'd pick fudge.)

Look, I can understand wanting to flee from anything that's been shoved down your throat. I might feel the same way if my experience and my goals (what goals?) had been different....I can also understand going after hard news for practical career reasons. By definition, a feature is never the lead story on a news program or on a front page of a newspaper. A features beat is no way, as everyone knows but doesn't say, to become a star. It's certainly no way to become an anchorperson, which may be the most boring job in news, but is still the one most people jump through hoops to get.

I had and have no objection to being a star. Even with all of the obvious prices paid, I'm sure stardom is swell. But if at any point it gets to be a choice between going for stardom or for the kind of work that makes you forget what time it is— work which at least occasionally makes you wonder, am I getting *paid* for this?—you've got to be a nitwit not to pick the latter.

By 1975, I had picked the latter—although I can't say it was a big, conscious decision. I just tried to keep doing what I liked to do, without worrying too much about where it would or wouldn't get me.

But here's the funny thing that happened: because what I liked to do was so unpopular, and because, therefore, so few other people did it, I began, I couldn't help noticing, to get noticed.

So altogether, not a bad life. A life, in fact, of luck and privilege. The surface had a particular sheen: an attractive, intelligent husband; an abundantly satisfying job; money (in spite of all that am-I-getting-paid-for-this-stuff, the answer was indeed yes—almost twice, in '75, what I started out getting in '71); a swell relationship with my mother (once I had broken free, I began really to *like* my mother); a fine pack of devoted old friends—Leo, Pat, Joanna, Molly, et al.—and a bevy of new ones, with all of whom we had countless gay (old meaning of the word) evenings, dining cross-legged on fat pillows on the floors of each others' living rooms.

And we laughed a lot, my husband, my parents, my friends, and I. And the older we got, the more we laughed. I'm not sure why. It wasn't that we were so happy. I certainly wasn't so happy.... Come to think of it, most of the laughter was about what had gone wrong in our lives. I guess laughing was a kind of resignation—the kind of resignation you don't have when you're young, when you think everything that's not good in your life can be fixed.

I was as happy, I figured, as anyone else I knew, and that seemed good enough. I tried never to be a pig about happiness. Besides, for what more could I have asked? Not more from my work, surely (well, I could have, but I didn't. I *never* stopped feeling underqualified and overlucky). I could have asked for more from my marriage, which had grown scrappy and remote; but that, too, seemed no worse than anyone else's. (It was, but I didn't know it.)

There was something peculiar about my marriage, though, and I did know that. The marriage didn't seem important. It was there—like the refrigerator—but it didn't seem central to either of our lives. Each of us was a career person with a difficult roommate. That's not the same, I knew, as being wed.

I had long outgrown the notion of marriage as being locked together, or as a way of being rescued from self. By the time I married Arthur, I didn't need to be rescued. I liked myself. But this was not the alternative I expected.

Even so, I was terribly fond of my difficult roommate/husband, and he of me and I think we both figured this—whatever it was—was the best we both could do. Besides, in the early seventies, among the people we knew in New York, the kind of marriage we had didn't seem *that* peculiar. "One of the nicest things about finally getting married," I heard a woman say around that time (maybe it was me) "is that it gets marriage out of the way, so you can get on with your work."

I talked tough in those days. I tried to feel tough, too. And I began to get pretty good at both.

When, suddenly, something came into my life that knocked both it and me upside down and over, and turned all of my allegedly firm insides into soup.

CHAPTER
20

Like love, cancer struck from behind. Out of nowhere, a lump on the side of the left breast. Hard little thing. Like a stone pea. Thought nothing of it at first. Fool internist thought nothing of it, too. "Come back in a year," he said. "Fine," I said, and skipped off to an appointment at the hairdresser's.

Six months later I am reporting, as it happens, on the mastectomy of Betty Ford. A follow-up story, about how women all over the country are all of a sudden rushing to mammographers to get their breasts checked. We shoot the stand-upper in the waiting room of the Guttman Breast Diagnostic Institute in New York:

... The terror that women feel is not unreasonable. What is unreasonable is that women still turn their terror inward. They think if they avoid investigating the possibility that they have the disease, they'll avoid the disease. But as cases of such prominent women as Betty Ford become known, other women are turning their fear into the kind of action that can save their lives.

"Is that a wrap?" says the cameraman.

"What? Oh . . . yeah," I say, slinging my shoulder bag over my shoulder, "it's a wrap."

Or is it? I think, giving my lump a little push with my index finger while nobody's looking. Maybe, while I'm here, I ought to get this thing looked at. Nah. No time. Besides, Dr. Fool said it was nothing—a cyst—not to worry. Separate yourself from the story, kid. This is about other people, not you. Relax.

But I can't relax. I sit in the editing room watching one nervous woman after another on the screen and it gets to me. So in half the time Dr. Fool said to come back, I go back, and this time he says oops, and sends me to a surgeon who says—I don't know what he says, exactly, because as soon as I get the gist, I pass out. The following Monday, April 7, 1975, I wake up in Beth Israel Hospital with my left breast gone.

Gone.

I'm brave at first (It's not really bravery; it's drugs and stupidity, but I don't know that and neither does anyone else.) It doesn't occur to me until I get home that more than a breast is involved here. Cancer is involved here. Cancer. My God, I could die. *I could die.*

Then I go a little crazy. I quit NBC. I leave Arthur. I run off with another man. Throughout all of this I have weird dreams, which I write down:

> I am a child and I have lost my arm. I must wear a horrid, pink, plaster-of-Paris thing, like the arms of my dolls. But my dolly's arms have fingers, and mine has none. So I must also wear a hook. Like hideous, bad Captain Hook in *Peter Pan*. I start to cry. I sob. The sobbing wakes me up.

> A young, handsome doctor is examining me. He touches my breast; then he moves his hand to the other side. He leaves his

hand on the flat place and looks at my face. He says nothing, but his look is sexy and tender. He leaves his hand there and continues to look at me. But I can't stay. I get up to leave, and I know, somehow, that I won't see him again.

When I write down the last one I am still in my marital home, sitting up in my marital bed, leaning on one of those big art books nobody ever reads but which make wonderful lap desks. I look at what I have written and I think, why am I writing this garbage down? But it's a phony question, because I know perfectly well why. Because it's good garbage and I know it. And the dreams are only a hint of more and better garbage to come. I'm a reporter and I know a story when I see one and this whole mess is a story and so what if it happens to be my mess. All the better. No research.

I don't write any more until I have made the break with Arthur and find myself parked for one day and night at my parents' apartment (they are in a daze) before running off with the Other Man. My mother asks her neighbor if I can borrow her typewriter and I type up my dream to make it look nice and I write an outline for a book and throw in another ten pages for good measure.

I do this in one day. It's strangely easy. The book has already formed in my head and it feels good to type it, even this much. I like the sound of the keys hitting the paper. It's such a clear, definite sound. It makes me feel less crazy. When the day began I wasn't altogether sure I wanted to do a book. But now I am sure. In a strange, private way. I feel very excited. I feel as if I'm pregnant.

Before I take off with my Amoroso to Philadelphia (it wasn't really Philadelphia, but I have to say Philadelphia so that no one will know who he is) I shove what I have written on my mother's neighbor's typewriter into an envelope and send it to my agent for her to sell. Then I fly away.

I am not so crazy that I am not nervous about everything. I am nervous about Arthur, about hurting him. I am nervous about the Amoroso, about him hurting me. I am nervous about Philadelphia. I am nervous about leaving NBC because I know I am burning a bridge; I know that in television, to disappear for more than a week is to die. Speaking of which, I am also nervous about that. I'm afraid that any minute cancer will recur and I will die.

The one thing I am not nervous about is this book which resides in my head. I am not at all nervous about that. I know it will work. I know I must write it. And I know with the certainty of a lunatic who hears voices that a publisher will want to publish it.

A month later the agent calls me with the news: no publisher wants to publish it. She has tried. She has received several polite, even complimentary letters. But nobody wants to publish a book about cancer. It's too depressing. No one will buy it. No one wants to read about cancer. "But it's not just about cancer. It's about—"

"I know, dear," says the agent, using the Talmey dear, "but they won't touch it."

Shit.

How can it be? How can it be when, for the first time in my life, I'm so sure?

Then, the next day, truly the next day, the heavens part and Genevieve Young drops out of them. Gene Young is an editor, she tells me on the telephone, at J. B. Lippincott & Co. and she is calling because someone has told her about the book and she is interested. "Tell me more about it," she says. I tell. I tell how I want to write about what it's like to get breast cancer, what it's been like for me. I tell her I want to do it without holding back because, otherwise, I say, what's the point. I tell her that some of the things that have happened are funny and that I want to write about them and I tell her I want to write about what a lousy sport I have been about getting cancer. "Good," she says cheerfully, "it doesn't sound Inspirational!"

She gets it, I think. She definitely gets it.

I was right. Soon after the telephone conversation she buys it. The advance is $15,000: low for a dirty novel, stratospheric for disease. That night a champagne cork hits the wall in Philadelphia (or wherever). One week later: another call from the agent. Another publisher, New American Library—presided over by another woman—wants the paperback rights, for over $100,000. You're joking, I say to the agent. But I know better. Agents don't joke about money. Another cork hits the wall near the Liberty Bell.

The paperback sale is very good, Gene Young tells me soberly, as if I need to be told, because the deal includes money for advertising the hardcover edition, which Gene says will launch the book properly. Yeah? Terrific! I say, too dizzy/happy to focus on details.

Now I have merely to write the book—or, since it is already written in my head, to type it. Thanks to cancer and the possibility of imminent death, I am no longer the tightwad I used to be, and so I go all out and purchase an expensive pumpkin and gray electric typewriter. It's beautiful. It hums. It makes me *want* to type.

So I type. And type. I type on a pretty antique desk in a pretty corner of the house near the Liberty Bell (it's not really near the Liberty Bell but I have to blah blah blah . . .). The Amoroso is rich and takes me to Europe and Africa. I enjoy the sights, and I'm mad for him, but for four hours each day I shut everything else out and type that book. I type in Rome, in London, and in a campchair outside our tent in the Kenyan bush.

Admittedly, typing the book isn't as easy as typing the outline. A book, I have by now discovered, is long, very long,

261

and even though it exists in my head in substance, there are still all those scenes to work out, all that pacing to do, all those adjectives to mine. I falter, too, over the sticky business of having to tell a lot of private stuff which, now that I'm slightly calmer, I find I don't like telling. But I can't figure out how to write about the thing honestly *without* telling.

"What do other writers do?" I ask Gene on our one transatlantic telephone call.

"They write novels," she says.

"Oh," I say, having not considered that. "Why don't I write it as a novel?"

"Because it wouldn't be as good."

We return to Philadelphia, where the days have grown shorter and darker, and I continue to type, once again on the antique desk. From June until December I type and then, at the end of one very dark day, the book is finished.

And so, it seems, is Philadelphia.

I go back to New York. Back to Arthur. That doesn't work. I go back to NBC. They put me on duty on Christmas Eve because I'm the only correspondent without a family. And they send me to cover a reenactment of Washington crossing the Delaware. People are dressed in costumes and are having a wonderful time. We film them having a wonderful time. It's 9 degrees. I am not having a wonderful time. All I want is for it to be over.

Suddenly, my father dies. A heart attack. I move in with my mother and we prop each other up. I love my mother. My mother loves me. It's the only good thing in our lives now, that love.

Except that book.

The book has been accepted. There is, however, one persistent problem with the book's end. The first version had me and the Amoroso walking off into the sunset, but we didn't. Quickly, when I got back to New York, I changed it to me and Arthur reconvening in the sunset. But we didn't. The publisher, meanwhile, was losing patience. "I wish you'd work your life out so that we can publish this book," says Gene, only half-kidding.

The next time we talk, I am forced to say that I am seeing Philadelphia again.

The time after, I am forced to say I am not.

"Okay," she says, "*don't* work your life out. End the book before you hit the sunset. Sunsets make lousy endings, anyway."

I take my mother and my beauteous pumpkin and gray typewriter to a spa in northern Florida. We bend and stretch in the morning and I kill the sunset in the afternoon. By the week's end it is done. A new closing paragraph has risen:

> I have made death's acquaintance. And however horrendous and premature that meeting was, I think it will have softened the shock of our eventually living together, whenever that happens. I hope it won't be soon. Because the peek at death has given me some new information about life, all of which has made me better at it than I was before. And with some more practice, I could get better still. If I don't have a recurrence of cancer and die soon, all I've lost is a breast, and that's not so bad.

So that's it, except for one more irksome thing I try to shake and can't. It bothers me that Gene is so uncritical, which, aside from the sunset issue and one or two other minor points, she has been. Of course it pleases me that she likes the book. I like it, too. But I *know* it must need more editing, more changes, than Gene has asked me to make (and I am too dumb to know that sometimes the best editing is the least editing). I had trusted Gene, who, by the way, turned out to be tall and beautiful and Chinese, but now I sort of don't. I want a second opinion and I know whom I want it from. Did I have the nerve to ask?

I have the nerve to ask.

I call Miss Talmey. Why of course, dear, she'd be delighted to read the manuscript and I should send it to her immediately. I hang up the phone and inhale all the air in the room. A week later the manuscript comes back. I slit the top of it with my finger. Okay, kid, I think to myself, you asked for it. I look at the first chapter. Nothing. The second. Nothing. No notes, no marks, nothing. Maybe she thinks the whole thing stinks. Then, about halfway through, on the right-hand margin, I see that handwriting—those perfectly curled letters, small and neat.

Her comment, which, as far as I can see, is the only one, refers to a sentence I have written about my father—how, when he was a child in Russia, he and his brothers and sisters hid under beds when the Bolsheviks came to the houses of the Jews. "Dear," reads the note in the margin, and as I read I can hear her voice, "*not* the Bolsheviks! . . . the Cossacks!"

Several months later, an extremely favorable review of the book appears in *Vogue* magazine: "unique," it says, "impressive . . . brusque, amusing and as honest as pain . . ."

The reviewer is Allene Talmey.

CHAPTER
21

Jokingly once, a friend of mine suggested that cancer was the best thing that ever happened to my career. I think it surprised her when I agreed. There are better ways, surely, to enhance one's professional well-being, but for me, in a variety of ways, cancer, having broken me, made me.

At some point early on, I think I just made a decision to use cancer. It had used me, after all. Knocked me down. Flattened me. Literally. When you're hit that way—hard and unexpectedly—you find yourself wanting to do what every kid in a playground who has ever been kicked around by the class punk wants to do: kick back. Or find *some* way to even the score.

If you go further than that and not only get even, but turn the calamity around—reshape it into something you feel deeply good about, proud of (it doesn't matter what)—my, what a sweet success. I'll never have a baby, so I don't know what that's like—and it's probably rude to compare a living creature to that which comes, originally, from wood; but occasionally, when I see a woman soaking up the warm rays of motherhood, it reminds me of what I feel for those two hundred and six pages about my disease.

What counts most of all are one's own inner swellings about one's small creation. But other people's swellings aren't bad, either. It's nice when people tell you your baby is cute, and it's nice when people—strangers, colleagues, friends (anyone, come to think of it)—come up to you and express concurrence with the shamelessly high opinion you hold of your own piece of work. Conversely, should a person, through whatever incredible lapse of taste or defect of character, *not* like your book, it's quite simply the end. Through Arthur, I knew a man, for example, whom I had always liked, even admired, until one day I found out that he couldn't stand *First, You Cry*. Since then, I have noticed a change in my feelings toward that man. I hate him. I'm not proud that I hate him. But fierce love for one's progeny has its ugly side; why pretend it hasn't? "I wish to burn every book that's not mine," my old colleague Ed Newman said to me cheerily one day, and I knew just how he felt.

In addition to the other pleasures which exist between hard covers, there is a special, odd joy that comes from people telling and writing you, not only that they liked your book, but that your book helped them. At first that reaction stunned and even embarrassed me, because writing that book, as I knew, if they didn't, had nothing to do with altruism. I wrote it because I felt like it, not because I thought it would do anybody, besides me, any good. But I began to feel less guilty and, therefore, more pleased about people reacting this way when, gradually, I began to understand why they did. If a person is going through some version of hell, it makes it easier, apparently, to hear or read about how someone else got through it—provided that person doesn't exaggerate, lie, or hide too much. People who are in a spot have a good nose for the straight story. They know when you're telling the truth, and it can help them because (a) your truth is probably like theirs, so they feel less alone, and (b) they figure if someone as vain, uncourageous, and ordinary as you got through it, so can they.

Anyway, to be the writer/recipient of this odd, but when you understand it, logical outcome of your typing is like getting a great present when it isn't even your birthday. Somehow, inadvertently, accidentally and unconsciously, you've done something as selfish as anything else you've ever done in your life, but it turns out *it has eased some people's pain*. Some trick! Some bonus!

Nothing sweetens success more than its improbability. I had had a hunch, an intense hunch, that I could write a pretty decent book about that mastectomy, but I had also been around too long to assume that a lot of people would buy it. That so many publishers had turned it down did not increase my optimism. And, until the agent brought it up, I never even fantasized about a movie. A movie? About cancer? I knew that movie audiences enjoyed large, improbable animals taking bites out of people; but parts of the body lost through a real disease was, I suspected, less thrilling. That Barbra Streisand wouldn't consider it came as no shock. That Mary Tyler Moore *would* struck me dumb.

Imagine sitting at home alone one night with your mother, having just finished cleaning the broiler pan, and the phone rings and you say hello and the voice on the other end says, "Hi, this is Betty Rollin," and giggles, and it's Mary Tyler Moore, and the joke is that she is going to do a two-hour TV movie of your book and star as you. Imagine, further, that the movie turns out to be *good*—not maudlin or dull or ponderous or cheap or "Inspirational" (Gene Young's word) or a lot of other awful things it might have been.

True, when I watched it—at home, on tape—it spooked me, because watching someone play you makes you feel dead. Also, because the film stuck so unusually close to the book, which, in turn, had stuck so close to what had really happened, it brought it all back; so I had to keep stopping the tape and going to the window for swallows of air. But so what. When I wasn't at the window, I sat there on the edge of my bed and felt proud, even victorious. To think what all of this had come from after all.

Before the movie there was the obligatory (obligatory, hell! I loved it) book-promotion tour—two, in fact, one for the hardcover, one for the paperback—five weeks, coast-to-coast, a city a day. By the time I got to Phil Donahue in Chicago, I had a fever and what felt like a permanently injured larynx. No matter. These days, if you are interested in anyone outside of your immediate family reading your book, you talk it up on television, and you are extremely grateful for the opportunity to do so.

Contrary to the myth, most of the interviewers seemed actually to have read the book—except Tom Snyder, who, it seemed, hadn't even read the flap and, I think, thought I had a bad heart—but who asked good questions, anyway.

Not that good questions are important. Most authors who go on television learn to do what politicians do: they say what they want, no matter what they are asked. Occasionally, however, one is bound to get cornered. It happened to me in Seattle without the interviewer's even meaning to do it. He was a young man, substituting, I think, for the show's regular host, and trying very hard to be winning. The interview had gone smoothly so far, when, suddenly, he leaned forward. From the look on his face, I knew he was about to ask something deep. "Miss Rollin," he said, furrowing his brow like a third-grader trying to spell *hippopotamus*, "your tumor . . . was it benign or malign?" "It was . . . not benign," I answered sweetly. (My second favorite question came from a woman in Boston who asked me if sex was better with one breast or two. I got out of that one by turning to stone.)

By the time the tour began I had moved out of my mother's apartment into a small but pretty place of my own, which hung over the Museum of Modern Art's sculpture garden. I hired a decorator, whom I ordered to use no color in the apartment darker than pink. I spent a fortune on furniture. I spent more money for one crystal ashtray—which, having wound up on a glass coffee table, therefore was rendered practically invisible—than I had spent on dresses only two years earlier. The bills stunned me, but they did not break me, the reason being—what could be nicer?—I seemed to be rich. I made a smart (okay, not smart, lucky) investment with the paperback money, and the hardcover was selling like crazy and lecture invitations, of all things, started coming in— from women's groups in the Midwest mostly—offering me monumental fees to speak (peppily) about surviving cancer.

My mail improved, too. Suddenly, there were as many invitations as bills, often from people I hardly knew. What did I care? Where I was invited, I went. After all, I was, once again, vaguely looking for a husband, and what better way than to attend the crowded parties of strangers?

During those months I went out with more men than a prom queen—and promptly worked that fact into my shtick on the lecture circuit. "I seem to be a lot more popular with one breast than with two," I'd tell the ladies in Dayton, and bring the house down. Crass? Commercial? Didn't give it a thought. All I knew was that cancer took from me and now it was my turn. Besides, I liked spreading the word (even though I wasn't totally convinced yet, myself) that losing a breast wasn't the end and that sex and sexiness had little to do with whether a piece of your body was missing. Even that piece.

Back at NBC, even though I had liked my job fine the way it was before the promotion tour, my television career started to pop and crackle like a Chinese New Year. All for the wrong reasons, natch. I was the same journalist I was before either *First, You Cry* or Mary Tyler Moore—but I accepted the new attention in a kind of affable daze (O'Brien, by this time, had grown positively sycophantic), even though I didn't trust it.

"Uh," says the producer of *Nightly News* the night after *First, You Cry* plays on CBS, "do you think it would be—uh—taking advantage of—uh—a situation if we ran that piece of yours on job-sharing tonight?"

Two months earlier, I had done a piece on part-time workers—mothers, mostly, who halved their jobs with other mothers as a way of handling the two roles without going under. The piece had been sitting on the shelf and might never have made the show—not because there was anything wrong with it, the *Nightly* producers told me, but because none of them could get excited about the subject. Why, then, had it been assigned? (That's a question one learned not to ask, because if it were answered it would make someone look stupid who was supposed to be smart.)

"Uh," I say, managing not to smirk, "sure, run it. This is show business," I add devilishly, "isn't it?" And the producer looks at me, unsure about whether I'm kidding, which is reasonable, because I'm not sure whether I'm kidding, myself.

And suddenly, right out of the proverbial blue, although they've been working on the show for months and, in fact, are perilously close to taping it, somebody gets the idea to make me the co-anchor on a three-hour documentary about the American family. As it happens, it's a subject I know something about and it's a show I'm as qualified to anchor as anyone; but I know and they know that I'm no more qualified this week—after being impersonated by Mary Tyler Moore—than last. Not, as I had always suspected but now I knew for sure, that knowing something about a subject had anything to do with being chosen to anchor a documentary about it. Anchoring, that most prestigious role of television journalism, does not, for the most part, require any skill but the ability to read a TelePrompTer. Hiring journalists to anchor is like hiring writers to type. (The difference is no one ever got rich and famous typing.) Okay, John Chancellor did more than read; and so does Dan Rather. But (a) many other anchors don't, especially local ones, and (b) Rather and the others *could* just read. They happen not to want to. Nor did I, on the documentary about the family. What I recited I wrote. I also put on my own eyelashes. But I didn't have to.

The "rewards" of my new station in life didn't stop there. For my next number, I was assigned to be a substitute co-host for Jane Pauley for three days on the *Today* show—an anchoring job which proved to require more than recitation. When the three days were over, I wound up not altogether sure what it *did* require—only that, whatever it was, I didn't have it.

CHAPTER
22

H ere's the bright side of doing the *Today* show (not unlike the bright side of vomiting): you lose weight.

End of bright side.

End, also, of analogy. Because (1) vomiting is shorter than the *Today* show, and (2) you usually don't know about it in advance.

The terror, which was the cause of the weight loss, felt familiar and I knew precisely why. Eight years earlier, when I had delivered myself of those theater reviews, I had had the same symptoms: loss of appetite, difficulty falling asleep, etc. The local news program, on which I did the reviews, was live. So was the *Today* show. Live. Not taped, not prerecorded, live. Worse, unlike the local news, it was live, not merely to the city, but to the nation.

"What are you afraid of?" said my mother. "What can happen?" "What can happen?" said my friends. "What can happen?" said my colleagues, all of whom saw me rapidly turning into a candidate for the lead in *The Incredible Shrinking Woman*. I heard them and I knew they were right. I knew that the worst thing that could happen was that I would make a horse's ass of myself in front of eight million people, seven million, nine hundred and ninety-nine thousand, nine hundred of whom I didn't even know. I knew there were worse things. I just couldn't think of any.

Not true. I could think of one. But it didn't help. Why, I wondered, didn't good old cancer, which had been so useful in dwarfing life's other catastrophes, have an effect on this one? It was like having a home insurance policy for everything, except an airplane falling on your house. Then an airplane falls on your house.

My efforts to survive the show were not helped by the hour at which it was necessary to rise. I don't look nice at five A.M. I don't look like anyone whom anyone else, given a choice, would want to look at. And by seven A.M., even with makeup covering my face like a shield, I didn't look a whole lot better. The parts of my face which had bones—the nose and the jaw, for example—they were all right. Mainly, it was the eyes, which puffed extravagantly, so that they looked like something on which to sit, rather than see out of.

My old college pal, Joanna Simon, whom I had always considered the Dr. DeBakey of cosmetic emergencies, gave me her puffed-eye prescription: upon awakening, wrap ice cubes in cloth and apply directly to eyelids....I figured fifteen more minutes of sleep wouldn't hurt, either. This I managed to get by first setting out every article of clothing I planned to wear the night before. Stick with the tried and true, Joanna had advised, so I auditioned everything in my closet and chose three dresses which felt like bathrobes and, I dearly hoped, didn't look like bathrobes. I put out breakfast the night before, too, cereal in a bowl, powdered instant coffee inside a cup—everything, in short, that wasn't liquid. Then, wedging my pillow in my neck so as not to wreck my hair, I went to bed.

It's dark at 5:15 A.M. It's dark and it's cold. On the first morning, I lurched into the bathroom, caught sight of my face in the mirror, woke up at once, and went running like a dog for his dish toward the kitchen for the ice cubes. No wonder they do test runs for space ships. Neither Joanna nor I had foreseen the following problem: when you hold ice cubes on your eyelids, you can't do anything else. And with the car coming at 5:45, there wasn't time not to do anything else. . . . Yes, they do send a limousine. But the way I felt, I would have preferred an ambulance. Ambulances have beds.

Curiously, once I got to the studio, which had no windows out of which to see the darkness, and which was populated with scores of technicians buzzing about as if it were three in the afternoon, it began to feel like three in the afternoon. I decided to try to speak. "HI!" I said to someone in overalls, startling myself a little by the volume (like turning on a radio without knowing the sound is on High), and headed for the makeup room. During the application of my left eye, Tom Brokaw ambled in and went into an immediate huddle with the producer—something about Castro having not arrived in the United States as expected, "so we'll switch to a weather lead."

Which meant, less than half an hour before air time, the entire opening of the show had to be changed. As far as I could tell from the script, the change wouldn't directly affect me, but it most assuredly would affect Brokaw, who, I noticed, looked as thrown by this new development as he might had he been told that the beef stew special was gone and that he'd have to have lamb instead.

If I were a man I think I might be jealous of Brokaw. He's smart, funny, handsome, nice, and, I assume, rich. On-camera, both on the *Today* show and now on *Nightly News*, he's perfect. He doesn't say dumb things. He doesn't get stuck. Except once in a while; and when he does, he doesn't look foolish. He looks cute. He doesn't even say uh.

When we were seated side by side in our little seats behind

the *Today* show play-desk, and as the man from Local #11 pinned our microphones on, Brokaw instructed me not to be nervous. He tried to be kind. He *was* being kind. But the kinder and calmer and more competent he seemed—and the kinder and calmer and more competent everyone else seemed (the only thing worse than being scared is if you're the only one who is)—the more frazzled and incompetent I felt until, finally, when the little red light in the camera went on and we were actually (oh, my God) on the air, and Brokaw turned to me and said how good it was to have me there and how are you?, instead of answering, "fine" or more to the point, instead of *answering*, I said GoodMorningTom like Betty the Talking Robot, and turned to the TelePrompTer and read my words as if in a trance.

Once into the show—sometime during a report about a high-pressure system over the Rockies—I began to feel corporeal again. But feeling corporeal was a long way from feeling good.

It might not have been so bad if, somehow, I could have practiced. But there is no way to practice the *Today* show. You do get a script in advance—they send it to your house by messenger at about eight each evening—so that you know the order and time of each segment, but, as I had just seen, the entire show can get flip-flopped at the last minute if an anticipated news event doesn't happen, as in the case of Castro, or if, say, a guest is late. The script also provides every word (including "Good Morning") that comes out of your and everyone else's mouth. Except that a television host who thinks of him or herself as a journalist pays as much attention to these words as anyone who fancies him or herself a creative cook pays attention to exact recipes in *The Joy of Cooking*.

By 6:30 each morning, a final version of the script has been placed on the desk in front of each person's chair, like place cards at a dinner party. A copy of the script goes on the TelePrompTer, which lives inside the camera. That way, the person on-camera can look into the camera lens and appear to be gazing into the eyes of the person watching at home, when, in fact, the person on-camera is gazing at a bunch of words being rolled by hand by a small friendly fellow named Charlie, wearing earphones, behind the set.

I sort of knew the tricks of reading a TelePrompTer: pause, not necessarily where the sentence ends, but here and there, as you do when you speak; don't stare as if you're reading an eye chart; if, by mistake, the camera moves too far away, don't scream "I can't see," but, instead, read from the script in your hand; et cetera.

But there were a few tricks I didn't know. In keeping with tradition, I, too, wanted to rewrite every word in the script. I hadn't read someone else's words since I had been an actress, and I wasn't about to begin again now. However, I could not figure out exactly when and how to make the changes. The week before I went on, I asked Jane Pauley, who told me her way of doing it was to scribble changes on the margins of her desk script as the show went along and more or less ignore the words on the TelePrompTer. This, I decided (wrongly), was too casual for me. Instead, I made script changes in advance—the night before—and duplicated them onto the TelePromp-Ter script in the morning, which enabled me, once on the air, simply to read.

And which enabled me simply to sound as if I were reading. The operation was a success but the patient died. I overlooked the fact that most of what is said into the camera is so brief—a word about what's coming up and an introduction to the next flock of commercials—that reading looks like reading, regardless of whether you've written your own words, and regardless of how good you are at reading them as they roll.

When it came to the interviews—Hal Holbrook, the actor;

the president of Tiffany; a woman who wanted head shops banned—I felt safer. Interviews I was good at. Interviews I could prepare for. So I prepared. And prepared. By the Friday before the Monday on which the ordeal was to begin, I knew everything about my interview subjects short of their mothers' maiden names. I had neglected, however, to absorb one small but pungent piece of reality: that the interviews were only five minutes each—less—and given that, the worst thing you can do is know too much.

I had done a zillion five-minute interviews in my time, but they were always five minutes *edited*—from at least thirty-five. There's a difference between five out of five and five out of thirty-five. In the latter you can go at least one inch below the surface, you can digress, you can grope, you can converse. And when it's over, you can pick the best of it. That's five out of thirty-five. When it's five out of five all you can do is: question, answer, question, answer, question, answer, good-bye, get the name right, hold the book up, and we'll be right back after a commercial. That's not an interview. That's target practice.

Of all stunned looks I've ever seen, none rivals that which passes across the face of a person who has just been interviewed on the *Today* program. Having answered two questions and having just begun to warm up, he has his microphone plucked from his lapel and his body nudged out of his seat so precipitously as to make him wonder if he has committed an indiscretion, and then, as he stumbles out of the area that's lit, he looks over at the monitor only to see a young woman who has already displaced him on the screen, extolling the virtues of cotton.

The interviews' brevity stunned me, too—the only difference being that, thanks to the Finger Man, I got stunned before the guest. The Finger Man, alias the stage manager, stands behind the chair of the interviewee in order to signal the interviewer when the time is almost up, which, as I've said, is almost immediately. One index finger, meaning one minute, would go up and I'd think, impossible!—and, at the same time, try to absorb what one minute meant—time for one more question? two? As my pulse rate rose perceptibly, I'd also try to figure out how exactly to guide the remains of the interview so that the person in front of me, who is unaware of the Finger Man, will shut up when the time comes. Barbara Walters told me once, long ago, that she used to signal people by gently kicking them; but I knew, when the time came, which it rapidly did—one finger became ten, signaling ten seconds left, then nine, eight—that (although I considered it) I could not kick the elderly president of Tiffany. Instead, I ended the interview by interrupting his final thoughts on table manners with a THANK YOU! which came out sounding like FIRE!

Smooth, very smooth.

Speaking of smooth, that is probably the number one priority on such a program. Whatever else you are—or are not—you must be a skater. You must glide, and as you glide, you must look happy. I never got the hang of saying "station break" and looking happy at the same time; I didn't smile *nearly* enough; and when I said that we would be back "after these announcements," I didn't sound sure.

All of these criticisms, by the way, were *my* criticisms. No one else told me what I was doing wrong, much as I would have liked them to.

"You were fine," said the producer curtly when I asked him to please criticize me after the first show. (In retrospect, I couldn't blame him for brushing me off since, the following week, *he* got brushed off the show—canned, that is.)

Meanwhile, I lusted for censure. I came from a tradition of writing and editing—of Allene Talmeys and Martin Goldmans and, most recently, Genevieve Youngs—and I knew what a difference good editing could make. Particularly when the territory is unfamiliar. Even in the theater, I remember, we had "notes" after each performance—sessions at which the director would tell us what we were doing wrong and right— so that we could adjust our performances the next night accordingly.

In television there is a different tradition. If they don't like what you do, they don't criticize you. They fire you. They couldn't fire *me* because I was only a substitute. Nor, for that same reason I suppose, was it cost-effective for them to spend so much as five minutes analyzing my performance. But for reasons of vanity and professional pride, even though I hated the assignment, I wanted to be wonderful.

"But how can I be wonderful," I wailed to my mother, "if they won't tell me how I'm terrible!"

"Maybe they won't tell you how you're terrible because you're not terrible!"

What else is a mother going to say?

Although the last thing on my mind during the three-day *Today* siege was the rest of my life, I couldn't help noticing where it had gone: out the window. For three days I experienced what it was like to be forty and not to be able to stay up with the grown-ups, and I didn't like it any more than I did when I was eleven. The difference was that when I was eleven and had to go to bed at nine o'clock, I only suspected I was missing all the fun. At forty, I *knew* it.

To live is to pay prices to get what you want. Had I coveted the *Today* show, or had the experience turned out to be enhancing rather than depleting (each show left me feeling as if I had spent two hours throwing quarters into a one-armed bandit without ever getting more than two bananas in a row), then *maybe* it would have been worth it.

All the same, I did manage to have one thirty-minute period on the program which was positively merry. I smiled—I think I even laughed once—I said "station break" as if I were saying Happy Birthday; and when I announced, "This is Today on NBC," you would have thought that NBC was the Land of Oz.

Toward the end of that thirty minutes I even began to feel a kind of runner's high—a palpable sense of joy that rose higher and higher until, heart thumping, I tore the ribbon on the finish line.

It was nine A.M. Wednesday (please, God, don't do this to me again—give me stakeouts, give me floods in Brooklyn, give me ...) and we were off the air.

CHAPTER
23

For my next number—yet another departure from the land of real people and from my decreasingly normal life as a features reporter—I was assigned to interview a super-celebrity, and I knew why. Aside from my new semi-hot-stuff status, I had something in common with the celebrity, which the fellows in charge clearly couldn't resist. Between us (ah, I could hear those executive wheels turning), me and the celebrity had two breasts.

Actually, for whatever imperfect reason it came to be, I was delighted and flattered and excited about the plan to pair me with the ex–First Lady, and I couldn't wait to meet her. Like most people—more than most people because of the experience we shared and how much her openness about it had helped me—I admired her and felt as affectionate toward her as any public person I could think of. So I did not greet the assignment with cynicism. I just left it that way.

More than anything I've done on television, interviewing Betty Ford—first for *Nightly News* and the *Today* show, and later for an hour special—made me wish I were a writer again. It wasn't because the interviews were so unpleasant— which they were. I had conducted far more unpleasant interviews in far more unpleasant places than the Fords' umpteen-room house in Palm Springs, California. It was the result of the interviews that bothered me—the fact that I had lost control, as I wouldn't have on paper. It was the fact that the Betty Ford who appeared on television wound up sounding the way the nation, her husband, her husband's staff, and the William Morris Agency wanted and expected her to sound (and, I confess, the way *I* had expected her to sound): sweet, modest, happy, intelligent, and, of course, honest. It was that that was not how she really was. It was that she—they—made monkeys out of us.

Altogether, I had four visits with Betty Ford. Each one was difficult, but I suppose the first was the most difficult. It was in May 1978, right after her release from a naval hospital in California, where she had undergone treatment for drug and alcohol addiction. Mrs. Ford's addiction to pills and alcohol had been made public, which some people saw as a further demonstration of her rare and wonderful honesty and others saw as a calculated effort on the part of the Ford people to take political advantage of a situation that might have turned into a political liability. Whatever it was, there was no question that, at this point, Gerald Ford was still thinking about having another go at the Presidency and there was no question that, if/when he did, his wife would be an important asset, assuming that her image was intact.

Shortly after Ford moved out of the Oval Office, NBC signed the President and his wife to a contract that would net the Fords about a million dollars. (Soon after that, the man who had made the deal was relieved of his duties as president of NBC.) It was now May 1978, and thus far NBC had received for their money two short interviews on the *Today* show, plus one one-hour interview, from Mr. Ford, and from Mrs. Ford, limited participation in a documentary film about the Bolshoi Ballet. The polite word used to describe Mrs.

Ford's performance in that documentary was "strange." Even with many retakes, her speech was unnaturally slow, her words slurred. She almost seemed drugged and/or drunk. Later, it turned out, she was.

Now, with her about to be released from the hospital, NBC began to press hard for an exclusive interview. Suddenly, it was granted, and, the following day, a producer, director, two four-person camera crews, and I converged on the Ford compound in Palm Springs.

Driving in from the airport, I looked around at Palm Springs. Everything was big and flat and beige. And hot. But the heat had no juice. It was dull, still, arid. The car, on the other hand, was air-conditioned and numbingly cold. We passed a number of no-colored, flat-roofed houses, and for every one of those there were four or more giant fast-food places, giant car lots, and giant neon signs and billboards. As we drove farther out, the houses got bigger and harder to see for the pools and tennis courts and golf courses surrounding them. There were almost no people in sight—except, of course, for occasional torsos in occasional cars—and, in the distance, pairs of men in pastel trousers on golf courses. Who, I found myself wondering, would want to live here? But I knew part of the answer: Bob Hope, Frank Sinatra, and Mr. and Mrs. Gerald Ford.

A long, wide public road leads to the Fords' and, once inside, there is a long, wide private road with a small guardhouse in the middle, not unlike the one at the White House.

"Right this way, folks," says the guard, smiling rather goonily as he gestures toward a large parking area. We pull over, park, and get out. For a moment, after the air conditioning, the oven-air feels good. A short, perky young woman comes over to greet us and introduces herself as Mrs. Ford's secretary. She, too, smiles widely (and continuously) and leads us into a one-story house across the road, which turns out to be a cluster of staff offices.

When I first saw Bob Barrett, who runs the Ford operation in Palm Springs, he was not smiling, and at first—only at first—that sufficed to make me like him. In his favor, I will say that Mr. Barrett wastes no time. We were hardly seated before he began to dictate the interview: "The way I see it, Betsy [*sic*], you'll ask her if it's nice to be back, she'll say, yeah, it's nice to be back; you'll say why, she'll say it's nice to be with the family again—y'know that sorta thing. You'll see if you can keep it to fifteen minutes, okay; we'd 'preciate it, 'preciate it." There was a minimum of eye contact during this recitation, and, now that it had ended, it was clear there would be no question period. I knew, as he must have, that the agreement called for more than a fifteen-minute interview and that it would be impossible to do what we had come the width of the continent to do—have a frank conversation with Mrs. Ford about her condition—in that length of time. I was about to speak up, when the producer gave me a don't-worry-he's-just-playing-bigshot signal. But I *was* worried. I didn't like having someone in a golf costume reciting both the questions and answers to an interview before (or after or during) the interview. Nor did I like what I sensed might be the consequence: that I'd have to be pushy with a sick person, who was being used by all of us.

The main house was a short drive past the guardhouse. The crew went in first and began setting up the camera equipment in the library. The producer, Barrett, the secretary, and I sat down to wait in the living room, which reminded me of all those oversized living rooms with oversized furniture in Beverly Hills. I felt myself growing less and less calm. The director and Barrett were handling their discomfort with one of those sports exchanges that men have: ". . . Did you see what So-and-so did in the eighth?" Meanwhile, on the overstuffed sofa, hands folded like nice girls, the secretary and I sat, smiling artificially at each other. After a few moments, she got up and excused herself, and then returned—smile intact—to say that Mrs. Ford would see me now. I stood up as if I'd been goosed. There was something about the tone. I actually felt frightened. Stop it, I shouted silently to myself. It didn't work.

Mrs. Ford received me—and the term fits precisely—in a small sitting room adjoining the bedroom. She was wrapped in a pink dressing gown—satin, I think—looking pale and fragile and glamorous, like one of those movie stars in one of those movies. She was holding onto the arm of a large, tanned man standing at her side: the ex-President of the United States. If you didn't know that, however, you'd think he had wandered in from the set next door, where they were shooting a Western.

After the introductions were made, I stopped feeling frightened. It's hard to be afraid once you realize that the person you're afraid of is equally afraid of you. "What are you going to ask me?" said Mrs. Ford in a whisper, like a third-grader, nervous about a test.

"W-well," I stuttered, not prepared for the terror in her eyes, "we can decide that together."

And then the bombshell: "You know," she said, "they didn't tell me . . . I didn't know you were coming . . . until just now . . . when you were in the driveway . . ."

"You . . . d-didn't?" I stuttered. I looked at the President, who was (you guessed it) smiling.

"It'll be fine, just fine," he said to her—or to me, I wasn't sure.

"Look," I said, turning back to Mrs. Ford, "I know this must be very difficult for you and—I had no idea they didn't even—that you didn't know we were coming—and I can imagine how you must feel—and, well, we'll do it in the shortest time possible and don't feel you have to answer anything you don't want to and ..."

Shut up, I said to myself. You're not her nurse. You're here to do an interview. "I'm not sure what to wear," said Mrs. Ford in a small voice, not letting go of her husband's hand. It was the first day of school and he was the parent and I was the teacher and Mrs. Ford was the six-year-old who wanted more than anything not to be left there. The secretary made a move then, and I sensed that was my cue to leave. I took it.

Betty Ford entered the library about an hour later in a pale blue dress, made up, coiffed, and smiling. It was as if a year had passed. She extended her hand to the director who, following a wise instinct, bowed. "What a pretty dress," I heard myself coo. "Thank you," she said, without a trace of tension. She sat. I babbled small talk. She babbled back and joked with the crew. They joked back. Finally, the clapboard snapped in front of our faces and the camera rolled. Simple, I said to myself, be simple and straight. This is the woman known for her honesty. Look her in the eye, ask her straight, and she'll answer you straight.

"You're just out of the hospital," I started quietly. "How do you feel?"

"Absolutely *marvelous*," she almost shouted, flashing most of her teeth. "I've never felt better in my life." Please don't lie to me, I thought. I know these people want you to, but don't. It's okay not to feel wonderful when you've been through what you've been through. Just say how you feel, okay? You don't have to say a lot, just something, one thing, that's true. I tried again. But the more I zeroed in, the cheerier—and phonier—she got.

Barrett, who had placed himself behind the camera, directly in my view, began making Cecil B. De Mille "cut" signals. I had just asked a question about the group therapy sessions at the hospital.

"It was one of the most interesting experiences I've ever had," she said.

"Really?" I jumped, thrilled with what sounded like the beginning of something. "How—in what way?" I said, leaning forward.

But Mrs. Ford lowered her head. "I'll talk about that . . . later," she said. Later? I thought, when later? And then it was over.

Later, I found out what later meant. Later meant she (they) were saving the juicy parts for her book, for which the paperback rights alone had just sold for a million dollars.

"That was *such* a good interview," said the secretary, as she walked us to the car.

"No, it wasn't," I said. "It wasn't good at all." She looked at me as if I had just relieved myself on the front lawn. "It was, in fact, a terrible interview. Mrs. Ford was in no condition to be interviewed. She wasn't prepared to talk about what has happened to her at all. She didn't even know we were coming, for God's sake. Her answers weren't honest. And whenever we started getting somewhere, she held back. I think the whole thing was a complete waste of time."

The interview ran the next morning on the *Today* show and that evening, on *Nightly News*. It was picked up and syndicated throughout the world. It was such a success that six months later I was chosen to interview Mrs. Ford for an hour show. "I get it," I said to the news executive who gave me the assignment, ". . . second prize is a *two*-hour interview with Betty Ford." He was not amused. Neither, come to think of it, was I.

CHAPTER
24

I know. I'm beginning to sound like a complainer. In truth, I felt more surprised than woeful. I had made the assumption that that which is considered a prize is necessarily a prize. I forgot that a reward can turn out to be a penalty, and, when you find out, how cranky that can make you, like having a lousy New Year's Eve. But I was old enough to know about New Year's Eve and I should have known about prizes, especially prize assignments in television.

When I caught on, I decided to engineer, if I could, my own prize. While I was still the golden girl (I did have the sense to know it wouldn't last) I thought I'd try to get something out of it I really wanted.

What I really wanted had to do with dying. Since the intrusion of cancer in my life, I had stopped thinking about death as a remote scourge that happens to old people, or to young people I don't know on highways. Not that I expected to die any moment, myself. But I knew, as I never knew before, that I could die and that, eventually, I surely would. (Most people don't know that, except in their heads, which doesn't count.)

So the subject began to grab me—not in a morbid way, but more as a practical matter of how best to deal with death when it comes. As it turned out, a lot of other people had been thinking about this, too—owing, no doubt, to the increase in cancer deaths and to the fact that, unlike many other kinds of death, victims of incurable cancer know it's coming.

Gradually, then more and more, attention began to be paid, not only to extending life near the end, but to improving its quality. Enter Elisabeth Kübler-Ross, whose book *On Death and Dying* was devoted to this goal; and enter Hospice, which put into practice the notion of helping terminally ill people to maintain their lives in comfort and with dignity—in their own homes, if possible. Enter also certain hospitals which, instead of treating dying people like lepers, began, instead, to treat them as they were: people who were near the end but who were still (very much, in some cases) alive.

I knew the story should be done. I wasn't sure how or on which show. It would get the biggest audience on *Nightly News;* but I couldn't see how to do it right in three and a half minutes, which was as long as any single piece could be. Unless (!) they ran it as a series—*two* or *three* three-and-a-half-minute pieces, running on successive nights. Unlikely, but if ever I had a shot at selling a bunch of pieces on death at the dinner hour, it was now.

As it turned out, I didn't even have to fight. I was almost disappointed. Fine, do it, they said, do two pieces, do three, whatever you want. And here's Ira Silverman to produce it. Which was like RCA saying to a songwriter, "Sure, we"ll record your song . . . and here's Barbra Streisand to sing it."

Ira Silverman had spent most of his work life trailing the Mob, with whom he was not popular. (Hence, the bulge in his back pocket, which was not his wallet.) However, like certain actors who can do comedy and tragedy equally well, Ira had a

Sensitive Other Side which didn't get much play on the Mafia beat. So he was as charged up about getting the assignment as I that he got it.

Together, then, we hit the research: read the books and the articles, made the calls, pondered the usual problems: how to focus, how to structure, how to find people—uncommonly difficult this time since we were looking for people who were dying; who, moreover, were having a relatively good death *and* who wanted to talk about it.

We decided early on not to fall into the ain't-it-awful trap. We agreed that the world did not need us to carry on about the ghastliness or sorrow of death, nor about society's clumsiness in dealing with it. Instead, without ignoring the bad news, we thought we'd focus on the good, new efforts being made—by individuals and institutions—to make the end of life better.

We made telephone allies of Hospice workers and hospital directors, who became scouts for us both for programs and for people who would illustrate what we wanted to say and show. They also helped us decide what we *wanted* to say and show.

We wound up with two Hospice stories—one about an elderly woman in New Jersey who was spending her last weeks propped up in her own bed at home, where she was able, when she felt well enough, to make it into the kitchen and turn out what I'm sure must have been the highest rising bread on her block (which, after the shoot, we got to eat); and another about a doctor in Connecticut, whose cancer had shrunk his previously athletic body almost in half, and who spoke unsentimentally but movingly of the Hospice worker on his case, who, he said, listened long after everyone else had stopped. "When people ask you how you are," he said in what was left of his voice, "they don't really want to know."

And his wife, looking small and bewildered in the corner of her living-room sofa, told us how much better she felt after the Hospice volunteer assured her that it really was all right for her to get angry at her husband once in a while. (It turned out he thought it was all right, too.) The further into the story we got, the more we veered off—appropriately, I think—into what happens to families of people who are dying, and how little of the right kind of attention is paid to them. "Sickness and death is rarely something that happens only to the person who is dying," said the Hospice nurse in Connecticut, a sweet, frail young woman who joined the program after seeing her own father die a lingering, painful "machine-connected" hospital death.

We wondered if any hospitals or institutions were doing anything innovative to lessen the horror of a child's death; and we found out some were—like Children's Hospital in Philadelphia, where they had a policy of allowing family members to stay in patients' rooms overnight; where they held group therapy sessions for dying children; where doctors and nurses stopped wearing uniforms once they realized uniforms scared some children; where staff members visited families of dying children—both before and after the death—and encouraged families to take the children home from the hospital for their last days or weeks, if that was what they wanted to do, and if it was possible to care for them at home. In every way, it seemed, the hospital treated the person—and persons—instead of treating only the disease.

We decided to use the Philadelphia hospital as our focus because the people there seemed to be working on every front, and also because the director had found a patient for us—an eighteen-year-old girl with bone cancer—who was willing to be interviewed. But before we went ahead, I wanted to know why. I wanted to make sure that what she expected from being part of our story was what we were able to give.

I called Dr. Audrey Evans, the director of the children's oncology ward, who, I sensed from previous conversations, would probably give me a straight answer. Which, in her neat

British accent, she did: "I think Janet is proud of how she and her family—and all of us, too, I suppose—have handled her illness, and she thinks it will help other people if she talks about it. Sick people rarely have the opportunity to feel useful, you know; and participating in your program will give her that feeling. She's quite looking forward to it!"

"When, then, should we begin to film?" I asked. "Is there one time that would be better than—"

She interrupted me: "I would say as soon as possible," and from her tone, I knew what she was saying. And it suddenly struck me what we were doing.

"I understand," I said, and hung up.

You're a reporter, I said to myself when we stepped off the elevator onto the oncology floor; act like one. The oncology floor was a sunlit place where the walls were full of color and the children's faces were gray. We were five: Ira and I, a cameraman and a sound technician, and Dr. Evans, who looked the way she sounded on the telephone: thin, fiftyish, tweedy, crisp—and soft around the eyes. Janet's room, she told us as she led the way, was at the far end of the corridor. I stopped just before we got to the door.

"What's the matter?" said Ira.

"Nothing," I said, lying. I felt queasy. Cut it out, I said to myself and put one foot in front of the other and, with the others, walked into the room. I was startled by how bright it was and how many people were milling about—a middle-aged man and woman, who I guessed were the parents, and a young man and woman, probably the brother and sister, and another young woman, in blue jeans, who turned out to be a nurse.

In the center of the room, in a big, high, white bed, lay the patient, Janet, a creature so wizened that, had we not been told, we would not have been able to tell either her age or her sex. Except for a few pale strands of hair, the scalp was bare; the body, swollen in the middle; the arms, emaciated; and the backs of the hands, sinewy and blue from intravenous needles. The face was pale and puffy and the eyelids were half-shut and only when her eyes looked at my eyes did I know that she was conscious.

Words came out of my mouth. I don't remember what they were. Some babble about the story and about how we hoped the interview wouldn't be too difficult for her. (Interview? I thought. How did anyone think we could interview her!) As I said whatever I said, she nodded and whispered what sounded like "okay," but then her eyelids shut all the way and her arm moved up slowly and her fingers grasped a small plastic cup attached to a pulley which came out of the wall and she put the cup—of oxygen—over her nose. As she inhaled, she closed her eyes and the room became absolutely still. Then, slowly, she removed the cup from her face, opened her eyes halfway as before, let her head roll to the side, and actually began to speak. The words came out in whispers and gasps, but they came out and they came out clearly. She said, "How—great—everyone—has—been," and how "lucky" she was to have people like her family and the hospital people around her. Lucky?

God.

I kept thinking each time she began to speak, sucking in air after every word, that she wouldn't make it to the end of the sentence. But she did. At some point, I shook hands with her mother and father, who looked like the most tired people in the world. But they smiled. And the sister and brother smiled and I smiled back. And I thought, none of them see her. This has happened gradually, so they don't really see her. At least, I hope they don't. Oh, I hope they don't.

Ira began to speak about arrangements—when we'd be

back, about how long it took to set up the camera—and the cameraman said something, too; we were all yammering absurdly, helplessly until, finally, we backed out and were in the corridor again.

I noticed a door with an exit sign and went for it. It was a stairwell. The door slammed behind me and it was suddenly quiet and cool and almost dark. I sat down on the top step and put my head down and wrapped my arms around my knees. I knew it was dumb to cry, and told myself not to. The door to the corridor opened and Dr. Evans walked in and sat down on the step next to me and put her arm around my shoulder and that did it. I cried and as I cried, Dr. Evans handed me tissues and I cried some more and she handed me more tissues and I kept trying to stop and finally I did. "I'm awfully sorry," I said. She told me not to be sorry and began to say some other things when the big door opened again and there was Ira— red-eyed and blowing his nose. I looked at him and he looked at me.

What have we gotten into? we both said without uttering a word. . . . I got up then and we went back out into the corridor.

I felt sick. I didn't want to go into that room again. I wanted air. I wanted out. I excused myself and went to the ladies' room and put the latch up inside one of the toilets and tried to decide whether to throw up. If you have to think about it, you don't have to do it, I told myself. I opened the latch and went to the sink and washed my face.

Idiot, I thought. What made you think that an eighteen-year-old dying of cancer could be anything but totally and unconditionally horrible? How can it matter what anybody does for her? Whatever they do, it's still unspeakable, catastrophic. I tried not to cry again, and did, anyway.

Wait a minute. I held on to the sides of the sink and looked down at the stopper; then I moved my head and looked at my eyes in the mirror. You're forgetting something. She wants this. She has something she wants to say. She thinks something good is happening in this hospital. So you will get your sniveling self out there and you will go back into that room and you will let her talk. Now.

Ira was standing outside the bathroom door when I walked out. He looked at me. "You okay?" he said.

"I'm okay. Let's do it." He nodded.

Back inside the room, I looked at the mother again. She had a plain, stark kind of beauty—hair pulled back, high forehead, high cheekbones, no makeup, no jewelry, flat heels, and a very straight back. She fussed about her daughter's hospital room as she might have at home—folding a sweater, a scarf, taking a magazine from a chair and putting it on a pile with others on the windowsill, placing a game of Scrabble in its box; moving things, fixing things, moving and fixing everything it was possible to fix—all the while as if she were connected by an invisible wire to the center of the room to the one thing she could not fix. Sometimes the wire seemed to pull her to the bed, and she would place the bent plastic straw resting in a water glass in her daughter's mouth, or smooth the covers at the foot of the bed.

Her husband, meanwhile, fussed not at all. He was a large, muscular man, and the room seemed too small for him. He sat in a wooden chair at the side of his daughter's bed, looking at the wall, at the ceiling, looking at her. Occasionally, he'd lean forward and say something to her. And he'd put his hand on hers—on the one without the needle.

Janet's mother had spent the night on a cot in the corner and, she told me, her husband had slept there the previous night, and her son the night before, and they had been rotating like that for weeks. The mother had dark circles under her eyes, but in a way that's hard to describe, she seemed all right. She seemed serene. They all did. There was, in fact, a strange absence of tension in the entire room. Movement, a lot of movement, but no tension. It was hard to figure. Then I realized they'd been living with this a long time. Living with dying. All of them, together. Holding Janet up. Holding each other up. And, it would seem, succeeding.

We began the interview. I had been worried about how to—whether to—use words like death and dying. I needn't have worried. As soon as she began to speak—in those small, terrible gasps—she used the words herself.

She said she knew she was dying and that she wanted it to be "out...in...the open....It means...a lot to me ...that...I can...share it...with my...family. In the hospital...they're...honest with me....I know what's ...happening...to me...but I don't feel...alone." She gasped then and her eyes rolled back. Dr. Evans pulled out the oxygen cup and put it over her nose and mouth. The camera clicked off. The cameraman wiped his face with his handkerchief.

Janet's eyes were open now. "We can stop if you want," I whispered to her. With the mask still on her face she shook her head no.

Then she signaled Dr. Evans to take the mask away.

"It's been...pretty...awful," she said with a half-gasp, almost a laugh. "But it would have been...worse...if they...pretended..." She needed oxygen again. Dr. Evans gave it to her. The room was still except for her breathing and the camera hum. I wasn't sure what to do. Then, suddenly, she waved the mask away again. "I know I'm...going ...somewhere," she said, smiling. "I hope...it's a nice... place." Then her head fell back on the pillow and she smiled, and for a moment I could see how pretty she must have been.

Later, we moved the camera into a conference room on another floor, and interviewed the parents. They said they were ready for what was going to happen. "We just want the time that she has left to be as good as we can make it—and it has been good," said Janet's mother, almost in a whisper, looking at her husband. He nodded: "In a way, now that we're near the end, this period has been the best we've had since this—nightmare—started. I guess it's that we're not fighting it anymore. Now we're—well, we want to be as close as we can now—and, as my wife says, make as much of the moments left—as we can. The hospital here—they've sure helped us do that."

When we went back into the room that evening to do some cover shots, they were all there playing a word game—Janet included. Now and then someone laughed. I noticed they touched each other a lot. One person would take another's hand, or put an arm around a shoulder; a small, natural kind of touching, of connecting.

We went back to New York and took a long time to edit. The usual frustrations. The usual having to leave out practically everything. But when we were through, the fragment left was as much about love and intelligence and tranquillity—about the good things of life—as it was about death.

By the time the piece aired, a few weeks later, Janet was dead. We stayed in touch with her family and they told us that they were able to bring her home for the last few days, and that she had died peacefully. Her father said how grateful they all were to us for "letting her" be on the program. "It gave her such a feeling of accomplishment," he said. "I don't know if a story like that does any good. . . . I guess you never know that. But it meant a lot to her. . . . She felt like she was using the illness, getting something out of it, you know, getting some good out of it . . ." Then his voice cracked. "That must sound pretty crazy . . ."

"No," I whispered. "It doesn't sound crazy at all."

CHAPTER
25

I don't believe in many things. I don't believe in Doomsday; I don't believe in astrology; I don't believe in God (at least not in a powerful and benevolent bestower of occurrences and weather, who keeps an "In" box for prayers); I don't believe in new theories about the Kennedy assassination; I don't believe in something for nothing; and, having passed my eleventh birthday, I don't believe in Prince Charming.

You remember Prince Charming. He is that perfect fellow on a horse—handsome, rich, kind, intelligent, and loving, who neither drinks nor pays alimony. Naturally, as one gets on in life and experiences higher dosages of reality, one forgets about Prince Charming and learns, instead, to keep an eye out for something attainable: a mortal man with whom you can live day to day, and whom you can love enough to absorb his crap. And who is willing to absorb yours. And should you find one of those, you consider yourself abundantly lucky.

When, after my divorce and my departure from "Philadelphia" I set out to find another husband, I felt practiced in and ready for compromise. Not about everything. Not about a sense of humor, for example, and not about monogamy. Nor, in order to catch or please a man, was I willing to masquerade as someone else. By now I liked who I was and felt too old to wear costumes.

But gladly would I have endured rotten moods, say, or hostile stepchildren. I was ready to greet short stature and moles with indifference, and poor taste in music and furniture with tolerance and respect. And were this less-than-Charming Prince slightly chauvinistic, due to faulty socialization, well, I could take that, too.

Then one evening, late in the fall of '77, I went to a party and met a man. He was handsome (blond, even), intelligent (brilliant, actually), and, I soon found out, loving, good-hearted, witty, and monogamous. He neither drank nor paid alimony. Nor were there any small children in the bushes waiting to sic me. He had never been married.

Wait a minute. Never been married? At forty-two? I'm not so dumb. I knew what that meant. That meant he was either a homosexual or a nut.

He wasn't a homosexual.

He wasn't a nut.

We got married. Our mothers cried. Leo cried. He cried. I didn't cry because I knew, in time, the Prince could turn out to be a frog. (As long as he was a nice frog, I was planning to be a good sport about it.)

During the first year of our marriage, I'd wake up each morning and roll over and look at him, wondering if this would be the day his ears would turn green.

They never did. So I stopped watching and, instead, I'd wake up and look at him and wonder how I got so lucky. The man, you see, is the genuine article. He has character, empathy, humor. He is kind, not only to me, but to friends, acquaintances, strangers, to my mother. He is honest; he likes children but is content not to own any; I look up to him, but except when I take my shoes off, he does not look down on me. He is romantic, but not gushy (Midwestern Protestants don't know how to gush); he is astoundingly smart—a mathematician by trade—but not pretentious. He is elegant, but not effete. He is classy, but not a snob. When he does the grocery shopping on his way home from the math library, he does not expect to be congratulated. He is abundantly sweet, but lets me know when I'm being a pain in the ass. Furthermore, he thinks I'm swell, too. Do you believe this?

I don't either.

Life isn't like this and people aren't like that, and books aren't like that either. Now I see why people write novels. If this were a novel, I would never have let this happen. It's corny, it's trite, and it ruins the point. The person in this book is supposed to go off into the sunset with a *job*, not a man— okay, maybe a job and a man, but not a man like *this*.

For a long while, I felt tricked. I went out and bought snowshoes, but the blizzard never came. I used to think that maybe my vision was askew—that maybe I see him as better than he is. I began to try to look for faults. That sort of worked. I began to notice, for instance, that the Midwestern Protestant reserve, which so charmed me at first, had its occasional down side. Example:

"Do you like this dress?"

"Uh-huh."

"What does 'uh-huh' mean?"

"Yes."

"Is that a *big* yes?"

"Uh-huh."

The second serious fault of my husband's—also the sort of thing you don't notice in the first flush of courtship—is that he thinks when you go to a restaurant you eat the thing you ordered.

"What're you doing?" he says as my fork spears his Stroganoff.

"I'm *tasting*," I say. "Want some of mine?"

"No," he says, "I like *mine*."

"I know you like yours, but you're supposed to share it and taste the other person's."

"Yeah?" he says. "What for?"

Here's the odd part: when we met, I needed a man, let alone a Prince, *less* than I had ever needed a man in my life. After all, I fell into this state of nuptial bliss at the age of forty-two, following one less-than-blissful other marriage, numerous less-than-blissful romances, and—largely to compensate for these "failures"—twenty-one years of career. Twenty-one years had passed since I fanned myself with a feather in that crummy theater on Bleecker Street, thinking I'll just do this until He (the Prince) comes. And he never came. Until Dan. Dan was a Prince. But his horse kicked me. So I got up and went on with career(s) until they became important to me, until they became me.

By the time I met my second husband, I no longer needed or wanted a Prince to whisk me away. I liked it where I was. I had worked hard to become what I had become. I didn't feel smug about it and I hadn't lost sight of the fact that the world could muddle along nicely without me and without anything I had ever done or would do, but I sure liked *doing* it!

So maybe one source of this strange (continual) marital euphoria, this feeling of getting so much from my husband, is that, in a sense, I need so little.

I don't need money, for instance. And that's nice because, although my husband is perfect, he is not rich. (College professors make about the same as garbage men. Nobody starves, but nobody rolls in clover, either.) But so what? I don't need his money. I have mine.

I don't need his identity, either. I have one of those, too.

I'm awfully proud of him and sometimes I like to be Mrs. Professor for fun and variety. But I remember what it felt like when I wanted (needed) to be Mrs. Dan. It's not the same.

I do not need my husband to provide a social world. I like his friends. I enjoy them, but I have my own friends, my own social world.

Although he is strong and I lean on him sometimes, I know if I didn't lean, I wouldn't fall down.

I don't need him to make my life interesting. It already is. I don't need him to make me feel: pretty, accomplished, worthy. I get that, in varying degrees on the outside, even when I don't deserve it.

I don't need, in other words, his stamp on my parking ticket.

Nor do I need him, as I used to need men when I liked and respected myself less, to put me down.

When we married—in the pastel living room I had purchased with the paperback rights of *First, You Cry*—I didn't even "need" to get married—at least not for any of those old societal reasons. The women's movement, remember, changed all that. In a decade I went from Freak to Role Model. As a single career woman, I had the same sense of "rightness" that women who got married out of college and had babies right away must have had twenty-five years ago. Which is to say, I had the bland, sweet comfort of conformity, without actually having conformed. So, not only didn't I need a husband. Neither society nor my mother (often interchangeable) was pushing me to get one.

But I wanted one. Why? Because I wanted someone to share my sandwich with. And it had to be marriage and not just living together because I didn't want him (or me) to eat and run. Besides, marriage is still what you do if you mean it. Even some homosexuals want to marry nowadays, and I think it's nice that they do.

302

I wanted very much to mean it. I wanted someone to be my family. I wanted someone with whom to celebrate this life (which I no longer took for granted). I can, I thought, be an independent woman and still have a partner. I can be strong, but I *want* to lean sometimes. I don't want to be a doormat, but I badly want to give.

I had a lot. I had half of what, according to Freud, is important in life: love and work. I had work. Now I wanted the other half. And when I got married on January twenty-first, 1979, I was finally ready — to give it and to get it.

CHAPTER
26

Particularly when it comes to matters professional, I've always been impatient with the if-you-had-your-way-what-would-you-want kind of question. First of all, who ever has his way? And if you got your way, you probably wouldn't *know* what you wanted. It's hard enough deciding what you want if you *don't* have your way. So, obviously, it's best not to think about such things.

Unless, of course, they happen.

One day, for example, in the spring of '79, while puttering about my office, having finished one assignment and having not yet begun on the next, I received a telephone call asking me to come to the office of the then president of NBC News.

Without any introduction, unless you call How-are-you-fine-thanks an introduction, he informed me that the then president of NBC, Fred Silverman, whom I had been introduced to once in a roomful of five hundred people, wished to give me four network hours in order to do four daytime specials of my own choosing (!) which would run quarterly during the upcoming year. I almost dropped my beeper. It sounded, as the corny line goes, like a dream come true; except I had never been so corny or so crazy as to have such a dream.

Wait a minute, I suddenly thought, why me? Never mind why me. What kind of a show? In the studio? Filmed documentaries? What kind of subjects? Who's the producer? Starting when? . . . To these questions the news president had no, that's right, no answers. "Think something up," he said in not so many words, "and write me a memo." I knew a departure cue when I heard one. I got up and walked out the door. Did I hear right? I think what I'm being told is, Here are four hours. Now go play.

Play what? I didn't know it at the time, but a (daytime) network hour is worth about $250,000. What I did know at the time was that network hours were not handed out like treats at a birthday party.

My office roommate at the time was a sane and sympatico young man who did science stories. I told him about my new assignment.

"That's great!" he said. "What kind of a show? In the studio? Filmed documentaries? What kind of subjects?"

"I don't know," I said.

That stopped him. "Who does?" he asked.

"I guess nobody," I said. "I guess I'm supposed to think something up."

He looked at me. "That's weird."

I looked at him. "You're telling me."

So I thought something up. What else could I do? Not think something up? Besides, once out of shock, I put my head in gear and started having a good time.

In about a week I sent a memo suggesting a concept for a show for and about women. Nobody had said anything about women, but I assumed that's mostly who's out there during the day. The memo said that there were a lot of magazine shows which all looked the same, so why don't we *not* do another one of those, and instead, as long as the audience is women, why don't we do a show that is specifically for and about them and why don't we avoid both cooking tips and celebrities and do ordinary women and what they're up to and why don't we call it *Women Like Us*?

Fine, said the grown-ups. Think up a first show. Fine? Think up a first show? Whatever you say, boss.

I thought up a first show. Another memo: how about if we find three women who represent the three ways women most often deal with their lives these days? A homemaker—a wife and mother who doesn't have an outside job; a wife and mother who *does* have a job; and a career-focused woman who isn't terribly interested in getting married and who definitely doesn't want children. And—get this, now—we'll find women who are all doing fine. And that way the show will say, hey, the 1980s are upon us and you can be a homemaker and here's somebody who's happy doing that. Or you can do the juggling act (if it doesn't kill you) and here's somebody who's happy doing that. Or if you want to, you can just have a career, and ditto. So, see, the first program will be about choices and about three women, each of whom has made a choice which is right for *her*. And the way we'll do it is, we'll film the three women doing what they do and *then* (I got so excited I began to stutter on paper) we'll bring them into the studio with an audience, you know, like Phil Donahue, and they'll answer questions. So what do you think?

Fine, said the grown-ups. Do it. Fine? Do it? Whatever you say, boss.

We did it. (They gave me a producer I loved—a smart and gentle man named Bill Turque.) It was fine. The three women were beautiful, shining, articulate, true. The one, I couldn't help noticing, I felt nearest to was the full-time homemaker. Isn't that odd? I think it was because, of the lot, she happened to be the happiest. Like me. (Is it possible? Yes, it's really true. Like me.) In the fall we launched another show—about women who have been wives and mothers and start careers late in life, and, conversely, women who have had careers and start motherhood late. That worked, too. Then we began the third show—about getting married: (1) the old-fashioned way (everybody's a virgin); (2) for the second time (everybody has children); and (3) after living together first (no virgins, no children).

I was having the proverbial time of my life.

Then came the revolution. The boss who kept saying "fine" was demoted. A new, straighter, tougher man came in. The news department picked up, but—especially after the Olympics were lost—the larger NBC began to falter. Poor Fred Silverman began to sweat—and then to fade. Somebody noticed that our show cost almost a quarter of a million dollars to produce. The End.

I started having lunch again. I went to Bloomingdale's. I invited my brother- and sister-in-law to dinner and made dessert instead of buying it. I began to think about getting slipcovers made for the living-room furniture. I began thinking about other things, too. Like writing. Most of all, I began to think about writing again.

I didn't want to write about cancer. I was sick of cancer. Still, it was the most interesting thing that ever happened to me, so I considered it. Until I talked to my hard-headed friend Pat in Cambridge. "Now, dearie," she said in a tone that I'd resent coming from anyone else, "I love you, but we've all had enough of that breast."

That did it. Okay, I thought, what is the second most interesting thing that ever happened to me? That was easy. Work. All those jobs. All that bluffing, learning on one's feet, all that bending, scraping—and all that exulting, too. All that love. What it was like at good old *Look* and glamour-pot old *Vogue*. I suddenly had a flash of Margaret Case and "Get the princess!" and laughed out loud. I thought about Pat Carbine. And Johnny Carson. And Janet.

I'll write it as a novel, I thought. Then I remembered I didn't know how to write a novel. The alternative was just to write it. So I did.

When I came up for air, I wrote a letter to the new tough-guy president of NBC News, informing him that I was ready to return to work.

No reply.

Hmmmm.

I wrote another letter.

No reply.

Hmmmm again. I got, as they say, the message. I brooded. I sulked. Then I got angry. Damn it, I thought. I've been at that place nine years. I didn't expect him to rejoice when he got my letter, but at least he might have replied. And if he doesn't want me back, that's his right, too, but I have a right to know why.

"I'm curious," I said when he finally deigned to see me three months later. "What is it about me you don't like?"

He looked up for a second, the way people do when they've just heard an unexpectedly loud noise.

"We don't have anything for you to do here right now," he said without any noticeable warmth.

I looked at him, at his white hair, his perfectly decent assemblage of features, and wondered how and when and why this man had become my enemy. "Well, I know there's no show for me like *Women Like Us*," I said quietly, "but there's *Nightly* and *Today*. . . .I *know* the producers of both of those shows want me to do features for them ..." By the silence that followed, I could hear him speak as clearly as if he had really spoken: Maybe *they* want you to do features, but *I* don't.

In truth, none of this surprised me. The man was a hard-news hawk. He had a reputation for not liking features, and I had felt from the start that he didn't like me. Maybe I should have let it go at that. But I didn't feel like letting it go. I felt like making him talk. At the very least, I felt like making him uncomfortable. I leaned forward.

"Is it my nose?" I asked sweetly.

"What?"

"Is it that you don't like my nose?"

He shifted in his chair. "I didn't know there was anything wrong with your nose."

"There isn't," I said.

Silence.

"Look," I said, feeling strangely heady now, "you'll probably never see me again. Why not tell me the truth? You needn't worry about hurting my feelings. I know I'm good at what I do. I also know that in this business somebody's bound to come along eventually who doesn't like your work....I admit it's rather inconvenient when the person who doesn't like your work *runs* the place ..." (small chuckle from me, zero from him) "*but* that's how it is...."(I shrugged, then paused, allowing him to interrupt me, which he did not.) "Anyway, I'd like to know what it is about my work that you don't like."

"We don't have anything for you to do here right now," he said, in a tone which remarkably duplicated the one he used the first time. I almost felt sorry for him. He was still fairly new at the job. (Neither of us was aware, of course, that in a short time he'd be out.) I'm sure he was trying to do his best. Doing his best just didn't happen to include rehiring me.

"I know that's the *official* reason," I said, giving it one last shot, "but I also know that when a news president values a correspondent, the news president finds the correspondent something to do. Now you have every right not to want to do that," I said. "All I'm asking from you is a straight answer about why."

I'm not a good cook. My timing is usually off. But that night at home I turned out a merger between lamb and eggplant that I knew was terrific even before my husband, who almost never says words like terrific, said it was terrific.

"You know," I said to him over dessert—an apple thing with a crust that wasn't bad, either—"I had this really rotten appointment today, my career in television is probably over, I couldn't even find out *why* it's over. I have every reason to feel perfectly awful and I don't. In fact, I think I feel good. Now why is that?"

My husband put his dessert spoon down and, through his small, round glasses, gave me his serious-professor look, of which I am most fond.

"You feel good because you got something off your chest with this guy, and because you think enough of yourself so that you're not about to go under because somebody comes along who doesn't think you're wonderful, *and* because you know *I* think you're wonderful" (small but noisy smooch here) "and because you know and I know that your television career *isn't* over. Can I have some more of that apple thing?"

See what I mean about him?

He was right about the television career. Not, by the way, that I want to work in television for the rest of my days, but I guess I want to quit when *I* want to quit, not when some new top of the totem pole decides to make me.

And speaking of new tops of totem poles, I suddenly

remembered an old one: thin, nice Richard Wald, who, when he was knocked off NBC's pole, moved over to ABC's.

I didn't call him because to call him myself would run contrary to a custom which television shared with nineteenth-century China, Japan, and *Fiddler on the Roof*: when you are seriously interested in romance, you employ the services of a matchmaker, which is to say in modern parlance, an agent. Reenter William Morris, alias Yentl, who took possession of my best lace handkerchief (the one with the word *Available* crocheted on its border) and dropped it outside Wald's office at ABC News.

It must have worked because he called me the next day.

"You know," he said, lingering indecently on each word, "you've always been a peculiar bird . . ."

"Ha," I said. "Thanks a lot."

". . . but I think I may have a cage for you. We'll take it slow at first. We'll have some dates. You'll do one piece, maybe two. Then we'll talk about getting married. How does that sound?"

We hung up and I leaned back in my desk chair, swung my feet up on the desk, and smiled. I don't know about marriage, I thought, feeling deliciously light-headed, but I'm definitely ready for a new romance.